KNOWLEDGE, CULTURE, AND SCIENCE
IN THE METROPOLIS:
THE NEW YORK ACADEMY OF SCIENCES
1817-1970

ANNALS OF THE NEW YORK ACADEMY OF SCIENCES
VOLUME 584

KNOWLEDGE, CULTURE, AND SCIENCE IN THE METROPOLIS: THE NEW YORK ACADEMY OF SCIENCES 1817–1970

SIMON BAATZ

THE NEW YORK ACADEMY OF SCIENCES
NEW YORK · NEW YORK
1990

⊗ The paper used in this publication meets the minimum requirements of American National Standard for Information Sciences—Permanence of Paper for Printed Library Materials, ANSI Z39.48-1984.

The cover art is an oil painting by Joseph Stella (1877–1946) entitled *The Voice of the City of New York Interpreted: The Skyscrapers* (1920–1922). It is from the Collection of The Newark Museum (Purchase 1937 Felix Fuld Bequest Fund) and is reproduced here with the permission of The Museum.

Library of Congress Cataloging-in-Publication Data

Baatz, Simon
    Knowledge, culture, and science in the metropolis : the New York Academy of Sciences, 1817–1970 / by Simon Baatz.
        p. cm. – (Annals of the New York Academy of Sciences, ISSN 0077-8923 ; v. 584)
    Includes bibliographical references.
    ISBN 0-89766-545-7. – ISBN 0-89766-546-5 (pbk.)
    1. New York Academy of Sciences—History. 2. New York (N.Y.)—Intellectual life—19th century. 3. New York (N.Y.)—Intellectual life—20th century. I. Title. II. Series.
    Q11.N5 vol. 584
    500 s—dc20   90-5649
    [506'.0747'1]   CIP

First printing: May 25, 1990
Second printing: January 28, 1991

                                        CCP
                        Printed in the United States of America
                        ISBN 0-89766-545-7 (cloth)
                        ISBN 0-89766-546-5 (paper)
                        ISSN 0077-8923

ANNALS OF THE NEW YORK ACADEMY OF SCIENCES

VOLUME 584

MAY 25, 1990

KNOWLEDGE, CULTURE, AND SCIENCE IN THE METROPOLIS:
THE NEW YORK ACADEMY OF SCIENCES, 1817–1970

SIMON BAATZ

CONTENTS

List of Illustrations

Preface

NEW YORK. LEON TROTSKY imagined it as a triumph of cubism, Le Corbusier praised it as a "catastrophe . . . a beautiful catastrophe," and Bertolt Brecht, in one of his more mordant poems, saw Manhattan as "empty canyons of lifeless stone columns." Few commentators have perceived New York as a city with a past; most would have agreed with Henry James that, in New York, "the new landmarks crush the old quite as violent children stamp on snails and caterpillars." New York is a city so preoccupied with the present and the future that the past has vanished, almost as if it had never existed.[1]

There are exceptions, of course, but those few remnants of the past that still survive in New York are curiosities, anomalies that, for idiosyncratic reasons, have been left behind in the rush towards the future. Against all odds, the spire of Trinity Church still stands, defiant against the skyscrapers; only a few hundred yards away is New York's finest example of Greek Revival, the Custom House on Wall Street. Yet the quaint incongruity of these examples eloquently demonstrates that the past contributes only vestigially to contemporary New York.

It is thus an especial surprise that the New York Academy of Sciences, originally known as the Lyceum of Natural History, is one of those few institutions in the city to have preserved the thread of continuity from

---

[1] Leon Trotsky, *My Life: An Attempt at an Autobiography* (New York: Charles Scribner's Sons, 1930), 270; Le Corbusier, *Quand les Cathédrales Étaient Blanches: Voyage au Pays des Timides* (Paris: Libraire Plon, 1937), 127; Bertolt Brecht, "Verschollener Ruhm der Riesenstadt New York," *Gedichte*, 10 vols. (Frankfurt am Main: Suhrkamp Verlag, 1960–1976), 3: 93, stanza 21; Henry James, *The American Scene* (New York: Harper & Brothers, 1907), 78–79.

the early nineteenth century onwards. Established when New York was little more than a small town at the southernmost tip of the island and during an era when science was exclusively the preserve of a few dozen naturalists, the Academy has successfully survived bankruptcy, fire, competition (from other, more recent, scientific societies), and the transformation of science itself into a vast international enterprise. The survival of the Academy into the late twentieth century has been neither guaranteed nor fortuitous; it has been a result of the Academy's successful adaptation to the changing urban context provided by New York City.

As a consequence, my account relies less on the internal aspects of the Academy (finances, structure, officers, and administration) and more on the external contexts that shaped the activities of the Academy and its members. This approach includes, *inter alia*, the changing relationships between the Academy and such institutions as Columbia University and the American Museum of Natural History, the function of science within the urban context during a period when New York became the unchallenged metropolis of the United States, and the necessary changes imposed on the Academy by the increasing specialization of knowledge.

The themes implicit in my account of the Academy's past are familiar to anyone conversant with the debate on methodology that has agitated historians of science during the past two decades. This debate informed the presentation of various chapters of the book to the April 1987 meeting of the New York section of the History of Science Society, the May 1987 faculty colloquium on the history of science and medicine at New York University, and, at Harvard University in July 1988, the forum for independent research in science and technology studies. Each of these three seminars was the occasion for lively discussion and helpful comment.

Throughout the book all quotations are accurately reproduced; spelling and punctuation, no matter how quaint or idiosyncratic, are given here as they originally appeared. Words originally underlined are here italicized. I have generally been faithful to contemporary names of institutions; thus, for example, the *New-York Times* is hyphenated before 1897. Those few exceptions to this rule include New York University (until 1895, the University of the City of New York) and City College (until 1928, the College of the City of New York). Columbia University was known throughout much of the nineteenth century as Columbia College; I have adhered to this distinction in the text.

During the past three years of research and writing I have benefited from the advice of several individuals; Christine Abbott, Charles Boewe, Nicholas Fitzgerald, Mary Louise Gleason, Bert Hansen, Christine Hoepfner, Robert Pates, and Claudia Sencer all offered thoughtful en-

couragement. The staff and officers of the Academy, most notably Bill
Bruce and William Golden, provided access to the Academy's archives
and facilitated the use of resources at the Academy's headquarters on
Sixty-third Street. The organizational skills of Bill Boland, Joyce Hitchcock, and Sheila Kane proved indispensable in shepherding the manuscript through the various editing stages. Sally Gregory Kohlstedt, as the
consultant to the history project, provided helpful encouragement and
support at every stage.

The idea of writing the Academy's history was first suggested by
Heinz Pagels, executive director of the Academy in 1985. It is therefore
tragically ironic that the manuscript was completed less than three
months after Heinz's untimely death in July 1988 while mountain-
climbing in Colorado. Heinz had maintained a keen interest in the
project; his suggestions and comments on successive drafts were always
stimulating and fruitful.

SIMON BAATZ
OCTOBER 1988

Prologue

THE DEVELOPMENT of American science during the early decades of the nineteenth century has been customarily portrayed by historians as a steady accumulation of resources. Indicators of the gradual expansion of science in the United States have included, most typically, the establishment of scientific journals, the founding of specialist organizations, the creation of scientific schools in the major colleges, and the appearance of national organizations for the promotion and advancement of science. Not until the second half of the century did science become a consciously organized research activity; similarly the systematic intervention of the federal government in the support of science was only apparent after the Civil War.[1]

That science, in the first half of the nineteenth century, won more adherents and found greater support among the literate classes is not a controversial proposition. Because the United States as a nation was itself inchoate and, in particular, because there was no one city that served simultaneously as the political, cultural, and financial center of the country, science flourished only in those few cities capable of providing intellectual activity with sustained support. In this sense the development of science during the period can be best understood through the use of a structure defined by the geography of the early American republic.

[1] The most comprehensive overview of the history of American science is Sally Gregory Kohlstedt and Margaret Rossiter, eds., *Historical Writings on American Science*, Osiris, 2d ser., 1(1985). For the classic account of the role of the federal government, see A. Hunter Dupree, *Science in the Federal Government: A History of Policies and Activities* (1957; reprint, Baltimore: Johns Hopkins University Press, 1986).

Science as a cultural activity first appeared in the three major urban centers: Philadelphia, New York, and Boston. On account of the distance between each of the three foci of science (it took almost two days, for example, to travel from New York to Philadelphia) and, as a consequence, the relative isolation of each city, the development of culture at each place was shaped by particular factors. The expansion of science in the early nineteenth century in each city was marked by determinants unlike those elsewhere; in this sense, the context for science was unique. Each city possessed a particular history shaped by highly variant economic, political, and cultural factors; it is scarcely surprising, therefore, to discover that science — a socially constructed activity — developed at a different tempo within each urban center.[2]

In Philadelphia the scientific community could boast an impressive tradition and a considerable number of institutions. The University of Pennsylvania was established by Benjamin Franklin in 1740; the medical school at Penn, after its founding in 1765, soon began to earn an enviable reputation as a center of science. In 1743 a second cultural institution appeared in Philadelphia: the American Philosophical Society, on account of its resources, its publications, and its later connection with the founding of the American republic (Franklin and Thomas Jefferson served respectively as the Society's first and third presidents), functioned as a scientific organization with a national scope. The tradition of science and medicine in Philadelphia was a crucial element in the city's subsequent rise to eminence as a center of culture and learning.

The city experienced a series of political and economic misfortunes in the early nineteenth century: in 1800 the federal and state capitals were moved to Washington City and Lancaster, respectively and, in 1825, the opening of the Erie Canal signalled the beginning of the end of Philadelphia as a major entrepôt. As a consequence the promotion of natural knowledge in Philadelphia served to compensate for the political and economic setbacks imposed on the city from outside.[3] Throughout the eighteenth century, Philadelphia had been a lively center of cultural endeav-

---

[2] For an incisive analysis of regional patterns of science in the early American republic, see John C. Greene, *American Science in the Age of Jefferson* (Ames, IA: Iowa State University Press, 1984), 37–127. Science in America continued to be dominated by the three cities even at mid-century; see Robert V. Bruce, *The Launching of Modern American Science, 1846–1876* (New York: Alfred A. Knopf, 1987), 32–42, 45–50.

[3] The term "natural knowledge" is used by historians to convey the idea of science as a cultural artifact. See Arnold Thackray, "Natural Knowledge in Cultural Context: The Manchester Model," *American Historical Review* 79(1974): 672–709.

or; largely on account of the efforts of Franklin, culture in Philadelphia possessed a scientific dimension unrivalled elsewhere. In the early decades of the nineteenth century this tradition of science combined with the local support of culture to produce a wide range and variety of scientific institutions.

The American Philosophical Society and the Academy of Natural Sciences commanded substantial resources: both institutions possessed a library, museum, and a healthy bank balance. Scientific societies devoted to particular specialties also existed; the Phrenological Society of Philadelphia, the Linnaean Society, and the Chemical Society of Philadelphia flourished at various periods with different degrees of success. Finally there were the medical institutions: the University of Pennsylvania Medical School, Jefferson Medical College, Pennsylvania Hospital, and a host of evanescent medical societies and lyceums all served a burgeoning community of physicians and medical students.[4]

The identity of Boston during the early nineteenth century derived from its prominence, throughout the previous century, as the leading entrepôt on the East Coast. The city patriciate, its economic welfare heavily dependent on shipping, consisted of a small group of mercantile families that had ruled Boston for several generations. Following the Revolution, when the British navy continued to obstruct American trade at every opportunity, Boston's mercantile class began to prize innovation in finding and exploiting routes to new markets. The continued success of trade for the local economy was dependent, therefore, on the patriciate's ability to transmit entrepreneurial skills to future generations.[5]

The most appropriate institution for the education of Bostonians was Harvard College which, throughout much of the eighteenth century, had differed little from such other private colleges as Yale, Penn, Princeton, and Columbia. In the decades after the Revolutionary War, however, Har-

<hr />

[4] The rich diversity of science in Philadelphia is discussed in Ian Inkster, "Robert Goodacre's Astronomy Lectures (1823-25), and the Structure of Scientific Culture in Philadelphia," *Annals of Science* 35(1978): 353-363; John C. Greene, "The Development of Mineralogy in Philadelphia, 1780-1820," *Proceedings of the American Philosophical Society*, 113(1969): 283-295; idem, *American Science*, 37-59.

[5] Frederic Cople Jaher, *The Urban Establishment: Upper Strata in Boston, New York, Charleston, Chicago, and Los Angeles* (Urbana, IL: University of Illinois Press, 1982), 15-20, 22-25. See also E. Digby Baltzell, *Puritan Boston and Quaker Philadelphia: Two Protestant Ethics and the Spirit of Class Authority and Leadership* (New York: Free Press, 1979), 207-245, passim; Robert F. Dalzell Jr., *Enterprising Elite: The Boston Associates and the World They Made*, Harvard Studies in Business History, no. 40 (Cambridge, MA: Harvard University Press, 1987), 7-8, 10-13.

vard was the recipient of many gifts; the college at Cambridge became a favorite of the patrician families who regarded Harvard as the ideal preparation for future entrepreneurs. By 1850, therefore, Harvard overshadowed all other American colleges; Harvard's library was three times the combined size of the libraries at Princeton, Penn, and Columbia; her total assets were three times those of Yale. Horace Binney, a prominent Philadelphia lawyer and a Penn trustee, wrote to a Boston friend in 1821 of the support that Harvard obtained from the "munificence of its patrons . . . there is nothing like it in any other State" and gloomily compared the situation at Penn with that at Harvard: "the revolution cost the University of Penns[a] her best friends. . . . I am not aware that this University has recorded a single offering except a sum of 3000 drs."[6]

While the Boston patriciate gave generously to Harvard, it did not, however, provide much support for the few scientific institutions in the city. The American Academy of Arts and Sciences, established in 1780, remained tabescent for several decades; both the Society for the Study of Natural Philosophy and the Linnaean Society of New England survived for only a few years. Science in Boston was weak and enervated; patronage for the city's scientific societies was sparse and infrequent.[7]

The cultural climate in New York City was, as in Boston and Philadelphia, *sui generis*. Unlike its two rivals, New York experienced a massive economic expansion during the early decades of the nineteenth century. The growth and subsequent diversification of the city's economic base was concentrated primarily in maritime trade, manufacturing, transportation, and banking; as a consequence the economic and political power of the colonial landholders was sharply reduced as new entrepreneurial groups came into existence in New York City.

By 1815 New York had become so important as an entrepôt that even

[6] Peter Dobkin Hall, *The Organization of American Culture, 1700–1900: Private Institutions, Elites, and the Origins of American Nationality* (New York: New York University Press, 1984), 182–197; Jaher, *Urban Establishment*, 32–33; Ronald Story, *Harvard and the Boston Upper Class: The Forging of an Aristocracy, 1800–1870* (Middletown, CT: Wesleyan University Press, 1985), 24–28; Baltzell, *Puritan Boston*, 252–255; Horace Binney to John Collins Warren, 15 January 1821, John Collins Warren Papers, Massachusetts Historical Society.

[7] Walter Muir Whitehill, "Early Learned Societies in Boston and Vicinity," in *The Pursuit of Knowledge in the Early American Republic: American Scientific and Learned Societies from Colonial Times to the Civil War*, ed. Alexandra Oleson and Sanborn C. Brown (Baltimore: Johns Hopkins University Press, 1976), 151; Linda K. Kerber, "Science in the Early Republic: The Society for the Study of Natural Philosophy," *William and Mary Quarterly* 29(1972): 265–276; Bruce Winchester Stone, "The Role of the Learned Societies in the Growth of Scientific Boston, 1780–1848" (Ph.D. diss., Boston University, 1974), 191–192, 215.

Boston merchants unloaded their goods at Manhattan. The concentration of trade at New York established the city as the overwhelming population center on the East Coast and, as a result, provided both farmers and manufacturers with a highly concentrated urban market. Paradoxically, however, the unprecedented growth and prosperity of New York meant an absence of patronage for cultural pursuits. Few individuals had either the time or inclination to sponsor science at a time when fortunes were to be made almost overnight. Thus New York, at least in the first half of the nineteenth century, never possessed the flourishing scientific societies that adorned the cultural landscape of Philadelphia. The most prominent scientific society in the city before 1817, the New-York Literary and Philosophical Society, had been founded in 1814 in imitation of the American Philosophical Society, but it remained a weak and faltering attempt and never attained the fame and success of its Philadelphia exemplar.[8]

Nevertheless, largely on account of the avocational interest in science of DeWitt Clinton, one of the city's most powerful politicians for much of the period, science was given very valuable support through the loan to the city's scientific and cultural institutions of the former almshouse building located on the south side of Chambers Street directly opposite City Hall. For New York's small coterie of savants the use of the almshouse, called the New-York Institution by its new occupants, was a magnificent gift that substantially increased the visibility of science within the city. The building itself, when cleaned and renovated, was substantial enough to provide rooms for several societies. On the first floor, the New-York Historical Society maintained a modest but valuable library and a capacious meeting room; the New-York Literary and Philosophical Society occupied a second meeting room; John Griscom — one of the city's leading scientific lecturers — carried out chemical experiments in a well-stocked laboratory and discoursed to attentive audiences in a lecture room; and finally, there was a display room stocked with natural history specimens collected by members of the Historical Society and the Literary and Philosophical Society. On the second floor of the New-York Institution there was a large museum run by John Scudder who made a decent living from the hundreds of citizens who trooped past his collections of butterflies, stuffed birds, minerals, and seashells. The American Academy of the Fine Arts occupied the third story with a display of paint-

---

[8] Edward K. Spann, *The New Metropolis: New York City, 1840–1857* (New York: Columbia University Press, 1981), 1–22; Jaher, *Urban Establishment*, 159–160, 173–178.

1. THE NEW-YORK INSTITUTION. This view from the northwest corner of Broadway and Chambers Street shows, on the right, City Hall and, on the left, the New-York Institution; the two-story building in the center is the city jail. During the 1820s several scientific and cultural organizations, including the New-York Literary and Philosophical Society, the New-York Historical Society, and the Lyceum of Natural History, occupied rooms in the New-York Institution. Note the sign advertising John Scudder's museum above the entrance facing onto Broadway. (From a water-color drawing [1825] by Arthur J. Stansbury. *Courtesy of the Museum of the City of New York.*)

ings that was possibly the finest collection in the United States, not excepting Philadelphia.[9]

The concentration of the cultural societies in one spot was one advantage of the arrangement; a second benefit was the location on one side of City Hall Park which, after the recent completion of City Hall on the opposite side of the park, had become the most fashionable place in the city. On public holidays crowds of well-dressed young men and women promenaded along the walkways; with the construction of grand houses for the city's wealthy elite taking place in the streets near City Hall, the city's savants reflected that the location of science was exactly where it should be: close to the center of political power and surrounded by wealth and luxury.

The celebrated poet, Fitz-Greene Halleck, used the city as a backdrop for his long, quasi-satirical poem, *Fanny*, about New York's political feuds; his references to science and learning are tangential to the main plot but remain a telling indication of the social prestige of culture during the mayoralty of DeWitt Clinton:

> We owe the ancients something. You have read
> Their works, no doubt—at least in a translation;
> . . . .
> 'Twas their misfortune to be born too soon
> By centuries, and in the wrong place too;
> They never saw a steam-boat, or balloon,
> Velocipede, or Quarterly Review;
> Or wore a pair of Baehr's black satin breeches,
> Or read an Almanac, or C*****n's Speeches.
>
> In short, in every thing we far outshine 'em.—
> Art, science, taste, and talent; and a stroll
> Thro' this enlightened city would refine 'em
> More than ten years hard study of the whole
> Their genius has produced of rich and rare—
> God bless the Corporation and the Mayor!
> . . . .
> I might say much about our letter'd men,
> Those "grave and reverend seigniors," who compose
> Our learn'd societies—but here my pen
> Stops short; for they, themselves, the rumour goes,
> The exclusive privilege by patent claim,
> Of trumpeting (as the phrase is) their own fame.

[9] Kenneth Nodyne, "The Rise of DeWitt Clinton and the Municipal Government in the Development of Cultural Organizations in New York City, 1803–1817" (Ph.D. diss., New York University, 1969), 98–99.

And, therefore, I am silent. It remains
To bless the hour the Corporation took it
Into their heads, to give the rich in brains,
The worn-out mansion of the poor in pocket,
Once "the old alms house," now a school of wisdom,
Sacred to S******r's shells and Dr. G******m.[10]

---

[10] [Fitz-Greene Halleck], *Fanny* (New York, 1819), stanzas 46, 47–48, 69–70. Halleck is referring to DeWitt Clinton's speeches, to John Scudder's shells, and to Dr. John Griscom.

1

Science in the Early Republic
1817–1844

INTO THIS FAVORABLE CONTEXT for the pursuit of science, a new organization, the Lyceum of Natural History, stepped—tentatively at
first but with growing confidence. The creation of the Lyceum in January
1817 was not a fortuitous event but was contingent on several factors.
First, there was the dominant role in the local scientific community of
Samuel Latham Mitchill, the principal founder of the Lyceum. Mitchill's
stature rested not only on his intellectual achievements but also on his
activity as a scientific entrepreneur; Mitchill established the first medical
journal in the United States, he was a leading spirit in the organization
of a prominent agricultural society, and he was an active promoter of
such technological innovations as Robert Fulton's steamboat.

Second, the creation of the Lyceum of Natural History was condi-
tioned on a specific organizational model. Until the establishment of the
Academy of Natural Sciences in Philadelphia in 1812, science in the
United States had been the exclusive preserve of patrician elites. Thus
membership in the two leading eighteenth century scientific societies,
the American Philosophical Society and the American Academy of Arts
and Sciences, was confined to socially prominent lawyers, bankers, and
clergymen—scientific achievement was no disqualification, to be sure,
but it was worthless if unaccompanied by an appropriate social status.
The Academy of Natural Sciences, by contrast, was democratic, egali-
tarian, and non-exclusive; the sole qualification for membership was an
interest in natural knowledge. The founders of the Lyceum of Natural History explicitly rejected the patrician model in favor of the more populist
pattern; the Lyceum's early concerns and activities were similar to those
of the Academy of Natural Sciences.

Third, the early years of the Lyceum were distinguished by the need
to locate sources of support outside the impoverished membership.

2. SAMUEL LATHAM MITCHILL (1764–1831). Mitchill was not only a scientific polymath with an extensive knowledge of chemistry, botany, geology, and ichthyology but was also a prominent politician who represented New York in the House of Representatives (1801–1804, 1810–1813) and in the United States Senate (1804–1809). In 1817 he founded the Lyceum of Natural History; Mitchill was president of the Lyceum until 1823. (From an oil painting [n.d.] attributed to Rembrandt Peale. *Courtesy of the Academy of Natural Sciences.*)

Since it had little or no connection with the New York patriciate, the Lyceum—by contrast to the older organizations that relied on the wealth of their members—had to rely almost exclusively on energy and enthusiasm to launch such ventures as a scientific periodical.

The scientific enterprise in the United States in 1817 was extraordinarily fragile—in New York City, for example, there were only a few dozen men who had any active interest in science. Thus it was a matter of good fortune that Samuel Latham Mitchill, an experienced savant with an illustrious national reputation, was the leading spirit behind the organization of the Lyceum; in less capable hands the Lyceum might have quickly perished. Mitchill, who, in 1817, was professor of natural history at the College of Physicians and Surgeons, had already managed to squeeze several careers into one very hectic and busy life. Mitchill's principal occupation was medicine, which he first learnt as an apprentice to Samuel Bard; in 1783, Mitchill began his formal studies at the University of Edinburgh where he received his medical degree three years later. In 1792, after his return to New York, Mitchill—in early recognition of his catholic appreciation of many scientific disciplines—was appointed to teach natural history, chemistry, and agriculture at Columbia College for an annual salary of two hundred dollars; one year later the Columbia trustees, impressed with his youthful energy, added botany to his list of duties.[1]

Mitchill's most enduring claim to intellectual achievement remains his role in proselytizing for the new system of chemistry recently propounded by Antoine Lavoisier in France. While Mitchill did not attack the phlogiston theory of Joseph Priestley with as much certitude as some other American chemists and even, for a short period, attempted to find a third way between the two systems, it is clear from a reading of his *Synopsis of Chemical Nomenclature and Arrangement*, published in 1801, that Mitchill rejected the theory of phlogiston. His importance as a participant in the debates on the nature of air lay chiefly in his role as founder and editor of the first medical journal to appear in the United States, the *Medical Repository*. In 1797, only a few years after Mitchill had begun teaching at Columbia, his position in the medical community was such

---

[1] Courtney Robert Hall, *A Scientist in the Early Republic: Samuel Latham Mitchill, 1764–1831* (New York: Columbia University Press, 1934), 22. For a biography of Mitchill by one of his closest associates, see John W. Francis, *Old New York or Reminiscences of the Past Sixty Years* (New York, 1858), 87–96. An unflattering appraisal of Mitchill's polymathy by a contemporary critic can be found in Chandos Brown, *Benjamin Silliman: A Life in the Young Republic* (Princeton, NJ: Princeton University Press, 1989), 297–298.

that his new journal received strong support and continued to flourish for many years. Since the appearance of the first number of the *Medical Repository* coincided almost exactly with the beginning in the United States of the controversy between Priestley and Lavoisier, and since Mitchill quickly made it clear that the pages of his journal would be open to anyone with something of substance to say, the *Medical Repository* soon attained great significance for the small communities of chemists in Philadelphia and New York who avidly read the various contributions from the leading American theorists: James Woodhouse, professor of chemistry at Penn; John McLean, professor of mathematics and natural philosophy at the College of New Jersey; Joseph Priestley (who, since 1794, had lived at Northumberland, Pennsylvania); Pierre Auguste Adet, a representative of the French government in the United States who resided at Philadelphia; and, of course, Mitchill himself.[2]

In addition to his medical journal, Mitchill also displayed his entrepreneurial nature in the establishment, in 1791, of the Society for Promoting Agriculture, Arts and Manufactures. This organization, which was essentially a local agricultural society, reflected first, Mitchill's vocational interest in agriculture, which he taught at Columbia; second, his family background—his father owned a large farm on Long Island; and third, a concern with an issue that was of great importance for a country that, at the time, was overwhelmingly rural.

In 1801 Mitchill resigned his chair at Columbia to begin a second career as a politician; he represented New York City in the House of Representatives from 1801 to 1804; Mitchill then moved to the Senate until 1809; and finally, he served a second term in the House from 1810 to 1813. Concurrently with his position as a representative and senator at Washington City, Mitchill also served in the state legislature at Albany until 1810. His terms of office as a federal and state representative did not prevent him from accepting an offer in 1807 to serve as the professor of chemistry at the College of Physicians and Surgeons, a medical school recently established in New York City by the New York County Medical Society.

Mitchill was a member of innumerable local organizations ranging from the avowedly comical Krout Club (Mitchill was elected Grand Krout in 1822) to the more dignified New-York Literary and Philosophical Society. The latter organization—the first scientific institution in New York

<hr/>

[2] My account of Mitchill's scientific interests is based on Hall, *Scientist in the Early Republic*. For a comprehensive treatment of his political career, see Alan David Aberbach, *In Search of an American Identity: Samuel Latham Mitchill, Jeffersonian Nationalist*, American University Studies, vol. 46 (New York: Peter Lang, 1988), 13–24.

City—was the dominant scientific society in New York until the appearance of the Lyceum in 1817. Since the Literary and Philosophical Society epitomized the patrician model on the local scene and since the founders of the Lyceum so clearly rejected it as an acceptable mode of science, it is worth our while to look at the history of the Literary and Philosophical Society in some detail.

While the Society was organized by three individuals whose scientific credentials were beyond reproach—Mitchill, the physician David Hosack, and DeWitt Clinton—it also enrolled many local worthies whose inclusion was determined more by social status than by intellectual achievements. The early members of the Literary and Philosophical Society included John H. Hobart, the Episcopal Bishop of New York; James Kent, Chancellor of the State of New York; Thomas Eddy, a wealthy Quaker philanthropist; and the politicians Rufus King and Gouverneur Morris. Thus the New-York Literary and Philosophical Society was, like the American Philosophical Society in Philadelphia and the American Academy of Arts and Sciences in Boston, a strictly patrician organization of the local elite. The first meeting of the Literary and Philosophical Society took place in January 1814 in the Mayor's office in City Hall; at the second meeting one week later the mayor of New York, DeWitt Clinton, was elected president of the Society. The Literary and Philosophical Society aspired to cover four areas of knowledge: history, literature, and moral philosophy; medicine, chemistry, and natural history; mathematics and astronomy; and finally, agriculture, manufacturing, and the "useful arts." There was, at some future date, to be a library and a collection of specimens of natural history.[3]

The Society's early election of DeWitt Clinton as its first president brought considerable advantages to the fledgling organization; thus in May 1814 a charter of incorporation was rapidly granted by the state legislature. Clinton's stature gave the Society immediate recognition: the mayor's first presidential address to the Literary and Philosophical Society, a review of the condition and progress of science in the United States, attracted great attention among the literati when it was published in the first volume of the Society's *Transactions* in 1815. Clinton had many political enemies, however, and, as a consequence, the Literary and Philosophical Society, much to the consternation of the members, was the object of constant attack from the Federalist press. The *American*, for ex-

---

[3] Jonathan Harris, "New York's First Scientific Body: The Literary and Philosophical Society, 1814–1834," *Annals of the New York Academy of Sciences* 172(1970): 331.

3. DEWITT CLINTON (1769–1828). Clinton served in the state legislature (1797–1802), represented New York in the United States Senate (1802–1803), and was mayor of New York City for the next twelve years except for two terms from 1807 to 1811. During his mayoralty Clinton was a prominent member and patron of many New York cultural, philanthropic, and educational organizations; he was elected an honorary member of the Lyceum of Natural History in December 1818. (From an oil painting [c. 1816] by John W. Jarvis. *Courtesy of the National Portrait Gallery, Smithsonian Institution.*)

ample, caustically questioned the character of men who could elect Clinton as their president and, in a pointed reference to both the Literary and Philosophical Society and the New-York Historical Society (of which Clinton was also a leading member), remarked that

> about twenty-five years ago, when the Royal Society of England was in the very zenith of its usefulness and lustre, Sir Joseph Banks was, by some management or accident, elected President, and the Society was filled with a herd of titled blockheads, of talking smatterers, of collectors, compilers, and butterfly hunters. . . . Something like this has taken place in our own city. . . . Mr. Clinton's management, aided by the weakness of some, the easy good nature of others, and the culpable and sullen indifference of the rest . . . has succeeded in getting the entire control of these bodies; and it has ever since sat like an Incubus upon them, pressing them down in a leaden death-like torpor.[4]

Clinton's enemies missed no opportunity to ridicule his scientific interests. Gulian Verplanck, one of Clinton's many adversaries, was the principal author of a series of sketches of the mayor that appeared at regular intervals in the Federalist press; it was a source of considerable discomfort for the target of Verplanck's sarcasm that the widespread popularity of the series warranted its subsequent appearance as a pamphlet:

> Of *Clinton* will I sing, and what sage Pell
> Hath told in swelling prose, in verse I'll tell,
> His martial deeds upon Hoboken's shore,
> His skill in conch-shells, and his Indian lore,
> Tell, how the learned all his works review
> In China, Sweden, Hayti, and Peru;
> How in yon hall, to science dear, and fame,
> Clinton and Newton, equal honours claim.

Verplanck also lampooned Clinton's stature as a leading member of the Literary and Philosophical Society; the poet wrote

> Of learn'd societies, that nothing need
> In every walk of science to succeed,
> Save more attention, and some more expense,
> And some more learning—and a little sense.[5]

---

[4] Editorial, *The American* (New York), 24 November 1819. For DeWitt Clinton's scientific accomplishments, see Jonathan Harris, "DeWitt Clinton as Naturalist," *New-York Historical Society Quarterly* 56(1972): 265–284; Vivian C. Hopkins, "The Empire State—DeWitt Clinton's Laboratory," *New-York Historical Society Quarterly* 59(1975): 7–44.

[5] "To the Author of Dick Shift," *The American* (New York), 30 October 1819; Robert W. July, *The Essential New Yorker: Gulian Crommelin Verplanck* (Durham, NC: Duke University

Since—on account of his association with Clinton—Samuel Latham Mitchill was also an occasional target of the poets, the controversies that swirled around Clinton in the byzantine world of New York politics may have given Mitchill second thoughts about putting all his scientific eggs into one basket; certainly it was true that the Literary and Philosophical Society was not the haven of peace and quiet for which the New York savant had hoped. Mitchill's concern was fueled not only by Clinton's political notoriety but also by the idea that there was an alternative institutional model for the organization of science—an alternative, that is, to the model provided by the august elitism of the American Philosophical Society.

In 1812 in Philadelphia a small group of obscure savants had organized the Academy of Natural Sciences which, as soon as it had abandoned its original grandiose plans of re-making the world through science, soon developed into a respectable, albeit small and impoverished, scientific society. As a consequence, only two years after its establishment, the Academy had attracted a sizable group of young men who, while interested in science, were socially unqualified to become members of the American Philosophical Society. Reuben Haines, who joined the Academy in 1814, was a typical recruit in the early years—Haines earned a living as a merchant, was a devout Quaker, and although he had not had the advantage of a collegiate education, he was deeply interested in science. More important for our purposes, Haines had married a young lady from New York, Jane Bowne, whom he had met through mutual friends among the Quaker community. Not long after he had joined the Academy Haines was elected secretary and was thus counted among the Academy's leading members.[6]

Since several prominent members of the New York scientific community belonged to the Society of Friends, Haines's Quaker background provided him with easy access to the small circle of New York scientists. In

Press, 1951), 68. Pell refers to Clinton's secretary; Hoboken was the site of Clinton's dueling activities. The pamphlet appeared as *The State Triumvirate, A Political Tale: And the Epistles of Brevet Major Pindar Puff*. Ibid., 273. For a persuasive analysis of the complex political feuds in New York politics at the time, see Alvin Kass, *Politics in New York State, 1800–1830* (Syracuse, NY: Syracuse University Press, 1965), 28–54.

[6] For the founding of the Academy of Natural Sciences, see Simon Baatz, "Philadelphia Patronage: The Institutional Structure of Natural History in the New Republic, 1800–1833," *Journal of the Early Republic* 8(1988): 117–120; Charlotte M. Porter, *The Eagle's Nest: Natural History and American Ideas, 1812–1842* (University, AL: University of Alabama Press, 1986), 3–7. Benjamin Say to Reuben Haines, 22 November 1813, Folder 192, Box 16, Series II, Reuben Haines III Papers, American Philosophical Society (hereafter cited as APS).

1812, while courting his future wife, Haines made several journeys to New York where he met many of the savants. In February 1812, for example, Haines attended lectures on botany at the Elgin Botanical Garden by the Quaker scientist, Caspar Wistar Eddy:

> Dr C. W. Eddy called at No 258 Pearl Street to invite us to attend a lecture he proposed giving yesterday morning on botany to which he had invited his Aunt Hossack and a select party of Ladies in addition to the Medical Students. We attended with T. Eddys daughters there were 10 ladies & 30 gentlemen present who I believe were all gratified. . . . *Elgin* Green house supplied the lectures with the requisite specimens.[7]

Within a short time Haines had become a familiar figure in the New York community. Samuel Latham Mitchill was one New York Quaker who took an especial interest in the young Philadelphian and it was not long before Haines was accompanying Mitchill to the Fulton Fish Market in search of new species; to a close friend in Philadelphia, Haines wrote in April 1813 that he had

> found various modes of employing myself here both agreeably and profitably. I have for instance availed myself of B D Perkins Collection of shells and Library to study *Conchology.* I have read two works on *Perspective* . . . and derived great pleasure from perusing Colemans 2nd Volume on the *internal structure of the horses foot.* But above all I have had the honour of standing in the Jaw of the Great Whale (*Balaena Mysticetus*) with the learned Saml L Mitchell—besides receiving a *private* lecture from him in the *New York Fish market* and yesterday attending his Introductory lecture to his course on Natural History at the New College.[8]

The friendship between Haines and Mitchill was central to the creation of the Lyceum of Natural History for, after Haines joined the Academy of Natural Sciences in 1814, Mitchill began receiving enthusiastic reports on the Academy's progress. Mitchill's admiration was excited by the Philadelphia success; as he wrote to Haines in February 1814: "I am glad to hear that the ingenious gentlemen of your city, have embodied themselves into an association for promoting Science. There is no country having pretensions to civilization, in which they who devote themselves to such investigations, have so much to expect as in this."[9]

[7] Reuben Haines to James Pemberton Parke, 25 February 1812, Folder 128, Box 14, Series II, Reuben Haines III Papers, APS.

[8] Reuben Haines to James Pemberton Parke, 5 April 1813, Folder 136, Box 15, Series II, Reuben Haines III Papers, APS.

[9] Mitchill to Haines, 8 February 1814, Folder 196, Box 16, Series II, Reuben Haines III Papers, APS.

At the same time as Mitchill was learning of developments in Philadelphia, Haines was relaying news of the New York scientific community
to his friends in the Academy of Natural Sciences. Thus, when Mitchill
informed Haines in 1813 that a petition had been presented to the City
Council on behalf of several cultural institutions for the use of the almshouse opposite City Hall, Haines suggested to his comrades in the
Academy that a similar effort might be successful in Philadelphia. Accordingly, in January 1814, at a meeting of the Academy, Haines took the floor
to talk about a "memorial written by John Griscom of New York and
presented to the corporation of the City Exhibiting the advantages which
would result from the establishment of a publick institution for the cultivation of general Science."[10]

The Academy of Natural Sciences was unsuccessful in persuading the
City of Philadelphia to grant a similar advantage to the local scientific societies; nevertheless when members of the Academy began a lecture-
series on science for the general public there was an immediate and enthusiastic response. In 1814 the Academy set up a committee to review
plans for a lecture-series on botany; at a subsequent meeting a report of
the committee was read which concluded that the "plan of lectures on
Botany for the use of the Ladies of Philadelphia . . . will be very honour-
able to the Society." An agreement with the Philadelphia Society for Promoting Agriculture for the use of a lecture-room was reached and within
a few weeks the two lecturers, John Barnes and James Waterhouse, were
speaking in front of an eager audience. The talks were very profitable for
the Academy; even though each member of the Academy was "permitted to introduce one lady" while the two speakers were given an un-
limited number of free tickets, enough ladies paid for admission for the
Academy to make a handsome profit. Samuel Latham Mitchill, who had
been watching the progress of the Academy with interest, sent his con-
gratulations to Haines on the successful inauguration of the botanical lectures: "I am glad to hear that your philadelphia damseles are indulging
their taste for Botany. It will be a charming employment for those whose
situation in life likens them to the lillies of the valley. . . . It would gratify
me highly to step in, and take a seat among these blooming daughters
of Flora."[11]

[10] Minutes of the Academy of Natural Sciences, 18 January 1814, Academy of Natural
Sciences (hereafter cited as ANS).

[11] Minutes of the Academy of Natural Sciences, 19 April 1814, 26 April 1814, 5 July 1814,
ANS; Samuel Latham Mitchill to Reuben Haines, 1 June 1814, Folder 196, Box 16, Series
II, Reuben Haines III Papers, APS.

An attempt at emulation on Mitchill's part in New York could not, however, be successfully achieved through the New-York Literary and Philosophical Society, an organization that explicitly eschewed any popularization of natural knowledge and relied instead on winning the support of the wealthy elite. Thus, in the latter part of 1816, Mitchill, stimulated by the positive example of the Academy of Natural Sciences and discouraged by the apparent torpor of the Literary and Philosophical Society, began to canvass his friends and acquaintances on the feasibility of establishing a new scientific organization.

He received the warmest response from the medical students at the College of Physicians and Surgeons—many of whom had first become acquainted with science through attending Mitchill's lectures on natural history. Since it was not probable that the Literary and Philosophical Society would soon open its doors to medical students who had yet to make their way in the world, Mitchill had a ready audience at the College of Physicians and Surgeons for his plans. This audience was eager to pursue science as an avocation and thus quickly responded to Mitchill's plan for a new organization. Accordingly on 29 January 1817, Mitchill convened a "meeting of a Number of Gentlemen favourable to the cultivation of *Natural Science* . . . at the hall of the College of Physicians & Surgeons, in Barclay Street." Mitchill was aware that his initiative might encounter resistance from those patricians most strongly connected with the Literary and Philosophical Society; as a consequence, he proposed merely that a committee be formed to consider the "adoption of measures for instituting a *Cabinet of Natural History*."[12]

This committee, which included Peter S. Townsend, a prominent physician, and Frederick C. Schaeffer, the Lutheran pastor of St. Matthew's Church, recommended, at a second meeting on 3 February, that a new scientific society was "perfectly practicable" and that those individuals interested in forming it "invite such of their friends as would probably unite with them" to a further meeting on the following Friday. It was not long before the Lyceum of Natural History (as the new organization was called) was engaged in adopting a constitution, looking for meeting rooms, and debating the conditions of membership. Within three weeks and after much discussion the constitution was formally ratified by a full meeting of the membership and, as the first significant act of the Lyceum, a group of officers was elected to run the society for the following year.[13]

[12] Minutes of the Lyceum of Natural History, 29 January 1817, New York Academy of Sciences (hereafter cited as NYAS). See also Kenneth R. Nodyne, "The Founding of the Lyceum of Natural History," *Annals of the New York Academy of Sciences* 172(1970): 142.

[13] Minutes of the Lyceum of Natural History, 3 February 1817, 24 February 1817, NYAS.

4. THE COLLEGE OF PHYSICIANS AND SURGEONS. The Lyceum of Natural History held its founding meeting on 29 January 1817 in a room in the College of Physicians and Surgeons on Barclay Street near Broadway. The Lyceum continued to meet at the college until 21 April 1817 when it moved into a room at the New-York Institution. (*Courtesy of the New York Academy of Medicine.*)

As everybody anticipated, Mitchill was elected to the presidency. The members also chose two vice-presidents, Frederick Schaeffer and the botanist Caspar Wistar Eddy; as corresponding secretary, the physician John Wakefield Francis and, as recording secretary, John B. Beck, a recent graduate of the College of Physicians and Surgeons. The new treasurer was Benjamin P. Kissam while the curators of the Lyceum's collections included John Torrey, D'Jurco V. Knevels, and Ezekiel R. Baudoine.[14]

The connection between the Lyceum and the College of Physicians and Surgeons was particularly pronounced. Almost all of the twenty-one men who signed the constitution of the Lyceum at the meeting of

[14] Minutes of the Lyceum of Natural History, 24 February 1817, NYAS.

24 February were recent graduates of the College while two, Mitchill and Francis, served respectively as professors of natural history and the institutes of medicine at the College. The link between medicine and science was based, in the case of the Lyceum, on Mitchill's position at the medical college; in a more general sense, science during the early nineteenth century was closely connected to medicine principally because, in an era when science was not part of the college curriculum but was taught only in the medical colleges, it was a general procedure for students interested in science to register for the medical degree. In addition, since there was no career structure for science and since employment as a scientist was exceptional, the choice of medicine as a profession was eminently logical since it enabled a savant to make a respectable livelihood while also providing him with the leisure for scientific studies.

Medicine was a resource for the Lyceum in a second sense in that the initial meetings of the group were generally held in rooms at the College of Physicians and Surgeons. This was not a desirable choice, however, because the medical community in New York was then divided into several warring factions; the Lyceum, if it continued to meet in the College rooms, ran the risk of becoming too closely identified with one of the principal factions. Fortunately, however, only a year before the creation of the Lyceum, the City Council had given the use of the New-York Institution to the various cultural groups in the city. If the Lyceum were to obtain a room in the Institution it would no longer be beholden to the College of Physicians and Surgeons and, more important, it would be able to emulate the Academy of Natural Sciences in building up a museum and holding public lectures.[15]

Fortunately for the Lyceum a ready solution to the problem of accommodation was available. Shortly after the establishment of the New-York Institution a small room had been ceded for the use of the United States Military Philosophical Society, an organization founded at West Point in 1803 that held peripatetic meetings for several years at various cities in the north-east wherever there was a concentration of military officers interested in science and literature. The organizing spirit behind the United States Military Philosophical Society was Joseph G. Swift, a former superintendent of West Point who, for several years after the War of 1812, was in charge of constructing the harbor fortifications at New York. Swift had heard of the establishment of the Lyceum of Natural His-

---

[15] On the medical disputes in the city, see Byron Stookey, *A History of Colonial Medical Education in the Province of New York, With its Subsequent Development (1767–1830)* (Springfield, IL: Charles C Thomas, 1962), 190–220.

22 ANNALS NEW YORK ACADEMY OF SCIENCES

tory and, in a letter written to Caspar Wistar Eddy in April 1817, volunteered the use of the room in the New-York Institution for the meetings of the Lyceum. The offer was immediately accepted, Swift was honored by a life membership in the Lyceum, and, on 21 April, the members met for the first time in the New-York Institution.[16]

The new arrangement proved valuable for the Lyceum for the members were anxious to begin a program of lectures, to collect a cabinet of natural history specimens, and to establish a library. The initial program of activities was ambitious; the Committee on Lectures, which included Frederick Schaeffer, Caspar Wistar Eddy, and Constantine Samuel Rafinesque, recommended that "every Resident Member shall within six months . . . read or cause to be read before the Society, a paper on any subject connected with Natural History, which shall be considered their *admission paper.*" For purposes of discussion, the Lyceum was divided into nineteen sub-divisions "in order that different gentlemen may be appointed to deliver Lectures thereon—so that the Lyceum shall have one Lecture on some one or other of the numerous branches comprehended under the term of Natural History." Leading members were to take responsibility for one or more of these subdivisions. Thus, Samuel Latham Mitchill was to oversee ichthyology, plaxology, apalology, and ecology; Constantine Samuel Rafinesque had charge of helminthology, polypology, atmology, hydrology, and taxonomy; John LeConte supervised mastodology, erpetology, and glossology; Frederick Schaeffer was responsible for mineralogy, Benjamin P. Kissam for ornithology, John Torrey for entomology, Peter S. Townsend for oryctology, D'Jurco V. Knevels for conchology, Caspar Wistar Eddy for botany, and James Clements for zootomy.[17]

Such an ambitious program was not to be realized; the members of the Lyceum, in their eagerness to avoid the apparent languor of the Lit-

[16] Ralph S. Bates, *Scientific Societies in the United States,* 2d ed. (Cambridge, MA: Massachusetts Institute of Technology, 1958), 42; James L. Morrison Jr., *"The Best School in the World": West Point, the Pre-Civil War Years, 1833–1866* (Kent, OH: Kent State University Press, 1986), 3; Swift to Eddy, 2 April 1817, in Minutes of the Lyceum of Natural History, 9 April 1817, NYAS; Minutes of the Lyceum of Natural History, 21 April 1817, NYAS.

[17] Report of the Committee on Lectures, in Minutes of the Lyceum of Natural History, 24 March 1817, NYAS. One member elected to the Lyceum during this period was subsequently unmasked as a British spy; Charles Hamilton Smith used his scientific activity as a cover for espionage for, as he wrote to his masters in Whitehall, "under pretence of botany and geology I could pursue my objects with comparative security." See Kenneth Bourne, "Mr. Smith: An Early Honorary Member," *New-York Historical Society Quarterly* 52(1968): 188.

erary and Philosophical Society, quickly overextended themselves—as a consequence the stipulation in the constitution that every member had to deliver a lecture was quietly dropped. The enthusiasm of the membership remained undimmed, however, and in May 1817, a proposal was put forward for the Lyceum's first scientific expedition. In August 1816, Mitchill's Philadelphia friend, Reuben Haines, had reported that he had "paid several interesting visits to the marle beds in the neighbourhood of Middletown and have some antediluvian remains to bring home with me—Oyster shells, Belemmites and a portion of one of the large bones of the mammoth weighing near 10 lbs."[18]

For the Lyceum members this was exciting news. They all knew of the spectacular exhibit of the mastodon that was on display at Peale's Museum in Philadelphia; if they were to emulate Charles Willson Peale and bring back to New York the skeleton of a second mammoth, their discovery would not only heighten the reputation of the Lyceum among the scientific community in New York but would also provide the Lyceum with a regular income from the thousands of curious citizens who would pay—as they did in Philadelphia—to catch a glimpse of a spectacular sight from the antediluvian past. Peale had been successful almost beyond measure; not only was his mammoth a sensation in the scientific world but, in addition, it had proved a lucrative investment as Philadelphians had flocked to see it for an entrance fee of fifty cents. A suggestion had even been entertained by a few New Yorkers that the skeleton (which Peale had discovered at Newburgh) should not have been allowed to leave New York State; the physician, David Hosack, remarked to Peale that he "was sory that I had got the bones I asked him wherefore, and he said they ought not to have let them go out of the State." Samuel Latham Mitchill was more generous—when Peale's son, Rembrandt, visited New York to display a second skeleton preparatory to making a grand tour with it in Europe, Mitchill announced the fact in his journal, the *Medical Repository*.[19]

Thus, in May 1817 Mitchill and Peter Townsend went, "under the sanction of the Society," to the area where Reuben Haines had previously discovered the mammoth bone. Their search was successful and on 2 June the members of the Lyceum of Natural History heard a report by Townsend in "which was given a history of their excursion and an account of

[18] Reuben Haines to Hannah Haines, 14 August 1816, Folder 146, Box 15, Series II, Reuben Haines III Papers, APS.

[19] Charles Coleman Sellers, *Mr. Peale's Museum: Charles Willson Peale and the First Popular Museum of Natural Science and Art* (New York: W. W. Norton & Co., 1980), 129, 147.

the discovery of a fossil Mammoth a part of whose remains they have brought with them . . . which were laid before the Lyceum. On motion the thanks of the Society were returned to Drs Mitchill & Townsend for their industry & zeal & the paper was ordered to be deposited in the archives of the Society." Two weeks later, news of another mammoth—this time in Ulster County—came to the attention of the Lyceum. The report mentioned that a local landowner, D. W. Wharry, had already secured permission for the Lyceum to "make the necessary digging and removal" and, for a second time, a committee was dispatched to make investigations.[20]

All this activity on the part of the Lyceum made a great impression on the New York intelligentsia. News of the Lyceum's spectacular discovery of the mastodon bones gave members of the New-York Literary and Philosophical Society cause to wonder if their own work were being overshadowed by the activity of the younger organization. John Pintard, secretary of the Literary and Philosophical Society, accurately reflected the consternation of the membership when he reported to his daughter that:

> a young assoc^n composing the Lyceum are doing wonders, chiefly young physicians that intelligent & most excursive of all the professional branches. Parts of a mammoth have been discovered by them & a subscrip^n is on foot to explore the Mammoths ground in hopes of recovering a complete skeleton, so that this city may boast as well as Phil^a of an exhibition of the wonderful extinct animal. I had contemplated this project for Scudders Museum, but we are anticipated thro' the zeal of these aspiring youths, who will eclipse the old Societies if we do not take care.[21]

Unfortunately a weak response to the Lyceum's subscription appeal (only $171 were raised) dashed the hopes of the members of rivalling Peale's Museum. A minor scandal within the Lyceum committee appointed to bring back the bones finished off the project; after a great deal of prodding, four members of the committee, James Clements, John Torrey, Ezekiel Baudoine, and Peter Townsend, could account for only $136 and on further inquiry were unable to explain the "apparent discrepancy of the several accounts and some unallowable expenses." The fifth member of the committee was nowhere to be found; Benjamin Akerly had made off with the remaining thirty-five dollars.[22]

[20] Minutes of the Lyceum of Natural History, 19 May 1817, 2 June 1817, 16 June 1817, NYAS.

[21] *Letters from John Pintard to his Daughter, Eliza Noel Pintard Davidson, 1816–1833,* 4 vols. (New York: New-York Historical Society, 1940), 1: 66.

[22] Minutes of the Lyceum of Natural History, 19 January 1818, NYAS.

This unfortunate conclusion to a promising business had a chilling effect on any remaining enthusiasm for dragging back mammoth bones to New York; Samuel Latham Mitchill tried periodically to beat the drum for a further expedition, even reporting on one occasion that a live mammoth had been spotted near Natchez, but no-one's heart was in a second attempt after Akerly's dispiriting abduction of their subscription money and the affair was quietly dropped.[23]

In later years the Lyceum flourished and prospered. In April 1818 the state legislature granted the Lyceum a charter; the act of incorporation was guided through the legislative process at Albany by Henry Meigs, a sympathetic state senator. A second success was an agreement reached with Horatio Bigelow to publish précis of the Lyceum's meetings in his monthly journal, the *American Monthly Magazine and Critical Review*. With great reluctance the members of the Lyceum had abandoned – for the moment at least – the idea of publishing a journal; notices of its activities in the *American Monthly Magazine and Critical Review* at least served the purpose of informing the local clerisy of the Lyceum's activities.[24]

In 1820 a small faction of physicians within the New York County Medical Society launched a campaign against the medical faculty of the College of Physicians and Surgeons on the ostensible grounds that the professoriate was abusing its monopoly on medical education in New York to charge exorbitant fees. The campaign was energetic and determined and, as a consequence, Samuel Latham Mitchill, who was then president of the medical college, found himself increasingly preoccupied with the battle against the insurgent faction (which counted among its supporters several of the trustees of the medical college). Since the College of Physicians and Surgeons received its charter from the state legislature, each side in the dispute looked for support from the representatives at Albany; thus Mitchill was forced to spend protracted periods of time at the state capital when the Senate and Assembly were in session.

The insurgents of the New York County Medical Society aimed eventually to replace the incumbent professors; with his professional position at stake, Mitchill became increasingly disinclined to preside over the affairs of the Lyceum. Consequently the leadership of the Lyceum passed to a triumvirate that guided the organization through the next decade with great aplomb. During this period the Lyceum went from

---

[23] Minutes of the Lyceum of Natural History, 20 July 1818, NYAS.
[24] Minutes of the Lyceum of Natural History, 14 July 1817, 26 May 1817, 27 April 1818, NYAS.

5. JOHN TORREY (1796–1873). A graduate of the College of Physicians and Surgeons and a founding member of the Lyceum of Natural History, Torrey served as president of the Lyceum from 1824 to 1826 and again in 1838. (From a miniature portrait [c. 1825] in ivory by Henry Inman. *Courtesy of the Frick Art Reference Library.*)

strength to strength—its accomplishments under the combined leadership of John Torrey, James Ellsworth DeKay, and William Cooper included the launching of a regular journal, the organization of a small, but creditable, museum, and the accumulation of a valuable and extensive library.

John Torrey, who was a founding member of the Lyceum, had begun his medical studies at the College of Physicians and Surgeons in 1815; he heard of plans to establish a new scientific society from his professor, Samuel Latham Mitchill, and was present at all of the early meetings of the Lyceum. Torrey provides the classic example of the usefulness of medicine as a profession for the study of science in the early decades of the nineteenth century. After he graduated from the College of Physicians and Surgeons in 1818, Torrey began a medical practice despite his very obvious desire to study natural history on a full-time basis. Since he spent most of his time either attending to the affairs of the Lyceum or studying botany Torrey was never a very successful physician; his small medical practice was sufficient, however, to enable him to live in modest comfort.

Torrey's zeal and enthusiasm for botany were so pronounced that, even though he was only twenty years old, Torrey was elected a curator of the Lyceum at its meeting of 24 February 1817. When the Lyceum voted to "compile and publish a Flora of the Country extending 30 miles round the City," Torrey volunteered to serve on the committee charged with organizing the task; within a short period, he had taken on the whole job by himself and within two years the Lyceum was able to announce to the world its *Catalogue of Plants*—written and compiled by Torrey and published by the Lyceum.[25]

In 1824, Torrey—despite his aversion to public speaking—secured a teaching position at the West Point Military Academy as professor of chemistry, mineralogy, and geology. Three years later he moved back to New York where he occupied the chair of chemistry at the College of Physicians and Surgeons. The latter position was undoubtedly prestigious— the College of Physicians and Surgeons was the oldest medical school in the city and many prominent New York medical men expected that, in years to come, it would rival both Penn and Harvard in prestige, enrollment, and faculty.

Torrey's appointment had an ironic and not altogether pleasant twist to it since Torrey was now a member of the professoriate that had supplanted the former faculty of Physicians and Surgeons which included Samuel Latham Mitchill and David Hosack, Torrey's former professors when he had himself been a student. The resignation, *en masse*, of the previous professoriate was a consequence of the battle that had begun in 1820 between two medical factions. In 1826 Mitchill and Hosack, together with John Wakefield Francis, John Griscom, and Francis Mac-Neven, formed a connection with Rutgers College in New Brunswick and established a new school in New York City called the Rutgers Medical College. Unfortunately, after four years of bitter wrangling, the Rutgers Medical College was defeated on account of the refusal by the New York legislature to give a charter to a medical college tied to a parent institution

---

[25] Minutes of the Lyceum of Natural History, 5 May 1817, NYAS; Asa Gray, "John Torrey, 1796–1873," *Biographical Memoirs of the National Academy of Sciences* 1(1877): 268.

in New Jersey. Thus the careers of two of the city's most eminent physicians ended on a sad note—Mitchill never recovered from this bitter
blow to his professional pride and died one year later while Hosack left
the city and his medical practice and retired to a country estate a few
miles north of New York City.[26]

Torrey's appointment in 1827 at the College of Physicians and Surgeons was not directly linked to the contretemps—he had been invited
by the new faculty to fill the chemical chair on account of his obvious competence, energy, and enthusiasm. For the Lyceum his appointment was
a welcome event since, as soon as he moved back to the city, he once
again became an active member, serving as vice-president of the Lyceum
for many years.

James Ellsworth DeKay was the second triumvir of the Lyceum during
the 1820s. Like Torrey, DeKay was a physician—he received his medical
degree from the University of Edinburgh in 1819—but he too practiced
medicine in a half-hearted way, preferring instead to spend his time at
the hall of the Lyceum chatting with his scientific friends and reading natural history books in the Lyceum's library. Before going to Edinburgh,
DeKay had been close friends with a bohemian group of young poets
and writers in New York City, most notably Joseph Rodman Drake and
Fitz-Greene Halleck. The latter, one of the principal authors of the series
of satirical poems—known collectively as *The Croakers*—that appeared at
regular intervals in the *Evening Post* throughout 1819, immortalized the
young DeKay in a sketch that nicely captures the foibles of the savant:

> The tea urn is singing, the tea cups are gay,
> The fire sparkles bright in the room of D.K.
> For the first time these six months a broom has been there
> And the house maid has brushed every table and chair;
> Drugs, minerals, books, are all hidden from view,
> And the five shabby pictures are varnished anew;
> There's a feast going on, there's the devil to pay
> In the furnished apartments of Doctor D.K.[27]

DeKay was elected to the Lyceum in 1819 after his return from Edinburgh; according to one reminiscent, he was a "short, square-built, dark-

---

[26] Christine Chapman Robbins, *David Hosack: Citizen of New York*, Memoirs of the American Philosophical Society, no. 62 (Philadelphia, 1964), 121–132; Henry Burnell Shafer, *The
American Medical Profession, 1783–1850* (New York: Columbia University Press, 1936), 82–85.

[27] To find out what transpired at DeKay's apartment that evening, read Fitz-Greene Hal-
leck, "The Tea Party," in *The Croakers*, by Joseph Rodman Drake and Fitz-Greene Halleck
(New York, 1860), 110–111. Halleck's poem, written in 1820, was first published in 1856; see
"Original Poems by Drake and Halleck," *The Home Journal*, 7 June 1856, 2.

complexioned man, of grave aspect, but very courteous in manner." He was also a model of efficiency for, in the years following his return to New York, he edited and published the *Annals* of the Lyceum, cataloged the growing library, and helped establish a modest natural history museum in the rooms of the Lyceum in the New-York Institution.[28]

William Cooper was the third member who ensured the Lyceum's survival and success during the 1820s. Like Torrey, Cooper had been one of that small band of young men who had followed Mitchill's lead in establishing the Lyceum. Cooper had been only nineteen years old when he joined the Lyceum; since he was one of those fortunate few who are blessed with wealthy parents, he never had to work for a living; thus he was one of the few founding members of the Lyceum with no connection to the medical world. Cooper used his free time to become an expert in zoology; although he published little, in later life he achieved a certain renown in scientific circles for a pioneering monograph on the mammals of South America; in recognition of his work Cooper became the first American to be elected a member of the Zoological Society of London. He was a stalwart member of the Lyceum; for the first two years he served as the recording secretary and in 1824 he was elected the treasurer of the Lyceum. He remained active in the Lyceum's affairs for the better part of fifty years; at his death in 1864 he was vice-president of the society.[29]

Cooper, Torrey, and DeKay constituted the triumvirate that, during the 1820s, controlled and organized the Lyceum's affairs with great success. At a time when science received little financial support from any section of society it is no small tribute to their competency that the Lyceum not only survived but continued to flourish and prosper. No better proof of this statement can be found than the publication of the Lyceum's journal, the *Annals*.

In the early nineteenth century the most potent symbol of success for the small scientific clubs that dotted the cities and towns of the northeastern seaboard was the publication of a scientific journal. Yet, because the number of scientists in the United States was so small and because the general audience for serious science was virtually non-existent it was almost impossible for a journal to pay its way. The history of the *Annals* was fraught with difficulties; the eventual success of the members in es-

[28] Herman Le Roy Fairchild, *A History of the New York Academy of Sciences* (New York, 1887), 85.

[29] Fairchild, *History*, 70–73; *Biographical Sketch of the Late William Cooper* (New York, n.d.), 5–8.

tablishing a permanent journal can be better appreciated by contrasting its survival with the early demise of a predecessor, Archibald Bruce's *American Mineralogical Journal.*

In 1810, when Bruce, professor of materia medica at the College of Physicians and Surgeons, began publishing a journal of science, he expected that it would not only endure but would also prosper. While the journal did attract considerable attention at first—Bruce wrote in 1811 that it had "greatly increased in circulation having within a very short time since received orders for its being sent to France Germany Eng. Scotland & Ireland"—once the novelty had worn off the *American Mineralogical Journal* became prohibitively expensive to continue as the number of subscriptions remained at a low level.[30]

By 1813 Bruce was clearly struggling to keep the *American Mineralogical Journal* in existence; since it was running in debt, Bruce was unable to hire any editorial assistance and the various tasks of printing, correspondence, and editing were proving to be heavy burdens. His declining health as well as his professional troubles (Bruce had left the College of Physicians and Surgeons to join the faculty of a rival medical school) contributed to the eventual demise of the journal; after 1814 no additional numbers appeared.

The second attempt at launching a scientific periodical in the United States came in 1817 when Benjamin Silliman, professor of chemistry at Yale College, established the *American Journal of Science and Arts*. Silliman was motivated to the task by the thought that, with the demise of Bruce's *American Mineralogical Journal*, the American scientific community had no means of communicating the results of their research; nevertheless Silliman began his endeavor with considerable reluctance: "[my] avocations are very numerous & I can hardly see how I can do justice to such an undertaking." Nevertheless, once publication had begun, Silliman was relentless in promoting the journal wherever he might find the possibility of support. The first number of the *American Journal of Science and Arts* was greeted with considerable enthusiasm and, much to his surprise, Silliman found that a second edition would be necessary: "the edition of No 1. is all gone except a few copies—we printed 1000 & shall print 1500 of No 2 & shall soon reprint No 1."[31]

---

[30] Bruce to Benjamin Silliman, 25 July 1811, Folder 1, Box 18, Silliman Family Manuscripts, Sterling Memorial Library, Yale University (hereafter cited as YU). A history of the journal can be found in John C. Greene, "Introduction," in Archibald Bruce, ed., *The American Mineralogical Journal* (1814; reprint, New York: Hafner Publishing Co., 1968), vii–xvii.
[31] Silliman to Parker Cleaveland, 6 October 1817, Parker Cleaveland Papers, Bowdoin

Within less than a year, however, the initial signs of success had begun to fade. Silliman's optimistic estimates of the journal's progress were soon replaced by anxiety over an expense that was not being met by the level of subscriptions. By July 1819 Silliman was warning his close friend, Parker Cleaveland, professor of mineralogy at Bowdoin College, that the "Journal is however in danger on the score of much expence & little return—a new plan must be adopted & I think N° 5 must be considerably delayed in order to accomplish it." Indeed, by August, the situation was edging perilously close to bankruptcy: the printer refused to produce the fifth number until he had received $2500 owed for the four numbers of the first volume. There was no problem with the contributions from aspiring authors who submitted more material than Silliman could deal with; unfortunately the laggard subscribers were not remitting their contributions: "I am ready to publish another number immediately if the publishers were not afraid to proceed till they have 2500$ for Vol 1 while not 1/3 of that sum has been paid altho there are 11 or 12 hundred subscribers." By December the journal had stopped appearing and the fifth number was indefinitely postponed until Silliman was able to assure the printer that he would receive prompt payment: "the Journal is now at a stand. . . . Negociations are going on for a new arrangement . . . it is temporarily suspended but is expected to issue again after possibly some months. . . . I can however promise nothing absolutely except strenuous exertions to carry it on."[32]

Silliman had learnt a painful lesson: the fickleness of the scientific public often masqueraded as enthusiasm. Twelve hundred subscribers had sent out for their copies of the first volume of the *American Journal of Science and Arts*; when it came to the reckoning, however, less than four hundred made good on their promises and sent on their remittances. Silliman was quick to realize, particularly after an acerbic conversation with his printers, that this situation could not continue: the journal would be received only by those savants who had paid in advance and even Parker Cleaveland was not immune from the stringent regulations: "Mʳ Converse, my manager & publisher, informs me that the work has not been ordered from your place, and we do not send them now unless they are unconditionally purchased by a previous application; any other plan we

College (hereafter cited as BC); Silliman to Isaac Lea, 6 November 1818, Isaac Lea Correspondence, ANS. ()

[32] Silliman to Cleaveland, 27 July 1819, Parker Cleaveland Papers, BC: Silliman to John Torrey, 13 August 1819, John Torrey Correspondence, New York Botanical Garden (hereafter cited as NYBG); Silliman to Torrey, 13 December 1819, John Torrey Correspondence, NYBG.

find will be ruinous and if the work cannot be maintained upon this it must stop."[33]

The size and extent of the American scientific community can be accurately gauged from the figures that Silliman provides. In 1819 the number of paying subscribers for the *American Journal of Science and Arts* was less than four hundred—as Silliman soon found out, this was barely sufficient support for his journal. Silliman, moreover, was only able to sustain it on account of his position as professor of chemistry at Yale; although the college never made any financial contribution to the expenses of the journal, his salary at Yale provided him with the funds and time needed for the publication.

For the Lyceum of Natural History, however, the task of publishing a journal was even more arduous on account of the Lyceum's strictly local influence. That is, because the Lyceum was an organization that relied solely on a New York audience for support, its subscription base was considerably lower than that for the *American Journal of Science and Arts* which was, in intent at least, a national publication. Thus, while Silliman's journal could count four hundred subscribers, the Lyceum was able to recruit, at the most, about one hundred and fifty supporters. The burden that this imposed on the Lyceum members can be clearly perceived in the inability in the initial years of the members to establish a periodical.

As early as July 1817 the Lyceum formed a committee of publication which recommended the "establishment of a Journal . . . whenever the accumulation of materials & funds shall render such a measure expedient." The same committee noted that the proceedings of the Lyceum should continue to appear in the *American Monthly Magazine and Critical Review* and also proposed that a "list of the specimens obtained [by the Lyceum] in Botany, Zoology Mineralogy . . . be inserted in a work about to be commenced by a member of this Society under the title of 'Annals of Nature'."[34]

This latter publication was a journal sponsored on his own initiative by Constantine Samuel Rafinesque, a founding member of the Lyceum. Rafinesque, even at this early period, had had a checkered career; originally from Constantinople, he had lived for two years in Philadelphia; in 1805 he was appointed the chancellor to the American consul at Palermo in Sicily; ten years later he returned to the United States where he passed the remainder of his life. The vessel on which Rafinesque returned was shipwrecked off Long Island and, having lost all his worldly

[33] Silliman to Cleaveland, 11 August 1820, Parker Cleaveland Papers, BC.
[34] Minutes of the Lyceum of Natural History, 14 July 1817, NYAS.

possessions, he was befriended by Samuel Latham Mitchill who secured for Rafinesque a position as a tutor. Thus, when the Lyceum was created in 1817, it was only natural that Mitchill should invite Rafinesque to participate in its initial meetings.

Although he was one of the most energetic and enthusiastic members of the Lyceum, serving on a variety of committees and giving numerous lectures on scientific subjects at the weekly meetings, Rafinesque soon developed a reputation as an incurable eccentric largely on account of his zeal for describing new species which, on many occasions, proved to be based only on incidental characteristics. John James Audubon, who knew Rafinesque well in this period, recalled the New York savant in an incident at his home which, while probably apocryphal, serves to illustrate both Rafinesque's reputation as a fanatical hunter for new species and Audubon's penchant for story-telling:

> every person I imagined was in a deep slumber save myself, when of a sudden I heard a great uproar in the naturalist's room. I got up, reached the place in a few moments, and opened the door, when, to my astonishment I saw my guest running about the room naked, holding the handle of my favourite violin, the body of which he had battered to pieces against the walls in attempting to kill the bats which had entered by the open window. . . . I stood amazed, but he continued jumping and running round and round, until he was fairly exhausted; when he begged me to procure one of the animals for him, as he felt convinced they belonged to 'a new species.'[35]

His reputation as an eccentric was supplemented by a suspicion within the New York scientific community that Rafinesque's science was occasionally spurious; even the mild-mannered Torrey, who rarely delivered a harsh judgement even in the intimacy of his personal correspondence, was skeptical about Rafinesque's abilities as a scientist: "Rafinesque gave me a . . . copy of his Flora of Louisiana. . . . His work is the most curious medley I ever saw. The author without ever being in the country whose plants he describes, has discovered 50 or 60 new species. This is doing business—it ought to make our botanists hang their heads. But Raf. will probably not stop here—I expect he will soon issue proposals for publishing the botany of the *moon* with figures of all the new species!"[36]

Thus, in light of Rafinesque's reputation, it was perhaps fortunate

[35] John James Audubon, "The Eccentric Naturalist," in *Ornithological Biography of An Account of the Habits of the Birds of the United States of America*, 5 vols. (Philadelphia, 1832–1839), 1: 457.

[36] Torrey to Amos Eaton, 21 March 1818, #4604, Miscellaneous Letters, New York State Library.

for the Lyceum that he shortly left New York to take up a position as professor of natural history at Transylvania University in Kentucky. Rafinesque's proposed journal, the *Annals of Nature*, was an abortive attempt to create his own publication outlet for his many putative discoveries in botany. Only one number of his journal appeared; in any case, it was evident to the more perceptive members of the Lyceum that a periodical controlled by Rafinesque would be an unacceptable alternative for the Lyceum.

A more acceptable model for the planned journal of the Lyceum was the periodical published by the Academy of Natural Sciences in Philadelphia. Since its establishment in 1812 the Academy had had plans for a journal; not until 1817, however, when a wealthy philanthropist, William Maclure, joined the Academy, was it possible for the members to produce a periodical. Maclure was soon involved in the Academy plans and, as early as March 1817 a committee set up to examine the feasibility of a journal reported in favor, a second committee began to collect subscriptions, and a third committee (which included Maclure) was charged with arranging "such papers as are now in the posession of the Academy . . . as may be thought deserving of publication, in order to commence the first N⁰ of the journal at an early period." The journal was ready for distribution by May and a fourth committee (with Maclure as one of its three members) was appointed for "the distribution of the journal at their discretion."[37]

While the Lyceum of Natural History, like the Academy of Natural Sciences, possessed energy and enthusiasm, it did not, unfortunately, count among its members a wealthy philanthropist like Maclure. Thus, despite valiant attempts, it proved impossible in the early years to publish a journal. In October 1817 the Lyceum's committee of publication reported that the "publication of any periodical journal was inexpedient at present." Eighteen months later the same committee was ordered to "prepare an abstract of the proceedings of the Lyceum and to select & arrange such communications as have been read before the Society, & offer the same to some respectable bookseller for publication, & that the said Committee report at some future meeting the terms & conditions upon which the same proceedings can be periodically published." After an exhaustive search, the committee, unable to find any bookseller, respectable or otherwise, willing to take the risk of publishing a scientific journal, could only recommend that the Lyceum should send a synopsis of its proceed-

[37] Minutes of the Academy of Natural Sciences, 4 March 1817, 11 March 1817, 18 March 1817, 25 March 1817, 20 May 1817, ANS.

ings to Benjamin Silliman who had generously offered to reserve some space in the *American Journal of Science and Arts*.[38]

With perseverance, however, the Lyceum was gradually able to accumulate the necessary financial and intellectual resources. A friendly rivalry with the Academy of Natural Sciences and a keen perception that the Academy's *Journal* was the best possible advertisement for the organization combined to spur the New Yorkers into action. By April 1823, John Torrey, the vice-president of the Lyceum, could tell his friend, the botanist Lewis David von Schweinitz, that "our *Lyceum* is in a flourishing state, but we need patronage greatly. If we had a Maclure among us we could do a great deal."[39]

By July of the same year the committee of publication reported on the "subject of printing a journal" and was happy to be able to recommend that the "same be published under the title of Annals of the Lyceum of Natural History of New York." Two months later the first number of the *Annals* appeared; the Lyceum triumphantly sent copies to several institutions including the Academy of Natural Sciences, the Wernerian Society of Edinburgh, the Philophuxian Society of Providence, and the Library of Congress. James Ellsworth DeKay, the corresponding secretary of the Lyceum, wrote exultantly to Adolphe Brongniart at the Jardin des Plantes in Paris, enclosing a "copy of the first number of the Annals of the Lyceum. . . . it is proposed to continue it monthly making two volumes a year" and discreetly hinting to the French botanist that he should contribute a paper to the new journal: "we shall be happy to receive communications from our Corresponding Members for the pages of our Journal."[40]

The appearance of the *Annals* immediately heightened the visibility of the Lyceum not only within the United States but also amongst the scientific communities in Europe and South America. In the early nineteenth century, when science was cultivated at the highest level only by small groups in the major urban centers, an international network of communication was promoted most effectively by an exchange of journals between learned societies. The Lyceum, through the publication of the *Annals*, became part of this international network and, as an examination

[38] Minutes of the Lyceum of Natural History, 13 October 1817, 3 May 1819, 16 August 1819, NYAS.

[39] Torrey to von Schweinitz, 11 April 1823, in C. L. Shear and Neil E. Stevens, "The Correspondence of Schweinitz and Torrey," *Memoirs of the Torrey Botanical Club* 16(1921): 178.

[40] Minutes of the Lyceum of Natural History, 21 July 1823, 29 September 1823, NYAS; DeKay to Brongniart, 30 September 1823, vol. 1, MS 1969, Adolphe Brongniart Correspondence, Muséum National d'Histoire Naturelle, Paris.

of the minutes reveals, the members were concomitantly better informed about the most recent scientific research. Thus, within two years after the first appearance of the *Annals*, a regular exchange was effected with groups as diverse as the Linnaean Society of Paris, the Academy of Medicine of Buenos Aires, the Royal Academy of Science and Art of Brussels, the Museum of Natural History at Marseilles, the Society of Natural History at Belfast, and the Royal Academy of Science at Uppsala. The Lyceum also received, in exchange for copies of the *Annals*, those scientific journals—such as David Brewster's *Edinburgh New Philosophical Journal* and André Étienne Férussac's *Bulletin des Sciences et de l'Industrie*—that were produced not by an institution but by an individual entrepreneur of science. It is hardly surprising, therefore, that Torrey, who had played a major role in bringing out the *Annals*, was able to write to his friend Amos Eaton, with a great deal of justifiable pride, that "our Annals . . . has done wonders for our society."[41]

The publication of the *Annals* was not achieved without a certain amount of travail. The cost of publishing always outran the income—after the first two years, for example, the committee of publication reported that "the expences incurred have been heavy." However, to the relief of the general membership, the reporter continued (in tortuous syntax) to say that "no debt has been contracted but what the means of the Society are sufficient to repay." In fact, while the first volume cost the Lyceum the grand total of $891.19 the income from the subscribers came to $424.42. If the income due from recalcitrant subscribers ($180.37) were added then the deficit due from publishing the *Annals* amounted to less than three hundred dollars. A rapid calculation enabled the members to perceive that "by a greater exertion to increase the subscription list [the *Annals*] might be made not only to repay its own cost but yield an additional revenue." Thus John Torrey, who had been elected president of the Lyceum in 1824, complained to a friend that the Lyceum, with regard to its publications, was still hampered by the lack of financial support: "we labour under great disadvantages for want of funds. If we had such a man as McClure to patronise us, the Academy of Philadelphia would not be before us many years. I send you a subscription paper for our Annals to circulate among such of your friends as you think will subscribe. We need some more subscribers to defray our expenses."[42]

Unfortunately the number of subscribers for the first volume did not

[41] Minutes of the Lyceum of Natural History, 17 May 1824, 12 July 1824, 16 August 1824, 25 October 1824, 22 November 1824, 17 January 1825, NYAS; Torrey to Eaton, 15 April 1824, Historic Letter File, Gray Herbarium, Harvard University.

[42] Report of the Committee of Publication for 1825, in Minutes of the Lyceum of Natural

significantly increase subsequently but remained around one hundred for several years yet the less proximate benefits were substantial enough for the Lyceum to continue publication. As the publication committee stressed in its report for 1826: "the Society becomes better known both at home and abroad. The objects for which we have associated assume a new interest among ourselves. Mutual information is imparted and received and the experience of the past year teaches that our efforts to contribute a share towards the advancement of the Natural Sciences have been received in a flattering manner by the Naturalists of Europe."[43]

In sum the *Annals* was a singular, albeit limited, success for the Lyceum during its early period. Yet the figures strikingly reveal that its existence relied on an extremely restricted base of support. Thus, in two years, the Lyceum had managed to obtain only 151 subscribers to the *Annals*, of whom only 106 were conscientious enough to pay on schedule. Thus the Lyceum, while apparently prosperous, was still in an extremely fragile position.

The limited base of support for science in New York was strikingly revealed when, in 1829, the Corporation of New York suddenly decided that it required the use of the New-York Institution. The city authorities needed the buildings on Chambers Street to house law courts and consequently asked the occupants, most of whom—like the Lyceum of Natural History—were paying only a nominal rent, to vacate the rooms "on or before the first day of August next." The sudden demand from the city for the removal of all the scientific and cultural societies from the New-York Institution was consequent upon the death of DeWitt Clinton during the preceding year. Clinton who, at the time of his death, was governor of the state, had also been an active participant in the affairs of several of the societies in the New-York Institution—at various periods, he had served as president of the American Academy of the Fine Arts, the New-York Historical Society, and the New-York Literary and Philosophical Society. Although Clinton was not a regular participant at the meetings of the Lyceum of Natural History, he considered his election as a member of the Lyceum in December 1818 as an event of "high gratification" and consequently extended his patronage to the Lyceum membership. When Clinton died in 1828, the New-York Institution lost a valuable

History, 27 February 1826, NYAS; Torrey to Lewis David von Schweinitz, 27 February 1824, Lewis David von Schweinitz Collection, ANS.

[43] Report of the Committee of Publication for 1825, in Minutes of the Lyceum of Natural History, 27 February 1826, NYAS.

friend who had consistently used his considerable influence to maintain the Institution as a center of scientific and literary culture. Deprived of Clinton's patronage the societies in the Institution were suddenly exposed to the whims of the City Council.[44]

Naturally enough the sudden request by the Common Council for the return of the New-York Institution caused a certain amount of consternation inside the various organizations. The Lyceum, for its part, initially hoped that the City would provide assistance "either by donation of a lot of ground or pecuniary aid," but more realistically began to explore the possibility of raising a subscription fund for the construction of its own building. Thus, on 4 May 1829 the members adopted the plan of offering individual shares in the Lyceum of one hundred dollars each; a stockholder would be "entitled to the use of the Library . . . he also shall be entitled for himself & family to free admission to the Museum; and to any public lectures which may be delivered in behalf of the Lyceum." The fine details of the plan were somewhat hazy; the members did, however, stipulate that a minimum amount of five thousand dollars had to be raised "otherwise the subscription to be void." Fortunately for the Lyceum the city authorities were behind schedule in arranging for the law courts to move into the Institution building and when Joseph Delafield, the president of the Lyceum, dutifully presented the keys to the mayor they were returned to the Lyceum "with the understanding that they are to be redelivered to him when called for by the Corporation."[45]

Coincidental with this happy extension of the Lyceum's lease came news of a proposal by influential members of the New York intelligentsia to establish a second university in the city. The establishment of New York University re-drew the institutional map of the city. It challenged the hegemony of Columbia College on the educational front, it provided a nexus for New York's small coteries of writers and artists, and in the early years at least, NYU gave a prominent place to science in the curriculum. The Lyceum of Natural History was intimately involved in the creation of NYU both through its individual members and as a corporate institution; the efforts of the Lyceum to introduce natural knowledge were ultimately unsuccessful yet the endeavor retains considerable interest in the history of education in the United States.

On 16 December 1829 a small group of prominent New Yorkers met

[44] Resolution of the Common Council of New York, 23 March 1829, in Minutes of the Lyceum of Natural History, 30 March 1829, NYAS; Minutes of the Lyceum of Natural History, 14 December 1818, 18 January 1819, NYAS.

[45] Minutes of the Lyceum of Natural History, 27 April 1829, 4 May 1829, 29 June 1829, 3 August 1829, NYAS.

to discuss the feasibility of a second college in the city. The project had the backing and support of New York's most influential citizens: three of the founders of New York University—James M. Mathews, Isaac S. Hone, and Myndert Van Schaik—were related to the city's wealthy mayor, Philip Hone; two of the original group of nine, John Augustine Smith and Valentine Mott, were prominent medical men; Jonathan Wainwright was the rector of Grace Church; John Delafield was a prosperous merchant banker; his brother, Joseph Delafield, was president of the Lyceum of Natural History; and Hugh Maxwell was the city's district attorney.[46]

The most significant name on the list was Joseph Delafield, a former lawyer who had served for several years as a commissioner of the federal government. Delafield was a mineralogist of high repute and, after John Torrey had resigned as president of the Lyceum of Natural History in 1826 to accept a teaching position at the West Point Military Academy, Delafield was elected in his place. His advocacy of New York University derived from the belief, common among members of the New York literati at the time, that Columbia College was little more than an academy that prepared its pupils for the professions; a classical education might be appropriate for lawyers and clergymen but it was of little use for manufacturers and merchants.

A second principal founder of NYU was John Augustine Smith who, like Joseph Delafield, was a leading officer of the Lyceum of Natural History, serving for several years on the finance and nomination committees and, from 1838 to 1846, as vice-president. In 1829 Smith was professor of anatomy at the College of Physicians and Surgeons and, as such, held a "very high position in the medical profession, and in society at large." His central position in New York literary and cultural life found expression in his activity as a leader of the Club, an exclusive, informal group of patricians that met weekly for polite conversation. The membership of the Club was restricted to twelve and, in 1829, when Samuel F. B. Morse left New York for a sojourn in Europe, Smith, charged with the responsibility of finding a replacement, wrote to Albert Gallatin, a former member of the United States Senate and Secretary of the Treasury, in the hope that the statesman would consent to become one of the apostles:

12 persons only are admitted, & there are at present three Gentlemen of the Bar—Chancellor Kent & Mes^{rs} Johnson & Jay; three Professors of Co-

---

[46] Theodore Francis Jones, ed., *New York University, 1832–1932* (New York: New York University Press, 1933), 9–10.

lumbia College Mes^rs McVickar, Moore & Renwick; the Revd Drs Wainwright & Mathews the former of the Episcopal the latter of the Presbyterian
church; two merchants Mes^rs Brevoort & Goodhue; & I have the honor to
represent the Medical Faculty . . . it may be safely avowed that for agree-
ableness of conversation there is nothing in N. York at all comparable to
our institution. We meet once a week—have no officers—no formalities—
invite when we can see them intelligent & distinguished strangers & after
a plain & light repast retire about eleven o'clock.[47]

The presence of Smith and Delafield among the group of nine men
that established New York University provided the Lyceum of Natural
History with a strategic role; the members were particularly anxious to
encourage the founders of NYU in a belief that science should occupy
a central position in the curriculum. Thus, at a meeting on 21 December
1829, the members of the Lyceum, noting the "low price at which [NYU]
shall impart instruction . . . [and] that literature & science . . . are at
present either confined to the more wealthy or . . . from the want of in-
structors is alike withheld from all . . . the Lyceum does therefore cordially approve of the contemplated establishment & will be at all times
ready to aid a design fraught with such incalculable & enduring good."
According to the first chancellor of NYU, James M. Mathews, the
Lyceum's early support was especially valuable since it provided a precedent that other institutions, most notably the New-York Historical Society and the New York Athenaeum, were to follow; thus the movement
for a second college in New York quickly gathered momentum: "the
Lyceum of Natural History, with a promptness and unanimity . . . led
the way in this important movement. . . . The Historical Society next followed. . . . The Directors of the New York Athenaeum . . . wait[ed] only
for a vote of the Patrons." Mathews, in his speech at a convention held
to launch the new university, hoped that the various literary and cultural
institutions in the city would formally unite with NYU—"thus may these
various Institutions, which, however excellent in themselves, have lain
hitherto like scattered or disunited columns, be erected into a Temple of
Science, equally perfect and magnificent as a whole, and harmonious in
the adaptation of its parts"—but his eloquent vision was to remain an un-
fulfilled wish.[48]

[47] Fairchild, *History*, 90; John Augustine Smith to Albert Gallatin, 20 November 1829,
#46, Gallatin 1829, Albert Gallatin Papers, New-York Historical Society. For an intriguing
account of the many literary clubs and salons in New York during the period, see Anne
Marie Dolan, "The Literary Salon in New York, 1830–1860" (Ph.D. diss., Columbia University, 1957), 32–43, 56–61.
[48] Minutes of the Lyceum of Natural History, 21 December 1829, NYAS; James M.
Mathews, *Recollections of Persons and Events* (New York, 1865), 200, 201.

As a consequence of the Lyceum's benevolent support, when a sub-scription campaign for the university had been launched and when it seemed that the new institution was, during the summer of 1830, about to take the step of purchasing a building, an offer was made to the Lyceum of the use of rooms in the new building on condition that the collections and library of the Lyceum were made available to the students and faculty of NYU. The members of the Lyceum, conscious that the City Council could reclaim the New-York Institution at any moment, imme-diately accepted this generous offer. Unfortunately the plans of both in-stitutions were stymied by the collapse of the university's subscription campaign and the incompetence of the first chancellor of NYU, James M. Mathews.[49]

The university did, at a later date, occupy a Gothic building on the east side of Washington Square. This gargantuan structure was, even by New York standards, highly idiosyncratic—for many years it served not only the university community but also a small army of bohemian artists and writers who lived as tenants in the upper rooms. One of the latter, Theodore Winthrop, in his novella *Cecil Dreeme*, satirized the vast crenel-lated building as Chrysalis College: "it's not a jail, as you might suppose from its grimmish aspect. Not an Asylum. Not a Retreat. . . . The Trustees fancied that, if they built roomy, their college would be populous; if they built marble, it would be permanent; if they built Gothic, it would be scholastic and mediaeval. . . . There it stands, big, battlemented, but-tressed, marble, with windows like crenelles; and inside they keep up the traditional methods of education."[50]

Although the Lyceum's arrangement for rooms with New York Uni-versity was never consummated, the early relationship between the two institutions did have the effect, in the initial stages at least, of placing science more emphatically in the center of the university curriculum. At a time when not a single American university paid much attention to science and relied on the rote learning of English literature, moral philos-ophy, rhetoric, and the classical languages, NYU's initial focus on science was almost unique. The innovative approach of the university had prac-tical benefits for the Lyceum membership: of the first faculty of five pro-fessors appointed in July 1832, John Torrey was selected to teach chem-istry and botany for an annual salary of five hundred dollars, Henry Vethake received the chair of mathematics and astronomy, and David B.

[49] Minutes of the Lyceum of Natural History, 12 July 1830, NYAS.

[50] Theodore Winthrop, *Cecil Dreeme* (Boston, 1862), 33–34. A detailed description of the NYU building is given in "The New York University," *New York Mirror*, 13 September 1834.

6. New York University. New York University was originally housed in this crenellated white marble building on the east side of Washington Square. Completed in 1835, it contained classrooms, studios, and, in the center, a Gothic chapel modelled after King's College, Cambridge. On the right are the twin towers of the adjacent South Dutch Reformed Church. (From a lithograph published by Henry Hoff in 1850. *Courtesy of New York University Archives.*)

Douglass was appointed professor of natural philosophy and civil engineering.[51]

The threat of imminent removal of the Lyceum from the New-York Institution and the failure to achieve the relationship that both NYU and the Lyceum desired, caused the members in 1830 to consider a third possibility: the construction of their own building in a central part of New York City. On this point the members were duly cautious; when a motion was first put forward for "the Appointment of a Committee to purchase ground for the erection of a building for the Lyceum" it was narrowly defeated by three votes. In April 1831 the Lyceum finally moved out of the New-York Institution and into a temporary home provided by the New York Dispensary at the corner of White and Centre streets.[52]

In the interim, the Lyceum, largely on account of the persuasive urging of James Ellsworth DeKay, decided to reconsider the possibility of building its own hall. In May 1831 the Lyceum voted to set the process in motion; during the next year the members discussed with the New York College of Pharmacy the "expediency of uniting . . . to erect a Suitable building for the Accommodation of both Institutions," and in the early part of 1833 the Lyceum, together with the New York College of Pharmacy and the Mechanics' Institute, presented a petition to the members of the Common Council "requesting their influence in presenting a memorial to the Legislature for the grant of certain lots of ground."[53]

Obtaining no response from the state legislature the Lyceum pressed on with its own plans. The subscription campaign was brought back to life; in 1834 John C. Jay, a curator of the Lyceum, reported to the members that seventy-seven shares had been purchased by sympathetic supporters and friends. Jay, a man of "somewhat nervous temperament," was the principal organizer of the subscription campaign and under his guidance, the plans for a new hall rapidly took shape. At the end of 1834 Jay, who had scouted out several interesting possibilities, recommended that members of the Lyceum purchase a "property on Broadway between Houston & Prince S^{ts}, & if they deem it expedient & for the Welfare of the Society that they . . . purchase 50^{ft} by 100^{ft} for the purpose of erecting a building thereon." At the public auction of the land the next January, Jay actually bought two contiguous pieces of ground, "one lot

[51] Jones, ed., *New York University*, 33.

[52] Minutes of the Lyceum of Natural History, 15 November 1830, 25 April 1831, NYAS; Fairchild, *History*, 32.

[53] Minutes of the Lyceum of Natural History, 16 May 1831, 19 November 1832, 5 February 1833, NYAS.

of ground 25 × 100 for Eleven thousand dollars . . . situated on the West Side of Broadway, the 3ᵈ Lot south of Prince Sᵗ [and] . . . the lot adjoining the above on the south Side, of the same dimensions & for the same price. The terms upon which both were bought were 10% on the day of Sale, 30% on or before the 15ᵗʰ insᵗ & the remainder to remain on bond & mortgage at 6% Interest payable half yearly."[54]

While it might have seemed to the casual observer that the whole business was proceeding smoothly, within the Lyceum there was a great deal of sharp controversy attached both to the purchase of the land and the construction of a building. As early as 1829 a sizable section of the membership had expressed considerable doubt that the Lyceum would be able to pay off the inevitable debt that such a purchase would necessitate. In May 1829, opposition—led by Jeremiah Van Rensselaer, the corresponding secretary of the Lyceum—had been declared with regard to the launching of the subscription campaign. When John C. Jay proposed, a few years later, that "a Committee of three to be appointed by the President be authorised to purchase [the land]" the Lyceum was again split down the middle; Jay's motion passed by a wafer-thin majority of two. When William Cooper proposed a resolution at the meeting of 26 January 1835 that the building committee could purchase land without having to call a public meeting of the Lyceum beforehand, the same polarization took place—Cooper's motion was carried by two votes.[55]

A sober consideration of the facts would surely, one might think, have persuaded the majority to adopt a more cautious attitude. In February 1835, the Lyceum had about fourteen thousand dollars; even before any construction had begun on the hall, therefore, the Lyceum—after spending twenty-two thousand dollars on the land—was already eight thousand dollars in debt. More significantly, the subscription campaign had raised, in six years, only seventy-seven hundred dollars; it was not probable that a great deal more would be obtained.

On 16 February 1835, Asa Gray, a young physician from Utica, attended his first meeting of the Lyceum while on a short trip to New York. Gray, a close friend of John Torrey, was impressed by the ambitious schemes of the small group of naturalists that met that evening at the New York Dispensary. He heard Jay announce that the Lyceum had been

[54] Minutes of the Lyceum of Natural History, 8 December 1834, 22 December 1834, 2 February 1835, NYAS.
[55] Minutes of the Lyceum of Natural History, 4 May 1829, 12 January 1835, 26 January 1835, NYAS.

able to get a loan of "Twenty five thousand Dollars on the follow⁸ Terms viz: $15,000 on Mortgage on the Society's Lots, & when the Society proceeds to build, a further Sum of $10,000." From that point on, the plans for the new building moved forward rapidly. An architect was appointed, the foundations laid, and, under the capable leadership of Jay, the new building was speedily completed, so that by May 1836 the Lyceum had moved its collections and library into the hall on Broadway.[56]

It was, without a shadow of doubt, a magnificent accomplishment for the Lyceum. On the first floor, in the interior of the building, there was a capacious lecture room and, on either side of the main entrance, stores that were intended to be let for commercial use. On the second floor, at the front, there was a large room "about 50 feet by 70, lofty and surrounded by a gallery" for the display of the Lyceum's natural history collections and, at the rear, there was a "spacious and comfortable room for the library and for the ordinary meetings of the Society." Finally, on the third floor there were a number of small rooms for meetings and for the superintendent and janitor of the building.[57]

The Lyceum's reputation as a scientific society was immediately increased; a symbol of its heightened prestige was the decision by Benjamin Silliman—by 1836 the doyen of American savants—to accept the invitation of the Lyceum to inaugurate the opening of the new hall by presenting a series of lectures on geology. A second consequence of the Lyceum's success was the application by a variety of scientific groups to use the Lyceum's rooms. In March 1836 the Phrenological Society of New York agreed to pay the Lyceum seventy-five dollars for the use of a room "on one Evening in the Week for one Year." Two months later the Mechanics' Institute and the Horticultural Society both petitioned the Lyceum for a similar arrangement; in October the American Institute asked for the "Use of the Museum Room"; and in November the American Society for the Diffusion of Knowledge requested the use of a small room for one evening a week.[58]

The Lyceum building, situated as it was in one of the more fashionable parts of the city and occupied by a variety of respectable scientific institutions, became a center of intellect not only in matters scientific but also (since science was then a part of general culture) in matters literary. In

[56] Minutes of the Lyceum of Natural History, 16 February 1835, NYAS; Fairchild, *History*, 39.

[57] Fairchild, *History*, 39.

[58] Minutes of the Lyceum of Natural History, 14 March 1836, 2 May 1836, 23 May 1836, 10 October 1836, 28 November 1836, NYAS.

ensuing years, literary groups as well as the small scientific clubs worked out an arrangement with the Lyceum for the use of its rooms—in 1837, for example, the "gentlemen composing the 'Authors' Club'," met on Tuesday afternoons in the library. As a consequence of its heightened prestige the Lyceum achieved a sense of stability, progress, and prosperity that it had rarely possessed—for the first time in many years the *Annals* appeared at a regular rate, the Lyceum lectures on science were well-attended, the weekly membership meetings were lively and interesting, and the museum collections—meticulously arranged by the curators—were displayed to their best advantage in handsome glass cases.[59]

One witness to the Lyceum's re-birth was Asa Gray who, following his graduation from the College of Physicians and Surgeons of the Western District, lived in New York City intermittently until 1838. In 1833 Gray's interest in botany had led to part-time employment as an assistant to John Torrey; Gray, then only eighteen years old, quickly formed a close friendship with Torrey, and for a brief period, boarded with Torrey and his family in New York. Gray's early career illustrates graphically the obstacles facing an aspirant scientist in the early nineteenth century; despite a winning manner and diligent application he was only able to get a series of temporary jobs teaching science. Gray left New York in 1834 to teach chemistry, mineralogy, and geology at the Utica Gymnasium and then at Hamilton College. The bankruptcy of the proprietor ended Gray's tenure at Utica and the position at Hamilton never matured into a permanent appointment and, at the end of 1834, Gray was back in New York City. There, despite the occasional loan from his father, Gray, with no prospects of employment, sank rapidly into debt; for much of 1835 he lived in a dreary boarding-house on Bleecker Street glumly wondering whether he should "give up all hopes from science as a pursuit for life."[60]

Gray's despondency was lightened at the end of 1835 by a ray of hope coming from the Lyceum of Natural History. In November 1835 the Lyceum, with its new building half-finished and anticipating the day when it would be able to display its natural history collections, informally advertised for a superintendent who would be charged with the care of the collections and the arrangement of the library. The salary was modest, only three hundred dollars a year, but the position also included the use of two rooms on the third floor of the building as an apartment.

---

[59] Minutes of the Lyceum of Natural History, 1 May 1837, NYAS.

[60] A. Hunter Dupree, *Asa Gray, 1810–1888* (Cambridge, MA: Harvard University Press, 1968), 50.

Gray, who had already given lectures at Lyceum meetings and had published two papers on botany in the *Annals*, was an obvious candidate
and, in the early part of 1836, he began quietly to push forward his application. On 11 January William Cooper nominated the young botanist
for membership in the Lyceum and on ballot Gray was unanimously
elected. During the next few weeks Gray energetically canvassed his
fellow-members for the job and very soon obtained a promise of the
position when it became available in May. When he eventually made the
move from Bleecker Street to Broadway, Gray was highly satisfied; his
days of penury were over and his career was launched:

> last Monday . . . a plan was completed which we have had for some time
> in contemplation. I became the Librarian of the N.Y. Lyceum of Nat. His-
> tory in February . . . and the society is now moving into their elegant new
> building in Broadway near Prince St. I am offered and shall accept, the situ-
> ation of Superintendent or Resident Curator.,—and have a fine apartment
> in the building and take the entire charge of the books and collections. Al-
> though the salary they can afford is small, yet it will be a fine situation for
> scientific pursuits and I think I shall be pleased.[61]

The increased visibility and reputation of the Lyceum gave it an enlarged stature not only in the city but also in the state. Thus when members of the state legislature began to contemplate the launching of a New
York geological survey in 1835, they turned to the Lyceum for advice. At
the same time, the members of the Lyceum, aware of the responsibility
that accompanied their new reputation, took pains to draw up a detailed
and comprehensive plan for the execution of the survey. The harmonious
relationship between the state legislature and the scientific institutions
in New York City and in Albany had a happy outcome: the New York
geological survey was one of the most significant surveys undertaken by
any state legislature throughout the nineteenth century.

During the 1830s a number of state geological surveys commenced operations; the Massachusetts legislature was the first to sponsor a survey
under the leadership of Edward Hitchcock in 1830 and during the next
few years several states followed suit. Tennessee and Maryland each
began a survey in 1831; four years later New Jersey, Connecticut, and Virginia all began state surveys; and in 1836 Maine, New York, Ohio, and
Pennsylvania commenced their surveys.

[61] Minutes of the Lyceum of Natural History, 11 January 1836, NYAS; Asa Gray to N. W.
Folwell, 25 February/3 May 1836. I am indebted to A. Hunter Dupree for a typescript copy
of this letter.

Generally the inauguration of a survey followed a period of agitation among the local scientific community. In South Carolina, for example, the initiation of a geological survey was part of a movement within the state to stimulate the local economy by improving transportation links between the seaport cities and the interior of the state (and, by extension, the western markets). The geological survey would, it was claimed, materially assist the agricultural, manufacturing, and mining sectors of the state economy. Thus, in December 1824, Lardner Vanuxem, a professor of geology and mineralogy at South Carolina College, was appointed state geologist for a period of two years at an annual salary equivalent to five hundred dollars. The appointment of Vanuxem was a consequence of the congruence of interests of the scientists and the politicians: several prominent members of the legislature, including the president of the state Senate, personally oversaw the creation of the survey.[62]

Similarly, in Pennsylvania the effort to organize a state survey was led by Peter Arrell Browne, a Philadelphia lawyer and a leading member of the Franklin Institute; Browne's efforts during the 1820s were prologue to the establishment of the Geological Society of Pennsylvania in 1832. In the spring of 1833 the Geological Society's agitation for a state geological survey that, it was claimed, would benefit the state economy by revealing mineral and coal deposits, resulted in a recommendation from a committee of the House of Representatives that a survey be established. The parlous condition of the state economy prohibited the realization of the proposal until 1836 when the legislature mandated a corps of geologists to make a "geological and mineralogical survey . . . to discover and examine all beds and deposits of ores, coals, clays, marls, and such other mineral substances as may be deemed useful or valuable."[63]

In New York, the Lyceum of Natural History first proposed, in a petition to the state legislature in 1829, that the representatives at Albany should "make provision by Law for a practical and efficient examination of the mineral formations of this state." The movement was led by George William Featherstonhaugh*, an emigré savant from Britain who, after living for a while in Duanesburg, had moved to New York City in 1829. Featherstonhaugh had long taken an avocational interest in geology and was on friendly terms with prominent members of the American and

[62] Anne M. Millbrooke, "State Geological Surveys of the Nineteenth Century" (Ph.D. diss., University of Pennsylvania, 1981), 32–40.

[63] Anne Millbrooke, "The Geological Society of Pennsylvania, 1832–1836," *Pennsylvania Geology* 7(1976): 7–11, 8(1977): 12–16.

* (pronounced FAN-shaw)

British scientific communities. Thus, when he moved to the city, it was only natural that he should immediately join the Lyceum. Featherstonhaugh quickly made an impression on the local literati particularly after he had given a public course of lectures under the aegis of the Lyceum on geology; Featherstonhaugh's lectures proved, by his own account at least, very successful: "my Lectures on Geology have produced quite a Sensation here—the novelty and dignity of the Subject . . . and a very advantageous arrangement of them in the Chapel of Columbia College, proved very attractive, and I am solicited in a very urgent manner to deliver a full course, which I probably may do in the course of the ensuing winter."[64]

Featherstonhaugh was perceptive enough to see that, with a certain amount of cajoling and suasion, the state legislature might be induced to support a geological survey. In New York State, moreover, there was a precedent for, in 1824, the patroon, Stephen Van Rensselaer, had sponsored a geological survey along the Erie Canal; written by Amos Eaton, founder of the Rensselaer Institute at Troy, the geological survey had been published to wide acclaim and had been distributed to interested members of the legislature. Unlike most other state governments in the United States at the time, the Assembly and Senate at Albany were not hostile or indifferent to science principally on account of the influence of DeWitt Clinton who, during his terms as governor, had sponsored lectures on science for the representatives. Finally, in Albany itself, a number of flourishing scientific societies—most notably the Albany Institute and the Albany Lyceum of Natural History—had taken root among the city's small coterie of intellectuals.[65]

In its campaign for a geological survey, the Lyceum of Natural History—under Featherstonhaugh's leadership—stressed almost exclusively the utilitarian and practical benefits of a state survey. On 19 Janu-

---

[64] Minutes of the Lyceum of Natural History, 2 February 1829, NYAS; Edmund Berkeley and Dorothy Smith Berkeley, *George William Featherstonhaugh: The First U.S. Government Geologist* (Tuscaloosa, AL: University of Alabama Press, 1988), 78; Featherstonhaugh to Benjamin Silliman, 29 April 1829, Folder 47, Box 20, Silliman Family Manuscripts, Sterling Memorial Library, YU.

[65] Greene, *American Science*, 93–94; Ethel M. McAllister, *Amos Eaton, 1776–1842: Scientist and Educator* (Philadelphia: University of Pennsylvania Press, 1941), 300–318; James M. Hobbins, "Shaping a Provincial Learned Society: The Early History of the Albany Institute," in *The Pursuit of Knowledge in the Early American Republic: American Scientific and Learned Societies from Colonial Times to the Civil War*, ed. Alexandra Oleson and Sanborn C. Brown (Baltimore: Johns Hopkins University Press, 1976), 126–141. For a discussion of the cultural context for science in Albany, see Mary Ann James, *Elites in Conflict: The Antebellum Clash over the Dudley Observatory* (New Brunswick, NJ: Rutgers University Press, 1987), 18–28.

ary 1829, the Lyceum appointed a committee of three members—Featherstonhaugh, James Ellsworth DeKay, and Timothy Dewey—to draw up a petition to "the Legislature on the subject of searching for Bituminous coal within the state." Two weeks later Featherstonhaugh presented the memorial to the members of the Lyceum for approval. Featherstonhaugh had seemingly left nothing to chance; after stressing the disinterested benevolence of the members of the Lyceum—"contributing . . . the means requisite for the establishment of a scientific Library and an extensive collection of objects in every branch of Nat. History; which is open at all times free of all charges for the gratification and information of their fellow citizens"—Featherstonhaugh went on in exhaustive detail to catalog the economic benefits for the state of a search for bituminous coal. If coal were discovered in New York State there would not only be a "new branch of industry" (coal mining) but, in addition, a halt could be called to the destruction of forests for fuel, the revenues of the Erie Canal would increase on account of transporting coal from the west to New York City, and the treasury would benefit from the eventual "exportation of [bituminous coal] from our state." On the latter point, Featherstonhaugh was supplied with the necessary facts: since 1821, six million bushels of coal had been imported into the United States. If the Lyceum were to receive funding to carry out a geological survey, this amount might eventually be "furnished from the coal-mines of this state, and supplied by the coasting trade from New York."[66]

Although the petition was adopted by the Lyceum and was presented to the City Council for endorsement before going onto Albany for consideration by the legislature, circumstances combined to halt its progress. Two months after Featherstonhaugh had made his report before the Lyceum, the city authorities asked the scientific societies to move out of the New-York Institution and in the general confusion and consternation that ensued, the geological survey was temporarily shelved. Then, in the summer of 1829, Featherstonhaugh suffered a grievous personal loss when a fire destroyed his country mansion and his library, personal papers, and possessions were reduced to ashes. As he reported to the British scientist, William Buckland, this disaster rendered Featherstonhaugh psychologically unfit to take on any scientific projects: "my Mansion at Featherston Park with my Library &c &c &c has been burnt to the Ground. . . . When I get engaged in anything important, a sense of the

[66] Minutes of the Lyceum of Natural History, 19 January 1829, 2 February 1829, NYAS. See also Michele Aldrich, "New York Natural History Survey, 1836–1845" (Ph.D. diss., University of Texas–Austin, 1974), 70–71.

desolate Life I am destined to lead comes over me, and I shrink from it."[67]

As a consequence, the geological survey remained a dormant issue for several years. In 1835, however, after various other states had begun geological surveys, the interest of the New York state legislature was reawakened by the enticing possibility that, as Featherstonhaugh had claimed six years earlier, there were vast mineral resources waiting to be exploited to the financial benefit of the state economy. A committee of the state legislature, set up to explore the possibility of beginning a geological survey, first contacted the Lyceum through James DeKay "for Information . . . as to the best Means of prosecuting a general Survey of the State." The Lyceum, flattered that the state legislature should consult the members, responded with alacrity and set up a special committee— consisting of DeKay, Jeremiah Van Rensselaer, and George W. Boyd—to report on the matter.[68]

The task assumed greater urgency later in the year when the members of the Lyceum heard that both New Jersey and Connecticut had ordered geological surveys. It did not go unnoticed by the Lyceum, moreover, that both states, by agreeing to fund the work of their respective surveys, were providing employment for a highly skilled scientific corps. The New Jersey survey, which lasted for four years, was led and organized by Henry Darwin Rogers, professor of geology at Penn, while the Connecticut survey was organized by James G. Percival, a graduate of Yale, and Charles U. Sheperd, a protégé of Benjamin Silliman. Thus the Lyceum, always aware of the precarious financial situation of science and eager to encourage the employment of the state's small scientific community, made the geological survey a matter of the highest priority. In November 1835 a second committee of the Lyceum was "appointed to prepare a Memorial to the Legislature praying that a geological Survey of this State be undertaken." The importance for the Lyceum of the task can be gauged from the membership of the committee; it included Joseph Delafield, president of the Lyceum, John Torrey, one of the most re-

[67] Minutes of the Lyceum of Natural History, 10 February 1829, 30 March 1829, NYAS; "Proceedings of the Lyceum of Natural History of New-York," American Journal of Science and Arts 16(1829): 355; Featherstonhaugh to Buckland, 27 June 1829, William Buckland Correspondence, Royal Society of London.

[68] George P. Merrill, ed. and comp., Contributions to a History of American State Geological and Natural History Surveys, Smithsonian Institution, United States National Museum Bulletin no. 109 (Washington, D.C., 1920), 327; Minutes of the Lyceum of Natural History, 13 April 1835, NYAS.

spected scientists in the state, and William Cooper, a member well-known for his generous support of the scientific cause.[69]

Joseph Delafield, who was well-connected to many of the legislators at Albany, knew the governor of the state, William Marcy, personally. At Delafield's suggestion the Lyceum presented its petition to Marcy directly, and, to give the request a greater weight, inveigled two other important New York scientific societies, the American Institute and the Mechanics' Institute, to join the Lyceum in its request. To bolster their case and to give the legislature an extra little push, two Lyceum members, William Cooper and John C. Jay, published a short pamphlet entitled *The Application of Geology to the Useful Purposes of Life* and pointedly distributed it to each member of the Assembly at Albany. All this work on the part of the Lyceum apparently paid off for, very soon, the members began to receive informal reports from the representatives at the state capital that the New York survey would soon receive a generous appropriation. Indeed the auguries of success seemed so promising that within a short time applications began to arrive at the Lyceum for the scientific positions on the survey; in addition, members of the Lyceum, suddenly aware of the pivotal role that they had played in establishing the survey and conscious that its eventual configuration would depend to a great extent on their recommendations to the state legislature, began jockeying among themselves to ensure that their own scientific disciplines would receive adequate support. Thus on 14 March 1836, John Torrey, who had played a leading role, made a bid for the funding of his discipline, botany, within the survey by making "some Remarks upon the intended general Survey. . . . These Remarks more particularly related to Geology, & Botany."[70]

In April 1836, when the Assembly made its report on the survey, the members of the Lyceum found that their efforts had been richly rewarded. The legislature, wishing to do a thorough job, had divided the state into four parts assigning to each a principal geologist and a corps of assistants. In addition, the legislature—in recognition of the Lyceum's role in establishing the survey—made provision for three independent investigations that were to cover the entire state. This measure, which

[69] Minutes of the Lyceum of Natural History, 7 September 1835, 14 September 1835, NYAS; George P. Merrill, *The First One Hundred Years of American Geology* (1924; reprint, New York: Hafner Publishing Co., 1964), 165–166, 168–170; Minutes of the Lyceum of Natural History, 23 November 1835, NYAS.

[70] Minutes of the Lyceum of Natural History, 7 December 1835, 21 December 1835, 28 December 1835, 11 January 1836, 18 January 1836, 25 January 1836, 1 February 1836, 14 March 1836, NYAS.

was unique to New York, ensured that the survey would stand as one of the most comprehensive surveys performed during the antebellum period. Lewis C. Beck was charged with organizing a review of the mineralogy of the state, John Torrey was responsible for surveying the botany of New York, and, finally, James Ellsworth DeKay supervised an examination of the zoology of the state. In part because it was organized in such a comprehensive fashion and also because the rock strata in the western part of the state proved extraordinarily propitious for providing the basis of a synthetic interpretation of geological formations in the United States, the New York survey was undoubtedly the most significant of the many surveys undertaken during the 1830s. The New York survey established the basic principles of stratigraphic geology, provided American geology with an adequate nomenclature, and demonstrated conclusively the significance of fossils in the correlation of rock strata. Under the subsequent leadership of James Hall, who successfully squeezed financial support from the legislature over many decades, the New York survey constituted one of the most impressive and significant achievements of nineteenth century American science.[71]

Unfortunately for the Lyceum, this spectacular success was somewhat dimmed by the sudden economic crisis that engulfed the country a few years later. Ever since 1836, when the Lyceum had moved into the new hall, the members had been troubled by the vaguely uncomfortable feeling that their outward appearance of prosperity masked a large debt. This sensation was exacerbated by a lingering resentment on the part of many members that the decision to construct the Lyceum hall had been reached over their protests and that several crucial votes had been decided by the slimmest of margins. As early as June 1836 John C. Jay, who, throughout the previous year, had been the unquenchable optimist on the building committee, advised the Lyceum to borrow five thousand dollars and to "pledge the faith of the Society to reimburse the principal with Interest at such times & in such Manner as may be agreed upon by the parties."[72]

The indignation of the minority was only increased when Jay, as chairman of the building committee, reported that, in order for the Lyceum to pay the interest on its loans, it should accept an offer from the proprietor of a local music academy for the "Use of the vacant Rooms

---

[71] Merrill, *First One Hundred Years*, 187–188.

[72] Minutes of the Lyceum of Natural History, 13 June 1836, NYAS. See also Minutes of the Lyceum of Natural History, 4 July 1836, 11 July 1836, NYAS.

on the second floor: the rooms to be occupied by a family & also as a Music School, with the Proviso that the Rooms are to be given up at the Expiration of the first quarter, in case the Music should prove an Annoyance, to the Soc." True, the music academy was offering to pay an annual rent of $600 but this was only a small compensation for the sacrifice of the scientific integrity of the members who had fondly imagined, a year previously, that they would have a library and meeting-rooms on the second floor; to their chagrin, the library remained packed up in boxes in the basement. Even worse was the news in April 1837 that the lecture-series sponsored by the Lyceum in a bid to generate some desperately needed income had signally failed in its purpose; the ubiquitous Jay, as a member of the committee on lectures, gave a "brief statement of the receipts and expenditures . . . from which it appeared that the nett proceeds would be little or nothing."[73]

In 1837 the American economy suffered its worst battering for twenty years: in reaction to a wave of inflation and land speculation during the previous year there was a sharp constriction of economic activity throughout the country. This economic collapse signalled disaster for the Lyceum since the subscription fund, which had been proceeding at a lackadaisical pace even during the economic boom of 1836, now came to an abrupt halt. The Lyceum, which had always predicated the construction of its building on the future success of the subscription campaign, was now confronted with a substantial debt and yet had no ability to generate income even to pay the interest on the debt.

As a consequence, the Lyceum, throughout 1837 and the first half of 1838, borrowed extensively on mortgage of the building so that by September 1838, the total debt had reached thirty-five thousand dollars. It did not help matters that, as a consequence of the economic crisis, the music school on the second floor had declared bankruptcy and that the proprietor was anxious to find out "what terms his lease of the Society's premises could be cancelled." During the following year a certain amount of relief was afforded the Lyceum by renting out virtually all the space in the building that was not absolutely required for the meetings. One of the stores that looked out onto Broadway was let for an annual rent of $750, a second store in the basement fetched a rent of $200, the lecture room was let "on Sundays for the purpose of a church at $350 per year, with the privilege of placing an organ there, if removed whenever the Lyceum shall require it," another one of the stores in the basement was

[73] Minutes of the Lyceum of Natural History, 8 August 1836, 3 April 1837, NYAS.

converted into a "confectionary store" for an annual rent of $175, and even
the cellar found a tenant who paid $50 a year for storing merchandise.[74]
   This highly unsatisfactory state of affairs continued until the early part
of 1843; by that time the Lyceum contained, in addition to various sundry
commercial enterprises, the New Jerusalem Church which now used the
large lecture-room not only on Sunday but throughout the entire week.
Despite the adroit maneuvers of the finance committee, however, the
Lyceum was unable to avoid the reckoning and, on 1 May 1843 the committee, in a special report, "stated that the affairs of the Society had arrived at such a crisis that something must be immediately done or the
Lyceum must cease to exist." Despite this prescient warning, members
of the Lyceum seemed peculiarly unaffected by the threat of foreclosure
on the building. For the next several months business carried on as
usual; a desultory attempt to reinvigorate the subscription fund briefly
interrupted the normal round of activity but in general the proceedings
continued as before: the lecturers read their scientific papers and displayed new specimens of birds, sea-shells, and minerals.[75]
   In October 1843 one of the principal creditors, William Pell—realizing
that no serious attempt was likely to be made to remove the debt—
ordered his solicitor to ask for the return of his previous loan of $10,000
which had fallen due on "the 20th Sep[t] last, with six month interest—
and stating if the money was not paid; proceeding would be commenced
against the Society to collect it." No longer could the members continue
to deceive themselves; in a sad postscript to the meeting of 9 October,
the president, Joseph Delafield, was "authorized to insert in the daily
papers an advertisement offering the building of the Lyceum at private
sale on terms to be agreed upon—for a sum not less than $45,000." Even
this was not sufficient for, at that price, there were no buyers. At the
public sale a few months later, members of the Lyceum watched their
proudest possession disappear under the auctioneer's hammer; they
stayed only until the price was sufficient to cover the accumulated debts:
"as soon as the amount was sufficient to cover the mortgages with interest the friends of the Society ceased bidding, and the property was
sold for $37,000."[76]

[74] Fairchild, *History*, 40; Minutes of the Lyceum of Natural History, 7 August 1837, 28
May 1838, 29 October 1838, 19 December 1838, NYAS.
   [75] Minutes of the Lyceum of Natural History, 21 December 1840, 1 May 1843, NYAS.
   [76] Minutes of the Lyceum of Natural History, 2 October 1843, 9 October 1843, NYAS; Fairchild, *History*, 43.

2

The Struggle for Survival
1844–1866

THE LOSS of the Lyceum building in 1844 was a serious blow to an organization that, only a few years previously, had seemed on the point of catching up with its old rival, the Academy of Natural Sciences of Philadelphia. The loss of the Lyceum hall on Broadway was not only a severe blow to prestige and morale but also, in a more immediate sense, threatened the very viability of the institution. What was now to become of the spectacular quantities of sea-shells, minerals, stuffed birds and animals donated by such illustrious scientists as John James Audubon and Samuel Latham Mitchill? Where would the books and journals—many of them from distant parts of the world—be stored and how would they remain accessible to the Lyceum membership? The loss of the Broadway building not only imperiled the past achievements of the Lyceum but also placed a question-mark over the Lyceum's ability to perform such essential tasks as the publication of the *Annals*. It was, moreover, doubtful that the Lyceum would receive further donations of specimens and books if there were no capability to utilize them.

For the following year the dispirited band of Lyceum devotees met at the home of the president, Joseph Delafield. The activities of this small group of savants were sharply curtailed: the weekly meetings were dominated by talk of the rueful loss as well as by schemes to raise a subscription for a second building. Over the summer months of 1844, the meetings were suspended; when the Lyceum re-assembled in October the members learned that some diligent campaigning by a handful of enthusiasts had raised just over one thousand dollars for a new hall; this pitiful sum—as most members tacitly acknowledged—was scarcely a promising augury of a rosy future. Nevertheless the building subscription drifted along until, by January 1845, it had reached the grand total of sixteen hundred dollars.[1]

7. JOHN WILLIAM DRAPER (1811–1882). A graduate of the University of Pennsylvania, Draper was appointed professor of chemistry at New York University in 1838. During his tenure at NYU, Draper made several discoveries relating to incandescent radiant energy; together with his colleague, Samuel F.B. Morse, he was also responsible for innovations in the chemistry of the photographic process. (*Courtesy of New York University Archives.*)

Fortunately for the Lyceum a new and more promising development was on the horizon, namely, the permanent establishment of the New York University Medical School under the leadership of John William Draper, a prominent local scientist who had already made a name for himself as a pioneer in the techniques of daguerreotypy. Draper, who became a leading member of the Lyceum of Natural History not long after his arrival in New York in 1839, had had an excellent education that served as an appropriate apprenticeship for his later career as professor of chemistry at NYU. A native of England, Draper had enrolled in one of the first classes at the University of London, where he studied chemistry, materia medica, and geology under the tutelage of Edward Turner, who, a few years later, was to serve as secretary to the Council of the fledgling British Association for the Advancement of Science. Draper's father, John Christopher Draper, owned two shares in the University of London and had hoped that his son would serve as a tutor at the university in addition to pursuing his scientific studies. Draper *père* died early the next year and any influence that might have attached to his proprietary interest died with him; Draper *fils* was only able to continue his studies at the university through the sacrifices of his mother and eldest sister.[2]

His educational experience at London was crucial for his later career in New York City in three respects. First and most obvious, Draper became a steadfast adherent to the cause of science which, even in a metropolis like London, was not, at the time, an obvious career choice for a young man with no independent financial resources. In Draper's case, the conversion seems to have been thoroughly intellectual; his teacher, Edward Turner, inspired his students with his enthusiastic devotion to chemistry and Draper long remembered how his own later researches on the analysis of spectral lines were a consequence of witnessing Turner's elegant demonstrations of the effect of light on the condensation of camphor.

The University of London was established in 1826 as an alternative to the hegemony of Oxford and Cambridge (which both excluded Dissenters); interestingly enough, NYU was established in 1831 in frank imi-

---

[1] Herman Le Roy Fairchild, *A History of the New York Academy of Sciences* (New York, 1887), 45.

[2] Donald Fleming, *John William Draper and the Religion of Science* (Philadelphia: University of Pennsylvania Press, 1950), 5–6. For Edward Turner, see Jack Morrell and Arnold Thackray, *Gentlemen of Science: Early Years of the British Association for the Advancement of Science* (Oxford: Clarendon Press, 1981), 486.

tation of the University of London. Just as London was a haven for those who were barred from the classical education offered by Oxford and Cambridge, so NYU—at least in its early years—aimed to teach science as a central part of the curriculum in sharp contrast to the almost exclusively classical education offered by Columbia College.[3]

The third formative influence exerted on Draper at the University of London was a consequence of its position in the center of a world metropolis. The hub of the British Empire was a nexus of intellectual trends and fashions that subsumed science as a single small part of an intellectual unity. History, philosophy, and literature were important components of Draper's life in London not as sterile disciplines solely to be studied but as guides to life—his studies at a college founded by the great utilitarian Jeremy Bentham reflected the cosmopolitan context of the city. Thus, in addition to his scientific courses, Draper also studied such subjects as the theory of jurisprudence; it was a happy coincidence that in one of these courses he was the class-mate of the young John Stuart Mill.[4]

On the completion of his education at London, Draper took a conventional step for a young man—he got married—and then, in the following year, he took the more controversial decision—at least for a well-educated gentleman with excellent prospects of success in his native country—to emigrate to the United States. After living in Virginia for two years Draper moved to Philadelphia to enroll as a student at the University of Pennsylvania Medical School where he studied chemistry with the celebrated Robert Hare. The medical school at Penn had long enjoyed an illustrious reputation and in 1834, when Draper arrived in Philadelphia, it was battling to sustain its fame against a local upstart, Jefferson Medical College, which, after a shaky beginning in 1824, was now successfully competing with its elder rival. As a consequence of the competition between the two Philadelphia schools, both Penn and Jefferson were improving their facilities and had recently extended the annual course of study to five months; this at a time when medical schools in other parts of the country were desperately lowering standards in an attempt to halt falling enrollments. Thus, on account of the reputation and high

    [3] H. Hale Bellot, *University College, London, 1826–1926* (London: University of London Press, 1929), 20–24; Theodore Francis Jones, ed., *New York University, 1832–1932* (New York: New York University Press, 1933), 12–13.

    [4] Fleming, *John William Draper,* 5–7. For an analysis that details the founding of the University of London by Dissenting professionals and Whig reformers, see Adrian Desmond, *The Politics of Evolution: Morphology, Medicine and Reform in Radical London* (Chicago: University of Chicago Press, 1989), 33–41.

standing of Penn, it was no small feat that Draper's doctoral dissertation (on the osmosis of gases through non-porous barriers) won a special commendation from the university medical faculty when it was presented in 1836.[5]

His distinction at Penn was a mark of later fame for, after teaching for a short time at Hampden-Sidney College in Virginia, Draper was nominated as the first incumbent of the chair of chemistry at NYU when proposals were being advanced in 1837 for the creation of a medical school attached to the university. A committee appointed that year to study the question reported in December that "the cause of Medical Science in this country requires that the period of study should be greatly enlarged" but, more realistically, recommended that "to require an attendance upon the instructions of the Medical Faculty for the full term of four years before conferring the degree of Doctor of Medicine would prove fatal to the hopes and prospects of the Faculty. They have therefore agreed to recommend that for the present the term be limited to a course of two years."[6]

The economic crisis of 1837 caused the postponement of all decisions about the medical school at NYU although, in the fall of 1838, while plans for the medical school were in abeyance, Draper received notice that he had been elected to the chair of chemistry in the collegiate department of the university. Draper, fearful that his acceptance might mean that he would forfeit the medical chair when it was eventually offered, postponed his decision. The university, anxious to win Draper, immediately reversed itself and offered him the medical chair at an annual salary of $750 together with the promise of a seven dollar fee for every student who paid tuition.[7]

Draper's acceptance of the chemistry chair at the NYU Medical School had a profound impact on the development of science in New York City for not only did he rapidly become—together with the surgeon Valentine

[5] Fleming, *John William Draper*, 7–9, 10–12; William Frederick Norwood, *Medical Education in the United States before the Civil War* (Philadelphia: University of Pennsylvania Press, 1944), 91–93. For a discussion of the medical culture of Philadelphia, see Simon Baatz, "'A Very Diffused Disposition': Dissecting Schools in Philadelphia, 1823–1825," *Pennsylvania Magazine of History and Biography* 108(1984): 203–215.

[6] Claude Edwin Heaton, *A Historical Sketch of New York University College of Medicine, 1841–1941* (New York: New York University Press, 1941), 2, 4; Robert J. Carlisle, "The University and Bellevue Hospital Medical College," in Jones, ed., *New York University*, 289.

[7] Fleming, *John William Draper*, 18–19; Carlisle, "The University," 291. For a more detailed account of the difficulties attending the creation of the NYU Medical School, see Norwood, *Medical Education*, 134–135.

8. THE STUYVESANT INSTITUTE. This building, which housed the New York University Medical School, was first used by the Lyceum of Natural History in April 1845. Six years later, in March 1851, NYU moved the medical school to a building on the outskirts of the city at Fourteenth Street; the Lyceum moved its collections and library to the new building in November 1851. (*Courtesy of New York University Medical Center.*)

Mott—a leader in the development of medicine at NYU but he also played a significant role in the life of the Lyceum of Natural History at a time when that organization was experiencing its deepest and most severe crisis. On 6 February 1845, only ten months after the Lyceum had sold its Broadway hall, the NYU medical faculty, which had recently purchased the building previously owned by the Stuyvesant Institute, offered the use of the "three front rooms of the second story . . . free of rent, for the term of ten years."[8]

This generous offer was not entirely unexpected by the beleaguered members of the Lyceum; after all, John William Draper had, for the previous five weeks, been acting as an intermediary between the two institutions and had even served on a Lyceum committee to consider the question. In addition, the members were aware that Cyrus Mason, another supporter of the Lyceum on the faculty of NYU, was preparing to make an offer that would include a payment of the debts of the Lyceum. Nevertheless the NYU offer, which included the gratuitous provision of "fuel, light and servants" was so munificent that a sizable section of the Lyceum membership expressed deep suspicion about the motives behind such generosity. Those founding members of the Lyceum who recalled their close association with the College of Physicians and Surgeons were apprehensive that the NYU Medical School, in its rivalry with Physicians and Surgeons, was intent on securing control of the Lyceum's collections and library in its bid for respectability and prestige.

John Howard Redfield who, as a school-boy, had first gazed at the Lyceum's collections when they were displayed at the New-York Institution, recalled that, as a young man of twenty-nine, he had attended the Lyceum meeting called to discuss the offer from NYU. According to his reminiscence, John Torrey, one of the few founders who still played an active part in the life of the Lyceum, was the leader of the opponents of NYU:

> many of these were friends of the old College of Physicians and Surgeons. . . . It soon appeared that old medical animosities were revived and that the Trojans of the 'Crosby Street School' feared the *Danaos et dona ferentes* of the newer establishment. No conceivable motive for such liberality could they see, unless to secure the prestige and reputation which might be derived from advertising the Lyceum of Natural History as part of their educational facilities; and fears were expressed that the professors of the new College would acquire the control and management of the Lyceum. The discussion was long and sharp—some things were said on both sides that

[8] Fairchild, *History*, 45–46.

would have been better unsaid—but finally a majority voted to accept the home that was offered them, whatever might be the risks.[9]

The vote in favor was consequent on the realization that the Lyceum—whatever the intentions of NYU—had no choice in the matter. Despite some skirmishing by the old guard during the next two months the membership held firm and repeatedly rebuffed attempts to reverse the earlier decision. Indeed, once the Lyceum had moved its collections and library into the medical college, the precarious financial position of the Lyceum was rapidly alleviated and the membership figures began a steady upward climb. Unfortunately the relationship with NYU was somewhat soured at the outset by "a wrangle about the degree of publicity allowed to the sign-board of the Lyceum" but in time even this contretemps was forgotten as the two institutions achieved a happy symbiosis.[10]

There is little doubt that the medical faculty at NYU did derive great benefit from its proximity to the Lyceum. In the rivalry with Columbia College, for example, NYU had carried off a remarkable coup and, more generally, in light of the deplorably weak condition of colleges in the United States at the time, the success of NYU in securing a magnificent natural history collection and a superb library of valuable books seemed all the more spectacular.

For John William Draper, in particular, the situation was close to ideal. As professor of chemistry on the medical faculty, Draper was more a scientist than a medical man and, as a listing of his research interests indicates, he had little concern with medical science. In this sense, therefore, the removal of the Lyceum of Natural History to the medical college was convenient for Draper, not simply because Draper was a central figure at the Lyceum, but also because the membership provided him with an audience for his scientific research. Draper was an important figure in two senses, first, because he was the archetype of the local, as opposed to the national, scientist. Second, Draper was one of the last polymaths on the New York scene; as specialization became increasingly the norm, the catholic range of Draper's achievements became exceptional. Because of the wide extent of his research and because Draper remained, for several decades, a leading figure in the development of New York science, it is worth our while to take a close look at the nature of the work performed by Draper at NYU and at the Lyceum.

Shortly before Draper moved to New York in October 1839 news of

[9] *Recollections of John Howard Redfield* (n.p., 1900), 287; Fairchild, *History*, 46.
[10] Fairchild, *History*, 47.

Louis Daguerre's photographic process reached the United States; the first American daguerreotype was taken by D. W. Seager in New York in September 1839, and from that moment on several scientists in Philadelphia and New York were occupied in perfecting the chemical process principally with an eye to the reduction of the time of exposure of the photographic plates so that portraiture could be more sharply defined. Draper, who had long been interested in the properties of light, immediately noticed that greater clarity could be achieved simply by shortening the distance between the plate and the lens; the principal problem, however, of making a photograph on a silver plate remained—that is, because the process took, at the very minimum, seven minutes, it was impossible for any sitter to remain stationary so that a sharply defined portrait was produced. The key to overcoming this difficulty was to increase the sensitivity of the plate and thus reduce the time of exposure.[11]

Draper's innovation in this respect consisted of keeping the plate covered after coating it with a mixture of iodine and chlorine. By April 1840 the photographic process had been so improved by this and other measures that Draper and his colleague at NYU, Samuel F. B. Morse, opened a photographic studio on the roof of the main building at NYU on the east side of Washington Square. Apparently the two savants did considerable business for they were able to charge the "very best people of the City" five dollars for each portrait.[12]

Draper, during the winter of 1839, also began to study various methods of astronomical photography. His first effort to take photographs of the moon, for example, relied on causing light from the moon to reflect from the mirror of a heliostat through a "lens four inches in diameter and fifteen in focus. With an exposure of half an hour [Draper] got an image one-sixth of an inch in diameter." His proficiency at improving the photographic plates was so great that, as Draper was able to announce to a meeting of the Lyceum on 23 March 1840—only a few months after daguerreotypy had been introduced to the world—he had, for the first time anywhere, achieved images of the lunar maria: "a portion of the figure was very distinct but owing to the motion of the moon the greater part was confused; the time occupied was 20′ . . . this is the

[11] Robert Taft, *Photography and the American Scene: A Social History, 1839–1889*, 2nd ed. (New York: Dover Publications, 1964), 15–17.

[12] Fleming, *John William Draper*, 22–23. See also Taft, *Photography*, 33. On the parallel work being done at the same time by Robert Cornelius and Paul Beck Goddard in Philadelphia, see William F. Stapp, "Robert Cornelius and the Dawn of Photography," in *Robert Cornelius: Portraits from the Dawn of Photography*, ed. William F. Stapp (Washington, D.C.: Smithsonian Institution Press, 1983), 25–44.

first time that any thing like a distinct representation of the moon's surface has been obtained."[13]

During the next decade Draper greatly extended his work on the photographic process to include more subtle considerations of radiant energy. His later discoveries during the next decade included the realization that only absorbed rays of light produce a chemical change in the plate; this phenomenon came to be called the Grotthuss-Draper law in recognition of the German scientist's own efforts in examining radiant energy. Six years later, in 1847, Draper demonstrated, first, that all solid substances become incandescent at the same temperature, second, that, as the temperature rises, solid substances emit rays of increasing refrangibility, and finally, that incandescent solids produce a continuous spectrum.

Draper's theoretical accomplishments were complemented by a series of experimental advances that have earned the New York scientist an enduring place in the pantheon of the history of science. Draper was the first scientist to photograph the diffraction spectrum with the use of a grating; he not only made the first photograph of the infrared region but also described three Fraunhofer lines; and, contemporaneously with Edmond Becquerel, Draper photographed lines in the ultraviolet.[14]

In 1850 Draper was appointed to the chair of physiology at the NYU Medical School and, with this change in his official duties, he began a series of works that eventually established his reputation as an elder statesman of the republic of letters. It is unclear what caused Draper gradually to abandon his studies in physics and chemistry; he retained, after all, his chair in chemistry. Whatever the reason, six years after his appointment as professor of physiology, he wrote his first major book, *Human Physiology, Statical and Dynamical*; this work, which remained a classic treatise on the subject for many years, was structured by the effort to consider physiology as an exact science.

At the same time as he was developing a keen interest in medical science, Draper was also extending his intellectual field of vision to history, political science, philosophy, and evolutionary theory. In 1863 his monograph *A History of the Intellectual Development of Europe* appeared; two years later Draper published his highly speculative *Thoughts on the Future Civil Policy of America*; at the end of the decade he brought out

[13] Fleming, *John William Draper*, 26; Minutes of the Lyceum of Natural History, 23 March 1840, NYAS.
[14] Fleming, *John William Draper*, 38–40. For a comprehensive and detailed account of Draper's scientific work, see George F. Barker, "John William Draper, 1811–1882," *Biographical Memoirs of the National Academy of Sciences* 2(1886): 356–372.

a three-volume history of the Civil War; and, finally, in 1874, Draper published his most famous and enduring book, *History of the Conflict Between Religion and Science*, a work that has earned him a minor, yet important, place in the ranks of nineteenth century American philosophers.[15]

Draper's intellectual journey over the course of four decades was certainly idiosyncratic—yet it remains evident that, in his early years at NYU and the Lyceum of Natural History, he was also highly representative of that section of New York's small community of savants and medical men that took little or no interest in the structural changes that were reshaping American science at mid-century.

From 1840 to 1850, at a time when Draper was conducting his most significant research, important institutional developments were transforming the nature and character of American science. Beginning in 1840 with the genesis of the Association of American Geologists and continuing into the next decade, science in the United States became increasingly a national, as opposed to a local, enterprise. The various discrete scientific communities in such urban centers as Philadelphia, New York, Boston, and Albany established liaisons with each other and, over a period of several years, gradually consolidated their initial efforts into a permanent national organization, the American Association for the Advancement of Science.

Concurrent with the formation of the AAAS a second development was also influencing the character of the scientific enterprise. The steady growth of the federal government went hand-in-hand with the funding of a number of scientific initiatives. In 1838 a major expedition under the command of Charles Wilkes was sent, under the aegis of the national government, to survey and chart the Pacific Ocean, to explore the southern and northeastern continental margins, and to carry out investigations in geology, anthropology, and natural history. On the return of the Wilkes expedition to the United States in 1842, the vast collections brought back by the explorers were stored in Washington with the idea of creating a museum of natural history. Contemporaneously with the return of the Wilkes expedition came the news that a wealthy Englishman, James Smithson, had bequeathed a legacy of half a million dollars to be used for the advancement of knowledge. For several years the disposition of the bequest was a matter of dispute, but in 1847 the money was finally settled for the establishment of the Smithsonian Institution.[16]

[15] Fleming, *John William Draper*, 56–64; Barker, "John William Draper," 373–375.
[16] William Stanton, *The Great United States Exploring Expedition of 1838–1842* (Berkeley

Both the appearance of government science and the consolidation of a national scientific community were radical departures from the past. The localized urban centers of science, each of which possessed its own educational and scientific institutions, were supplemented by a series of national institutions that would, in ensuing decades, greatly alter the function and role of the local societies.

In this changing context of science, John William Draper epitomized the essence of the local savant who relied heavily on such institutions as NYU and the Lyceum of Natural History for support but who eschewed the new national societies. Draper in this respect stands in contrast to his close friend, William Cox Redfield, who was not only a leading member of the Lyceum, serving as vice-president for six years, but was also a member of the inner council of the AAAS, serving as the Association's first president at its establishment in 1848. Draper, in his adherence to the local institutions that provide him with valuable support, shunned the new societies such as the American Association for the Advancement of Science. In this respect he stood alongside such Philadelphia scientists as George Ord, vice-president of the Academy of Natural Sciences, who vehemently attacked the appearance of federal science: "no scientific institution in our country will flourish under the patronage of the government; for the moment an appropriation is made for its advancement, a host of vagabonds, *soi-disant savants*, will rush forward, thrust aside modest men of merit and obtain the prize."[17]

Draper's abstention from the politics of science is even more striking when we consider the strong link between New York City and the founding both of the American Medical Association and the American Association for the Advancement of Science. Thus, in May 1846, the first national convention of physicians met in New York City at the Stuyvesant Institute to consider three reforms in medical education: the improvement of the training of apprentices, the extension of the semester from four to six months, and the creation of state licensing boards. There were a few conspicuous absences from the meeting: no representatives were present, for example, from Penn, Harvard, or Jefferson Medical Col-

---

and Los Angeles: University of California Press, 1975); Nathan Reingold and Marc Rothenberg, "The Exploring Expedition and the Smithsonian Institution," in *Magnificent Voyagers: The U.S. Exploring Expedition, 1838–1842*, ed. Herman J. Viola and Carolyn Margolis (Washington, D.C.: Smithsonian Institution Press, 1985), 243–253; A. Hunter Dupree, *Science in the Federal Government: A History of Policies and Activities* (1957; reprint, Baltimore: Johns Hopkins University Press, 1986), 66–90.

[17] Ord to Titian Ramsey Peale, 16 March 1843, Ord-Peale Correspondence, Peale Papers, Historical Society of Pennsylvania.

lege. The most bizarre aspect of the meeting, however, was the opposition to the convention from the medical faculty at NYU; in March 1846, only two months before the meeting was to convene, Martyn Paine, professor of the institutes of medicine at NYU, warned that, as far as the nascent AMA was concerned, there *"is an aristocratic feature in this movement of the worst omen."* Despite the fact that the convention was meeting in the rooms of the NYU Medical College on Broadway, the two delegates from NYU who did appear at the conference, Granville S. Pattison and Gunning S. Bedford, professors of anatomy and obstetrics respectively, restricted their contribution to the proceedings to proposing as the first order of business a motion that "this Convention adjourn *sine die.*"[18]

The hostility of the NYU medical faculty to the establishment of the American Medical Association was prompted by an obscure dispute with the New York State Medical Society and, since the professoriate was united in its antipathy to the meeting, the absence of John William Draper from the convention is not as surprising as it might otherwise appear. Draper's abstention from the proceedings of the American Association for the Advancement of Science is surprising, however, particularly in light of the prominent role that his close friend and Lyceum colleague, William C. Redfield, assumed in the organization.

On joining the Lyceum of Natural History in 1837, Redfield played an active role in its affairs and soon became a member of the inner circle that decided policy. In 1845 he was chosen a member of the committee (together with John William Draper and Martin Zabriskie) to negotiate the removal of the Lyceum to the new medical building of NYU on Broadway; for a brief period, he served as editor of the *Annals* and, in 1847, he was elected vice-president of the Lyceum, a position he held for the next six years.[19]

As a child, Redfield had had little more than a rudimentary education and, at the age of fourteen, he became a mechanic's apprentice. Even at this early age, Redfield was a voracious reader "eagerly devouring every scientific work within his reach." According to one account, his early struggle to better himself was sustained despite all the obstacles that pov-

---

[18] Nathan Smith Davis, *History of the American Medical Association from its Organization up to January, 1855*, ed. S. W. Butler (Philadelphia, 1855), 30, 33. See also "National Medical Convention," *New-York Daily Tribune*, 6 May 1846. On the reform movement in American medicine that led to the founding of the AMA, see William G. Rothstein, *American Physicians in the Nineteenth Century: From Sects to Science* (Baltimore: Johns Hopkins University Press, 1972), 108–121.

[19] Fairchild, *History*, 45, 53, 121.

9. WILLIAM COX REDFIELD (1789–1857). An autodidact, Redfield was elected a member of the Lyceum of Natural History in 1837; he later served as vice-president (1847–1854) of the Lyceum. An expert on meteorology, Redfield was elected president of the American Association for the Advancement of Science at its inaugural meeting in 1848. This engraving, by A.H. Ritchie, appears in Herman Le Roy Fairchild, *A History of the New York Academy of Sciences* (New York, 1887), facing page 80. (*Courtesy of the New York Academy of Sciences.*)

erty was able to throw in his way; without the means to purchase even a lamp, Redfield was forced to study by the light of a "common wood fire in the chimney corner."[20]

In the early years of the nineteenth century, when educational insti-

[20] Denison Olmsted, "Biographical Memoir of William C. Redfield," *American Journal of Science and Arts*, 2d ser., 24(1857): 355.

tutions were confined to the large urban centers, scientific learning was transmitted in rural areas of the country either by way of itinerant lecturers who went from town to town giving popular talks on physics, mechanics, and chemistry, or through the efforts of indigenous self-help groups that slowly and patiently accumulated such resources as a library and experimental apparatus. In Upper Middletown in Connecticut, where Redfield served his apprenticeship, a group of young men, known collectively as the Friendly Association, met at regular intervals to exchange ideas and discuss the latest scientific news. The work of the Friendly Association was supplemented by the library of a local physician who served as a valuable contact to the wider worlds of American and European science. Redfield, as a leading member of the Friendly Association, quickly won a local reputation as an acolyte of science; nevertheless it would have seemed, at the time, highly improbable that he would eventually become an elder statesman in the American scientific community. Redfield himself did not envisage such a future but settled down to a humdrum life in Upper Middletown "eking out a scanty income by uniting with the products of his trade the sale of a small assortment of merchandize."[21]

According to his son—the author of a biographical memoir of the father—Redfield first became seriously interested in meteorology after traveling through Connecticut shortly after a violent storm; the percipient mechanic noticed that, at Middletown, at the commencement of his journey, the fallen trees pointed towards the northwest—on arriving at Berkshire, however, he found that the trees now lay toward the southeast. After making careful observations and inquiring when the gale had hit a particular area and in which direction, Redfield concluded that the gale had occurred as a progressive whirlwind, that is, a whirlwind advancing along a given path at a variable rate.[22]

A chance encounter with Denison Olmsted, professor of natural philosophy at Yale College, led to the publication of the main points of Redfield's theory of storms in the *American Journal of Science and Arts* and very soon he had been accepted into the scientific community. From 1831—the year when his first article appeared—until his death in 1857, Redfield systematically refined his theory of storms on the basis of calculations made from log-books of ships caught in storms at sea. By studying the observational data and by collecting accounts of sailors caught in the storms, Redfield was able to postulate that inside each whirlwind air

[21] Olmsted, "Biographical Memoir," 357.
[22] *Recollections*, 46–47; Olmsted, "Biographical Memoir," 360.

moves in the form of a spiral—descending to the base externally and ascending internally; that the direction of revolution of the whirlwind is always from right to left when above the equator and from left to right below the equator; that the velocity of rotation increases from the margin towards the center of the spiral; and that the whirlwind advances at a velocity greater than the velocity of revolution.[23]

Redfield's theory of storms, at first sight an apparently arcane and esoteric concern, caused a minor commotion within the scientific community principally because it was at variance with the theories advanced by two eminent Philadelphians, James Pollard Espy, professor of mathematics at the Franklin Institute, and Robert Hare, professor of chemistry at Penn. Nor was the debate a purely academic dispute since it was confidently believed—by the three protagonists, at least—that, with a scientific and precise knowledge of cyclones and hurricanes, it would become possible to predict their effects in time to remove shipping from the trail of destruction that generally accompanied whirlwinds. As the debate unfolded in the pages of such publications as the *Journal of the Franklin Institute* and the *American Journal of Science and Arts*, and as the question was increasingly perceived as a practical problem for commerce, so Redfield's scientific reputation began to rise. Redfield's articles on storms began to appear not only in such nautical almanacs as *Blunt's American Coast Pilot* and the *United States Naval Magazine* but also in such publications as the *New York Journal of Commerce*. In 1835 the debate crossed the Atlantic with the appearance of articles from the Americans in the *Philosophical Magazine* and, in 1836 and 1840 respectively, appearances by Hare and Espy at meetings of the British Association for the Advancement of Science, presumably to argue their case and win support from the British scientific community.[24]

In 1824, long before he had attained his later celebrity, Redfield was appointed an agent of the Middletown Steam Navigation Company and, as such, traveled frequently to New York where, after his commercial business was completed, he spent his evenings at meetings of the Lyceum. Although he was only intermittently in New York, Redfield soon became

[23] Olmsted, "Biographical Memoir," 362–363. Redfield also earned a certain renown for his research on fossil fishes; he wrote several articles on Triassic fishes for the *American Journal of Science*. See George Gaylord Simpson, "The Beginnings of Vertebrate Paleontology in North America," *Proceedings of the American Philosophical Society* 86(1942): 167.

[24] Olmsted, "Biographical Memoir," 364–365. For the debate between the three scientists on the nature of whirlwinds, see Edgar Fahs Smith *The Life of Robert Hare (1781–1858): An American Chemist* (Philadelphia: J. B. Lippincott Co., 1917), 462–476; Morrell and Thackray, *Gentlemen of Science*, 379, 416.

a familiar figure at the New-York Institution and quickly won the respect of such savants as Samuel Latham Mitchill and John Torrey.[25]

In later years Redfield's eminence as a meteorologist, as well as his public position as vice-president of the Lyceum, served to place him in a central position when the AAAS was established in 1848. The movement to create the AAAS did not appear first in the urban centers of science but at the periphery of the scientific world—among those savants, like Edward Hitchcock of Amherst College and Parker Cleaveland at Bowdoin College, who were isolated in remote areas far from any scientific institution. This is not quite as surprising as it might at first appear for in each of the three major centers of science—Philadelphia, New York, and Boston—conditions were sufficiently propitious at midcentury for the pursuit of science that additional scientific societies were felt to be superfluous.

Thus in Philadelphia many institutions of every sort catered for the large community of savants. The American Philosophical Society covered a wide range of disciplines from anthropology to physics and, in a very real sense, was the legitimating organization for that part of the city's patrician elite interested in natural knowledge. The Academy of Natural Sciences had, by 1845, a research collection of fauna and flora that was clearly pre-eminent among American scientific societies. The Academy's publishing program—based largely on research done in the collections at the Academy's hall on Seventh Street—consisted of a regular journal as well as intermittent monographs by the members.[26]

In New York City the situation was somewhat dissimilar since only one scientific institution existed there for much of the first half of the nineteenth century. After the debacle in 1843, when the Lyceum lost its building, there was a temporary slump in activity but, largely on account of the arrangement with NYU, a gradual consolidation of resources took place—a process led by such members as Redfield and John William Draper—so that very quickly the Lyceum was holding weekly meetings, publishing issues of the *Annals*, and expanding its large museum collections in natural history.[27]

[25] *Recollections*, 167.

[26] Whitfield J. Bell Jr., "The American Philosophical Society as a National Academy of Sciences, 1780–1846," *Proceedings of the Tenth International Congress of the History of Science* 10(1962): 165–177; Charlotte M. Porter, "The Concussion of Revolution: Publications and Reform at the early Academy of Natural Sciences, Philadelphia, 1812–1842," *Journal of the History of Biology* 12(1979): 273–292.

[27] Fairchild, *History*, 47–48. For a more pessimistic view of New York science at the time, see Robert V. Bruce, *The Launching of Modern American Science, 1846–1876* (New York: Alfred A. Knopf, 1987), 45.

In Boston there existed two distinct foci of science: first, the academic community at Harvard College and second, the more public sphere of scientific institutions in the city. Although Harvard possessed a nugatory scientific tradition throughout much of the first half of the nineteenth century, in 1847 the situation changed with the donation by the textile manufacturer Abbott Lawrence of fifty thousand dollars to establish a scientific school comparable to the medical and law schools. Although Harvard was not the first university to institutionalize science in this way—the first scientific school at an American university had been established at Penn in 1816—Harvard's effort was the first that received sufficient financial support. With the creation of the Lawrence Scientific School at Harvard, a coterie of eminent scientists, including Louis Agassiz and Eben Horsford, was attracted to Cambridge. In addition, the scientific culture at the college was supplemented by the work of the American Academy of Arts and Sciences and the Boston Society of Natural History, both of which possessed large collections and a reputable library.[28]

The original initiative for the AAAS, therefore, came not from the urban centers (where science was flourishing and where the scientific institutions were adequate for local needs) but from a handful of scientists scattered at rural outposts where scientific organizations were either nonexistent or inadequate. In 1840 the initial hesitant step was reinforced by the decision of several geologists employed in state surveys to create the Association of American Geologists, an organization that—in imitation of the British Association for the Advancement of Science—was to meet peripatetically at annual intervals. In 1843 the organization was expanded to include naturalists and, finally, in 1848, the Association of American Geologists and Naturalists became the inclusive American Association for the Advancement of Science.[29]

Although the Lyceum of Natural History had played a significant role in the creation of the New York state geological survey—the Lyceum had petitioned for a survey as early as 1829 and two of its leading members,

[28] Bruce Winchester Stone, "The Role of the Learned Societies in the Growth of Scientific Boston, 1780–1848" (Ph.D. diss., Boston University, 1974), 466–478; Howard S. Miller, *Dollars for Research: Science and its Patrons in Nineteenth-Century America* (Seattle: University of Washington Press, 1970), 77–81. On the Faculty of Natural Sciences at Penn, see Edward Potts Cheyney, *History of the University of Pennsylvania, 1740–1940* (Philadelphia: University of Pennsylvania Press, 1940), 205–207.

[29] For the pre-history of the AAAS, see Sally Gregory Kohlstedt, *The Formation of the American Scientific Community: The American Association for the Advancement of Science, 1848–60* (Urbana, IL: University of Illinois Press, 1976), 59–77.

John Torrey and James Ellsworth DeKay, were in charge of the botanical and zoological components of the 1836 survey—control of the administration and planning of the survey was increasingly centered in Albany, the seat of the state legislature. Moreover the Lyceum scientists employed by the survey, for a variety of reasons, did not continue their explorations for more than a few years. Hence it was not until the late 1840s that the Lyceum became involved with the organization of the AAAS.[30]

In 1848, William Barton Rogers, the central figure in the AAGN and the foremost individual in the creation of the AAAS, was corresponding with William C. Redfield to ask him to distribute circulars among local scientists. Redfield responded enthusiastically, and very soon he had become a pivotal figure in the group of twelve men that not only created the AAAS in 1848 but also carried the organization successfully through its early years. Partly because he was perceived to be neutral on the constitutional issues that divided various groups within the nascent Association and partly because he had performed sterling work in the early planning stages, Redfield was a leading candidate to assume the presidency of the AAAS. The one element that distinguished him from his co-founders was his prominent role in the Lyceum of Natural History; no other candidate for the presidency of the AAAS occupied a comparable office. Thus in Philadelphia on 20 September 1848, when the Association met for the first time, William Cox Redfield was unanimously elected president.[31]

The establishment of national scientific societies and the increasing involvement of the federal government in the support of science was only a part, albeit a very significant part, of the gradual transformation of the scientific enterprise in the United States at mid-century. The other aspect of this transformation was the growth of science at the local level, a growth that manifested itself both in the creation of new institutions for science and in the enlarged role for science within pre-existing institutions. In New York City this second aspect appeared to a qualitatively greater degree largely because New York was the commercial and economic metropolis of the nation; the relatively novel perception that science was now an important dimension of American life, both in its consequence and effects, was the stimulus for the consolidation of science where it had previously had an ephemeral existence.

[30] George P. Merrill, ed. and comp., *Contributions to a History of American State Geological and Natural History Surveys*, Smithsonian Institution, United States National Museum Bulletin no. 109 (Washington, D.C., 1920), 335.

[31] Kohlstedt, *Formation*, 86, 102, 201, 206; Olmsted, "Biographical Memoir," 370.

In the first four decades of the nineteenth century, very few scientists were able to earn a respectable living *qua* scientists. A small number of men—less than twelve at any one time—were able to earn a salary as professors of chemistry at the nation's leading medical schools: Benjamin Silliman at Yale, Robert Hare at Penn, John White Webster at Harvard, and John William Draper at NYU all succeeded in this respect. The majority of would-be scientists, however, had either to find a wealthy patron to sponsor scientific research or to earn a living by taking a full-time job and practicing science as an avocation.

By mid-century this situation was changing—an expanding educational system provided increased opportunities for scientists; the federal government not only sponsored scientific expeditions but also employed a growing number of scientists in the various regulatory bureaux that were being established; and finally, a small number of scientists were able to earn a living through a connection with industry. Last, but not least, numerous institutions that explicitly catered to science were created at mid-century: the Lawrence School at Harvard in 1847, the Cooper Union of Science and Art in 1859, and the Sheffield Scientific School at Yale in 1861 all reflected this change in the relationship of science to society. The creation of a variety of scientific institutions in New York during the second half of the century bears testimony to the increased relevance of science. Additionally, science, to a greater and greater extent, became a part of the educational program at the colleges in New York, in particular, at Columbia College and New York University.

For the Lyceum of Natural History, the increased significance of science was a missed opportunity; on account of the loss of the building on Broadway, the Lyceum was restricted in its range of operations. The Lyceum, unable to make the quantum jump to its own building, was continually held hostage through its dependence on other societies, and, as a consequence, its participation in the scientific renaissance was greatly inhibited. The use of the rooms occupied by the Lyceum at the NYU Medical College were always contingent on the goodwill of the university and, as the medical school gradually began to win a reputation and an increased enrollment, so the tenancy of the Lyceum became more problematic. As a consequence, the Lyceum spent a disproportionate amount of time at mid-century in attempts to find itself a niche in the topography of science within the city.

At the beginning of 1850 the New-York Historical Society, an organization that, like the Lyceum, was having difficulties in adapting to the new age, proposed that the members of the latter "join them in petitioning the Legislature to make an appropriation towards the erection of a building for the two Societies." The Historical Society had even gone so far as to draw up a memorial to the state legislature and, by dint of perseverance, had succeeded in persuading the Assembly at Albany to vote for a measure to provide the NYHS with a suitable building in New York City. Unfortunately the petition died in a committee of the Senate but the Lyceum, stimulated by the Historical Society's initiative, decided to take matters into its own hands. Consequently on 4 February a committee of the Lyceum was formed to "devise some plan by which the Society will be permanently established in a fire-proof building."[32]

The importance that the subject commanded can be gauged from the standing of the individual members of the committee. William C. Redfield took time away from his professional affairs to chair the Lyceum committee while the other members of the committee included J. Carson Brevoort, vice-president of the Lyceum from 1854 to 1864, and Oran W. Morris, the indefatigable librarian who faithfully served the Lyceum in that capacity for almost twenty years.

One of the most energetic members of the committee, however, was a relative newcomer to the Lyceum. Wolcott Gibbs had been elected to the Lyceum in 1840 in his junior year at Columbia College. On his graduation in 1841, Gibbs studied chemistry with Robert Hare at Penn and then returned to New York to enroll at the College of Physicians and Surgeons. Gibbs's purpose in obtaining his medical degree was to learn chemistry—this ambition was realized more fully by a European tour lasting two years; Gibbs studied analytical and organic chemistry at Berlin and Giessen and then finished his tour with a stay at Paris where he attended lectures by Henri Regnault.[33]

In sum, his education was altogether quite superlative. When Gibbs returned to New York in 1848, he was offered the position of assistant professor of chemistry at the College of Physicians and Surgeons. This appointment was an enviable opportunity for any young man at the beginning of his career not only because such a relatively visible position would undoubtedly lead to a wider fame but also because Gibbs would be working with the professor of chemistry, John Torrey, who was one of the leading scientists in the country at the time.[34]

In 1849, however, a new opportunity presented itself to Gibbs. In that

[32] Minutes of the Lyceum of Natural History, 28 January 1850, 4 February 1850, NYAS.

[33] F. W. Clarke, "Wolcott Gibbs, 1822–1908," *Biographical Memoirs of the National Academy of Sciences* 7(1913): 5–6; Edward W. Morley, "Oliver Wolcott Gibbs, 1822–1908," *Proceedings of the American Philosophical Society* 49(1910): xxi–xxii.

[34] "Wolcott Gibbs," *Science*, 18 December 1908, 875.

10. WOLCOTT GIBBS (1822–1908). Educated at the University of Pennsylvania and the College of Physicians and Surgeons, Gibbs was appointed professor of chemistry at the Free Academy (City College) in 1849. He joined the Lyceum of Natural History in 1840; in later life Gibbs was elected president of the National Academy of Sciences and of the American Association for the Advancement of Science. (*Courtesy of City College Archives, City University of New York.*)

year, the educational and scientific topography of New York was changed by the appearance of a third major college. Just as the creation of NYU some twenty years earlier had supplied opportunities for employment for the scientific clerisy, so the establishment of the Free Academy (later to be named City College) was to provide for the employment of a small cadre of scientists. The creation of the new school did not occur without some controversy; the founders explicitly pointed to the torpor of Columbia and NYU as sufficient reason for a third college. More tellingly, as the proposal pointed out, both of the older schools offered only a classical curriculum that prepared young men for the professions but provided nothing for those who wished to enter into manufacturing; as a committee of inquiry of the Board of Aldermen put it: "[the] design is to offer the idea of a College, which, while it shall be in no way inferior to any of our colleges in the character, amount, or value of the information given to the pupils; the courses of studies to be pursued will have more especial reference to the active duties of operative life, rather than those more particularly regarded as necessary for the Pulpit, Bar, or the Medical Profession. . . . an Institution, where Chemistry, Mechanics, Architecture, Agriculture, Navigation, physical as well as moral or mental science, &c, &c, are thoroughly and practically taught, would soon raise up a class of mechanics and artists, well skilled in their several pursuits."[35]

The college rapidly became a political issue; the friends of Columbia and NYU in the state legislature at Albany did all in their power to prevent its incorporation. The *Commercial Advertiser*, a newspaper generally sympathetic to the Whigs, complained that the citizens of New York would not tolerate a new tax to support a third school, while the *Evening Mirror*, a Democratic publication, caustically remarked on the true nature of the opposition: "we do not see how any intelligent man can oppose a plan like that, for a Free Academy. Some are afraid that it will injure Columbia College and the University, but if those institutions rest upon so ticklish a foundation as to be upset by such a rival, the sooner they are got rid of the better." William Cullen Bryant, editor of the *Evening Post*, urged a "vote for a free Academy," while James Gordon Bennett, publisher of the *New York Herald*, argued that the new college "will be too honorable to New York—to our State—to our country—to the age—to be now rejected."[36]

[35] S. Willis Rudy, *The College of the City of New York: A History, 1847–1947* (New York: City College Press, 1949), 13.

[36] Mario Emilio Cosenza, *The Establishment of the College of the City of New York as the Free Academy in 1847: A Chapter in the History of Education* (New York: College of the City of New

For Wolcott Gibbs the establishment of City College was an opportunity not to be missed. Its future seemed secure—with the guarantee of funding from the state legislature City College seemed to hold out better prospects than either NYU or Columbia. Additionally, since the faculty would be at liberty to develop the curriculum, the appointment as professor of chemistry would allow the incumbent considerable latitude with respect both to teaching and research. For Gibbs, who was chiefly interested in analytical chemistry, it was thus a wise move to resign his assistant professorship at the College of Physicians and Surgeons and join the City College faculty.[37]

Since Gibbs's official duties were comparatively light, his appointment at City College was doubly fortunate for the Lyceum of Natural History; Gibbs was able to devote a considerable amount of time to serving on the most important committees of the Lyceum and to concentrating his efforts on that great desideratum, a permanent home where the museum collections could be displayed and the library rendered more accessible. Soon after his appointment at City College, Gibbs was elected a curator of the Lyceum and also served on the finance committee; as he was drawn into the small circle that controlled the Lyceum, he, together with the more percipient of his colleagues, realized that only an energetic and vigorous campaign for funding would succeed in winning support. This, in February 1850, Gibbs was largely instrumental in proposing the establishment of a *"building and sustaining fund . . .* the purpose and object of this subscription . . . shall be to raise and increase the fund aforesaid to the amount of at least Thirty-thousand dollars."[38]

The appeal to the local patriciate mentioned the "uses and advantages derived from natural science," but stressed more particularly that, while science was sponsored not only in Europe but also in rival American cities, in New York great opportunities for establishing a reputable natural history museum were being ignored: "Public patronage carefully encourages [science] in Europe, and at home we have the proof of its importance by the liberal appropriations made for Natural History surveys in many of the states. The Natural History Societies in Philadelphia and

York Press, 1925), 43–47; Editorial, "The Free Academy," *Evening Mirror* (New York), 5 June 1847; "A Free Academy," *Evening Post* (New York), 27 May 1847; Editorial, "Education in New York and Boston—Ought we not to have a Free Academy?" *New York Herald*, 31 May 1847.

[37] In 1854 Gibbs was a candidate for the chair of chemistry at Columbia; for an intriguing account of the contretemps over his appointment as professor of chemistry at Columbia College, see Milton Halsey Thomas, "The Gibbs Affair at Columbia in 1854" (M.A. thesis, Columbia University, 1942).

[38] Minutes of the Lyceum of Natural History, 25 February 1850, NYAS.

Boston are established in their own buildings, through the liberality of their citizens. This feature alone gives them a constantly increasing advantage."[39]

If the members of the Lyceum had been able to foresee the catastrophe that awaited them in the near future they would undoubtedly have pressed their efforts harder until the connection with NYU had been irretrievably broken. As it was, the subscription fund was only moderately successful; after twelve months the members concluded that an insufficient amount had been donated to the Lyceum—those subscriptions that were received had to be returned. Fortunately the apprehension that the Lyceum would lose its lease in the Stuyvesant Institute on Broadway proved unfounded; the NYU medical faculty, having witnessed a considerable increase in enrollment, had decided to buy a much larger building on the outskirts of the city at Fourteenth Street. Happily for the Lyceum, there was sufficient space in the new medical college for the museum collections, which were subsequently transferred in November 1851.[40]

As this action by the NYU medical faculty demonstrated, it remained a mark of distinction to be linked to the Lyceum in such a tangible fashion. Indeed the next decade bore witness to a series of attempts by other scientific institutions—most notably Cooper Union and Columbia College—to lure the Lyceum away from NYU. Thus, in 1852, Peter Cooper, a New Yorker who had made his first fortune by supplying track to the Baltimore and Ohio Railroad, put in motion the process for establishing a new scientific institute in New York City. Cooper—described by one contemporary as "a peculiar-looking . . . person, under the medium size, with a sharp, thin visage, a profusion of brown hair, very little gray eyes, [who] always wears gold spectacles"—was involved in a variety of lucrative and profitable enterprises: he owned a wire factory at Trenton, several blast furnaces in Pennsylvania, a glue factory at New York, and some iron mines in northern New Jersey. In later life he was appointed president of the North American Telegraph Company and served as a candidate of the Greenback Party on the Board of Aldermen of New York.[41]

[39] Report of the Committee on the Address to Citizens, in Minutes of the Lyceum of Natural History, 11 March 1850, NYAS.

[40] Fairchild, History, 48–49.

[41] Howard Carroll, Twelve Americans: Their Lives and Times (New York, 1883), 86–90; Julius Henri Browne, The Great Metropolis: A Mirror of New York (Hartford, CT, 1869), 641; J. C. Zachos, The Political and Financial Opinions of Peter Cooper (New York, 1877), 4–13;

In 1852 Cooper set aside $300,000 from his personal fortune for the establishment of a Union of Science and Art (later to be known simply as Cooper Union). Although he was no scientist, Cooper, in his youth, had been greatly interested in the natural world and profoundly impressed by the displays of animals and birds that he had seen at Scudder's Museum. His great regret had always been that, as a young mechanic serving an arduous apprenticeship, he had never had the time or the resources to study science in any systematic manner. The Cooper Union, therefore, was built expressly to enable the artisans and mechanics of New York to acquire a scientific education as cheaply and as effectively as possible. The plans for the new institution included a six-story building with the "upper story being occupied as an observatory, with choice astronomical . . . apparatus," a large lecture hall, an exhibition room, a library, a refectory, small rooms for the discussion of scientific theories, and, on the roof, a garden where acolytes of natural knowledge could relax and enjoy the music of a hired orchestra.[42]

Cooper's plans had necessarily to be modified as the scheme matured: the roof-garden, for example, never appeared. The principal problem in establishing and maintaining Cooper Union, however, was the cost. Thus, when the building was completed in 1858 it had consumed more than twice the original estimate. Cooper was willing to devote his fortune to the cost of the building but balked at committing the necessary sums for the teaching staff and for the upkeep of the building. A partial solution was found by letting out the first two stories as commercial space for stores and offices; central to the realization of the scheme was the proposal that the Cooper Union, as an educational institution, be allowed to operate tax-free.[43]

This was a tricky question for the state legislature which was not, by any means, sure to grant a tax-exempt status to an institution that contained commercial properties. Thus, as part of his campaign before the legislature, Cooper was anxious to stress the beneficial and philanthropic dimensions of his enterprise; consequently, in an effort to bolster his case and to render the Cooper Union a more attractive proposition generally, Cooper approached the Lyceum of Natural History in June 1853 with an

"Peter Cooper: His Early Struggles and Final Triumph," *Irish World* (New York), 9 September 1876.

[42] "A Princely Donation—A New Popular Institution," *New-York Daily Times*, 27 November 1852; Allan Nevins, *Abram S. Hewitt* (New York: Harper & Brothers, 1935), 177–178; Edward C. Mack, *Peter Cooper: Citizen of New York* (New York: Duell, Sloan and Pearce, 1949), 245; Carroll, *Twelve Americans*, 99–102.

[43] Nevins, *Abram S. Hewitt*, 178; "From Albany," *New-York Daily Times*, 12 January 1857.

"intimation . . . of his desire that the Society shall be accommodated with rooms in the building." Members of the Lyceum, surprised and flattered by the interest of the distinguished philanthropist, were inclined to accept the offer especially after the medical professoriate at NYU had indicated that, with respect to the "renewal of the lease held by the Lyceum . . . the Faculty declined to renew it." The officers of the Lyceum, concerned that they were about to be expelled from the NYU Medical School, were somewhat relieved by the firm declaration of Peter Cooper in October 1854 that "it was his intention to give the Society rooms for the Library and Collections."[44]

A series of severely cold winters, the financial panic of 1857, and competing demands on the construction company from several other major building projects in New York all conspired to postpone the opening of Cooper Union until May 1858. In the interim the state legislature approved Cooper's application for a charter as a tax-exempt institution. Unfortunately, however, the enormous cost of completing Cooper Union and fitting it up for operations—a total amounting to almost seven hundred thousand dollars—made Peter Cooper hesitant to allow the Lyceum as much space as the members felt was necessary for the display of the collections; Cooper preferred to rent the space to commercial tenants. Although he did make a revised offer in 1859, the Lyceum, having just paid NYU the rent for two more years, was reluctant to incur the costs of moving and, moreover, was not keen to be put once more in a dependent situation that offered less space than the members required.[45]

The decision of the Lyceum to remain in the NYU building on Fourteenth Street was strengthened by the sudden announcement that space might be found for the Lyceum in the new Central Park. In 1856 a Board of Commissioners appointed by the New York Supreme Court to regulate the construction of a park in the middle of Manhattan began its deliberations. The proposed park was a feasible project for a variety of reasons: it would employ many thousands of laborers who had been laid off as a consequence of a recent economic recession; it would provide valuable breathing space for a rapidly growing population that already numbered almost eight hundred thousand; and, after five million dollars had been paid out by the state legislature as compensation to the former owners of the land, no politician was going to risk his seat by obstructing

[44] Minutes of the Lyceum of Natural History, 20 June 1853, 26 June 1854, 16 October 1854, NYAS.

[45] Mack, *Peter Cooper*, 245; Minutes of the Lyceum of Natural History, 7 November 1859, NYAS.

11. COOPER UNION. Founded in 1858 by Peter Cooper, the Cooper Union was organized to provide a scientific education for mechanics. In 1875, when this photograph was taken, there were two thousand pupils studying metallurgy, analytic and synthetic chemistry, engineering, architectural drawing, photography, and design. (*Courtesy of the New-York Historical Society.*)

such a worthwhile endeavor. Largely because the project was never controlled for any significant length of time by Tammany Hall, there was a minimal amount of corruption involved in creating Central Park and, under the supervision of Frederick Law Olmsted, the construction of the larger part of the park was successfully completed by February 1861.[46]

The Board of Commissioners, by virtue of the authority granted by the Common Council, had the right to dispose of any buildings that were enclosed by the new park. Most were torn down soon after they were

[46] Laura Wood Roper, *FLO: A Biography of Frederick Law Olmsted* (Baltimore: Johns Hopkins University Press, 1973), 126–128.

purchased but for a while it looked likely that the Lyceum of Natural History would be invited to use the State Arsenal building on Fifth Avenue opposite Sixty-fourth Street as a headquarters. Members of the Lyceum were optimistic about effecting the transfer especially after seven additional commissioners were named, several of whom—including Washington Irving, George Bancroft, Charles A. Dana, and Stewart Brown— were known to be prominent supporters of the Lyceum.[47]

In 1857 the Republican party obtained a majority on the Board of Commissioners—to deflect the criticism of the Democrats that the plunder of the funds would now begin in earnest, the board elected James E. Cooley, a reform Democrat, as president of the Board of Commissioners. In November 1858 Joseph Delafield, president of the Lyceum, met with Cooley and, much to the satisfaction of the members of the Lyceum, was able to report that Cooley had "proposed to accommodate the Lyceum in the building formerly occupied by the Arsenal and that the building would be made as safe against fire as possible." Early in the new year, one of the commissioners, John Gray, informed the Lyceum that a "Committee had been appointed by the Commissioners to confer with the . . . Lyceum" and, a few weeks later, asked for "information respecting the Library, Cabinets and Condition of the Society."[48]

Unfortunately for the Lyceum, the construction of Central Park, given its enormous expense, had always, from its inception, been a delicate issue; that the project had succeeded thus far was a testimonial to the competency and honesty of the commissioners. In the fall of 1859, when Andrew Haswell Green, a prominent lawyer and formerly president of the Board of Education, was appointed comptroller of the Central Park, the work was run even more efficiently. Green was by nature a rigorously economic individual; his parsimonious nature was exacerbated by constant pressure from the state legislature to reduce the costs of construction of the park. Frederick Law Olmsted, whose mandate included the daily supervision of the work, was constantly at odds with Green over his reluctance to spend money: "not a dollar, not a cent is got from under his paw that it is not wet with his blood and sweat. . . . [He has] a constitutional reluctance to pay where it is possible to avoid or postpone, or neglect payment." Thus when the Board of Commissioners, in its third annual report, proposed the establishment of an observatory, a museum of natural history, a botanical garden, and a zoo inside the park, Green

<hr />

[47] Roper, FLO, 127–128.

[48] George Alexander Mazaraki, "The Public Career of Andrew Haswell Green" (Ph.D. diss., New York University, 1966), 31–32; Minutes of the Lyceum of Natural History, 1 November 1858, 17 January 1859, 7 February 1859, NYAS.

was careful to remind the commissioners that their "duty is confined to the construction, maintenance, and regulation of the Park; and while institutions of this kind are desirable . . . the means for their establishment, maintenance and arrangement, should be derived from other sources."[49]

As a consequence the plan to renovate the State Arsenal for its eventual transfer to the Lyceum was repeatedly postponed. In December 1859 Henry Stebbins, the new president of the Board of Commissioners, wrote, in response to letters from the Lyceum, that the "delay has been caused from no indisposition on the part of the Committee to meet your views, but by the state of our finances which was thought would not warrant an expenditure on Architectural Structures until the more important matters were completed." Six days later, Stebbins, who had been waiting on a decision from Albany on the allocation of additional funds for the park, had to report to the Lyceum that the Board of Commissioners would be able to renovate the Arsenal building "so soon as the Legislature of the State shall place them in a position to incur the necessary expense, which we hope will be at an early day in the session."[50]

For the Lyceum members the issue seemed to drag on endlessly; all the commissioners and even the principal architects, Calvert Vaux and Frederick Law Olmsted, expressed their desire to see the Lyceum housed in Central Park but the expense of renovating the Arsenal—now estimated at forty thousand dollars—had necessarily to be borne by the state legislature. In February 1861 the Lyceum members heard the gloomy news that although "new plans had been prepared with especial regard to the views of the Lyceum" by the Board of Commissioners, it was determined by the legislature that "now the sum is limited for the completion of the Park itself, and no appropriation can be made . . . by the Commissioner to carry out the project." A bill was in a committee of the Assembly to reduce the scale of the project and although Stebbins remained the eternal optimist—"the desired appropriation will be at once made"—it was clear to all that the Lyceum, in its search for a permanent home, was to be once again frustrated.[51]

Although the members did not know it, the apocalypse—year zero for the Lyceum—was only a short period away. With the advent of the Civil

[49] Roper, FLO, 145–146; Mazaraki, "Public Career," 72, 87; John Foord, The Life and Public Services of Andrew Haswell Green (New York: Doubleday, Page & Co., 1913), 53, 62.

[50] [Henry G. Stebbins] to Thomas Bland, 18 December 1859, in Minutes of the Lyceum of Natural History, 9 January 1860, NYAS; Stebbins to Bland, 24 December 1859, in Minutes of the Lyceum of Natural History, 9 January 1860, NYAS.

[51] Report of the Committee on Accommodation, in Minutes of the Lyceum of Natural History, 4 February 1861, NYAS.

War, however, any possibility of raising funds for a Lyceum building seemed as remote as ever. The Lyceum's diligent and long-serving librarian, Oran W. Morris, expressed the hope of all the members when, in his annual report for 1861, he rhetorically demanded whether "some of the Capitalists and Bankers of our Metropolis will from their abundance aid the cause of Science and furnish us with a commodious fireproof building in which to deposit our invaluable collection of books and objects of Natural History." Not surprisingly—in 1861—the capitalists and bankers had more pressing and urgent matters to consider and the following year Morris was again heard to lament that the "public spirit of our citizens has been directed towards saving the country rather than to fostering science."[52]

Towards the end of that year, however, the promise of aid and assistance did arrive—from an entirely unexpected quarter. At Columbia College there had been a strong spirit of renewal and reform ever since the dissension in 1854 among the trustees and faculty over the appointment of Wolcott Gibbs to the chair of chemistry. A majority of the Columbia trustees had voted against Gibbs (even though he was clearly the most competent candidate) on account of his Unitarian beliefs. This refusal to hire Gibbs (who later had a distinguished career at Harvard College) stung a small group of trustees into action. Led by George Templeton Strong and Samuel Ruggles they waged an energetic campaign to reform Columbia. Thus, immediately after the Gibbs affair, Ruggles circulated a highly critical pamphlet entitled *The Duty of Columbia College to the Community*. In his tract, Ruggles compared Columbia, founded in 1754, with the University of Göttingen, established in the same year. The comparison was damning and a severe jolt to his fellow-trustees.[53] Whereas Göttingen, situated in a small village, had over fifteen hundred students, eighty-nine professors, and a well-deserved international reputation as a center of research and teaching, Columbia, despite its situation in a great metropolis, had only 140 students, six professors, and the reputation of a rigid and intellectually austere classical academy. Ruggles, in his pamphlet, pointed out that, with the recent establishment of the Free Academy (City College), Columbia's perilous situation was likely to get worse before it got better. City College threatened to become everything

---

[52] Report of the Librarian for 1861, in Minutes of the Lyceum of Natural History, 25 February 1861, NYAS; Report of the Librarian for 1862, in Minutes of the Lyceum of Natural History, 24 February 1862, NYAS.

[53] For a trenchant account of the significance and effect of Ruggles's essay, see Thomas Bender, *New York Intellect: A History of Intellectual Life in New York City* (New York: Alfred A. Knopf, 1987), 271–275.

that Columbia was not: based on the popular will, lavishly funded by both city and state, and democratic (in the sense that it was open to all who were qualified).

While Ruggles did not attain any of his reforms at Columbia immediately—they were to be realized a few decades later—he did shake the trustees up to the extent that they made some drastic changes. The most dramatic move was the purchase by the trustees of the building of the Deaf and Dumb Asylum on Forty-ninth Street at Madison Avenue; in May 1857 the college moved from its old site at Park Place to the new quarters. The spirit of renovation and re-birth at Columbia was such that, a few years later, the trustees began to give serious consideration to the possibility of luring the Lyceum of Natural History away from the medical school at NYU (where the Lyceum still occupied three large rooms). Columbia was perpetually haunted by the frightful possibility that either NYU or City College (or both) might overtake Columbia in enrollment, funding, and prestige. Thus, in light of the fact that Columbia now occupied a spacious site (albeit opposite the Bull's Head cattle yards at Forty-ninth Street and Fifth Avenue) and, aware of the Lyceum's desire to move to better and more secure quarters, the College trustees began making cautious enquiries to see if the Lyceum would move uptown.[54]

Among the college trustees who were active in the matter, none was more determined than George Templeton Strong while, for the Lyceum of Natural History, it was Thomas Egleston, a recent graduate of the École des Mines in Paris and a member of the Lyceum since 1861, who pressed the issue. Strong and Egleston first formally discussed the removal of the Lyceum to Forty-ninth Street in December 1862. Egleston, who was also angling for Columbia to support his own independent idea of a mining and engineering school, apparently suggested the removal only of the Lyceum's mineralogical collection to Columbia, a suggestion that "met with favor from several of the Trustees of the College." Few Lyceum members were fully aware of the private scheme that Egleston was quietly hatching; nevertheless they were discerning enough to sharply remind him that "no separation of the Society's Collections is likely to be permitted."[55]

Whatever the motives behind Egleston's maneuver the door to an

[54] Horace Coon, *Columbia: Colossus on the Hudson* (New York: E. P. Dutton & Co., 1947), 75–76. On the reforms at Columbia, see also Frederick Paul Keppel, *Columbia* (New York: Oxford University Press, 1914), 6–11.

[55] Minutes of the Lyceum of Natural History, 22 December 1862, NYAS; Report of the Committee on Accommodations, in the Minutes of the Lyceum of Natural History, 5 January 1863, NYAS.

agreement with Columbia had been opened and, although the Lyceum still cast a longing glance at the Arsenal building in Central Park, further negotiations with the college continued. In March 1863 Charles A. Joy, who was both a member of the Lyceum and a professor of chemistry at Columbia, met with the president of the college, Charles King, and two of the trustees, Gouverneur Ogden and George Allen. Joy was able to report back to the Lyceum that Columbia was now interested in providing the land for a building on the college grounds; on making further enquiries, the Lyceum was gratified to discover that the trustees envisaged a "Building . . . to occupy a site say 60 feet on 4th Avenue by 40 on 49th Street and of three stories in height." Unfortunately the Columbia trustees were not able to donate the necessary funds but as George Allen pointed out, there was a sentiment among the trustees that a building fund would succeed: "Mr. Allen expressed the willingness not only of himself but of others of the Trustees to take an active part in raising such funds; he as well as others connected with the College feeling a deep interest in carrying out the object."[56]

One week later, the members learned that the proposal from Columbia had been broadened to include not only the Lyceum but also "various Societies engaged in the study and promotion of Science. . . . The building to be erected by means of funds raised by public subscription — the College being the recipient of the monies, and remaining the owners of the building." At further conferences between Columbia and the Lyceum, however, it soon became clear that while the two sides were both eager to have the affair consummated, the obstacles to raising the necessary money during the turmoil occasioned by the Civil War were simply too great. The Columbia proposal was gradually abandoned, and the Lyceum was reluctantly forced to sign an extension of its lease with the NYU Medical College.[57]

It says a great deal about the public perception both of higher education and of science that so little support was forthcoming for the college's plans to house the Lyceum. Indeed the whole sorry saga of the Lyceum's fruitless efforts at mid-century to get permanent accommodation reveals, with especial clarity, that — by sharp contrast with later decades — science was, for most citizens, a peripheral concern largely restricted to a handful

[56] Minutes of the Lyceum of Natural History, 2 March 1863, NYAS; Report of the Committee Appointed to Confer with Columbia College, in Minutes of the Lyceum of Natural History, 16 March 1863, NYAS.

[57] Report of the Committee on Accommodations, in Minutes of the Lyceum of Natural History, 23 March 1863, NYAS. See also Report of the Committee on Accommodations, in Minutes of the Lyceum of Natural History, 6 April 1863, NYAS.

12. Fire at the Academy of Music, 21 May 1866. The fire at the Academy of Music broke out on the night of 21 May 1866; after spreading to adjacent blocks, it caused extensive damage. This lithograph (which first appeared in *Harper's Weekly*, 9 June 1866, 360) shows the gutted building; the roof has collapsed and the interior is destroyed. (*Courtesy of the New-York Historical Society.*)

of enthusiasts. The story of the Lyceum's efforts to find a home did not end with the Columbia enterprise but finished three years later when the Lyceum was struck the hardest blow imaginable, a blow that ended forever the dream of creating, from the Lyceum's collections, a great natural history museum in New York.

On the night of Monday, 21 May 1866, an arsonist set fire to the Academy of Music, a large opera house on the corner of Fourteenth Street and Third Avenue. As the night watchman was making his rounds and preparing to close the hall at the end of the evening's performance, he noticed thin streams of smoke issuing out of the stage. By the time the firemen arrived, "flames [were] bursting out in the basement beneath section F of the parquette. [The firemen] at once directed several streams upon the fire, and in a short time there was every indication that the fire would be got under control before inflicting much damage." That was not the end of it, however, for as the chief engineer of the Fire Department walked about the house, checking that the fire had been thoroughly extinguished, suddenly he "was electrified at discovering flames rapidly darting upward from fires which had been kindled by some person in the second and third circles." Almost immediately after spotting the new outbreaks of fire, the "gas which had been lit to enable the firemen the better to work went out, and all were enveloped in darkness."[58]

Sadly, in the confusion that followed, two firemen were trapped on the stage, and, blinded by the billowing smoke, were suffocated before they could reach the exit doors. The death toll could have been considerably higher for eighteen other firemen were trapped inside the Academy but were quickly rescued: "cries were heard proceeding from beneath the steps leading into the Academy from Irving-place. Axes were at once procured and the wooden steps were dashed away by strong and willing hands, and from the gloom and smoke were drawn 18 half suffocated firemen amid the cheers of their comrades."[59]

The efforts by the fire companies at saving the Academy were fruitless. The fire had been set so well that the building was soon enveloped in a huge conflagration and within ten minutes after the first alarm the fire had spread throughout the Academy. According to one witness the flames "went from tier to tier, licking up everything. Balcony after bal-

[58] "The Great Fire: Total Destruction of the Academy of Music," New-York Tribune, 23 May 1866. See also "The Academy of Music and Other Buildings Destroyed: The University Medical College in Ruins," Evening Post (New York), 22 May 1866.

[59] "The Great Fire," New-York Tribune, 23 May 1866. See also "Disastrous Conflagration: The Academy of Music and College of Surgeons Destroyed," New-York Times, 22 May 1866.

cony went down with a rush, and the interior of the theater, which a short time before had contained a large audience, was nothing but roaring, living, crackling, howling fire."[60]

Very soon the whole block of stores on Fourteenth Street between Irving Place and Third Avenue was ablaze. After the Academy of Music had been destroyed, the Ihne Piano Factory—with the "exception of one piano"—went up in smoke to be followed in rapid succession by a restaurant, a pork butcher's store, a lager-beer saloon, a second piano-factory, a paint store, a clothing store, a second saloon, the St. James Evangelical Lutheran Church, and innumerable private dwellings all of which suffered damage to varying degrees from the fire.[61]

Immediately to the east of the Academy of Music and facing onto Fourteenth Street was the NYU Medical College which contained, on the first floor, the Mott Surgical Museum; on the second floor a "large and valuable collection of anatomical and pathological specimens"; and, on the third floor, the lecture-rooms and the operating theater. The collections of the Lyceum of Natural History—comprising many thousands of items including, *inter alia*, John James Audubon's collection of birds, an unrivalled mineralogical cabinet with specimens obtained by the New York State Geological Survey, and Samuel Latham Mitchill's ichthyological collection—were stored in the basement of the medical college. Everything was destroyed by the fire—a strong south-easterly wind blew sparks from the Academy of Music onto the roof of the medical college and, in a few short minutes, the collections of the Lyceum were reduced to a pile of ashes.[62]

When the fire had been brought under control several hours later a hasty estimate of the damage was given. By unanimous consent those individuals connected with the Academy of Music had come off worse. While the directors were covered with adequate insurance to begin plans for rebuilding almost at once, several other unfortunates were not so lucky. The operatic entrepreneur, Max Maretzek, had lost the "scores, vocal, instrumental and choral parts of over 80 complete operas, the entire [collection] of his vast and expensive wardrobe, and all his scenery, properties, &c. These could hardly be replaced for $150,000 for they were the accumulation of the labor of years. On these . . . there was an insurance for barely $10,000." The manager of the Academy of Music, Eugene

[60] "Description of the Fire," *New-York Tribune*, 23 May 1866.

[61] "The Great Fire: Details of the Disaster—Losses and Incidents," *New-York Times*, 23 May 1866. See also "The Great Fire: Further Particulars," *Evening Post* (New York), 22 May 1866.

[62] "The Great Fire," *New-York Times*, 23 May 1866.

THE STRUGGLE FOR SURVIVAL

Grau, was also a "heavy sufferer . . . he did not insure either the music, the dresses, or the properties, for the operas which he produced; all of which perished in the flames on Monday night. His losses are calculated to be between $30,000 and $50,000, on which there was no insurance."[63]

Less dramatic but equally severe was the loss sustained by the Medical College; while the Academy of Music could be rebuilt, there was no possibility of restoring the various medical collections—including the Mott Surgical Museum—that had perished in the fire. John William Draper, professor of chemistry at NYU, had lost his "expensive chemical apparatus . . . [as well as] delicate and costly instruments . . . [and] the notes and books of a large amount of unpublished experiments." His son, Henry Draper, professor of analytical chemistry at the university, was relatively fortunate: the younger Draper suffered only the "loss of a telescope mirror which had cost many months of labor."[64]

The heaviest loss for the city's scientific community, however, was the destruction of the collections of the Lyceum of Natural History. The Medical College was able to find space within Bellevue Hospital and the congregation of St. James Lutheran Church was able to accept an offer to hold its services at the Tabernacle Baptist Church on Second Avenue, but the Lyceum, bereft of its collections, was now no more than a shadow of its former self and certainly could no longer have any pretensions to constitute a natural history museum. Reporters for all of the city's major newspapers regarded the loss of the Lyceum collections as a severe blow to the cause of science in New York—a writer for the *Evening Post* expressed both regret at the loss and resolve for the future when he prophetically editorialized that the "fire in Fourteenth Street ought to be a lesson and a warning. The Mott museum, the Lyceum collection, the preparations of numerous distinguished anatomists, the telescopic mirrors of Draper—the work of years—were consumed in a few minutes. . . . What we want in New York is a great fire-proof building, sufficiently capacious to afford shelter to all the societies which possess valuable collections."[65]

[63] "Destruction by Fire of the Academy of Music," *New-York Times*, 23 May 1866.

[64] Editorial, "The University Medical College," *New-York Times*, 25 May 1866; "The Great Fire," *New-York Tribune*, 23 May 1866.

[65] "The Lyceum of Natural History—A Severe Loss," *Evening Post* (New York), 25 May 1866.

3

A Rivalry for Resources
1866–1887

IF THE LOSS of the Lyceum building in 1844 had had the taste of gall then the destruction of the natural history collections savored of the most bitter hemlock. For the tiny handful of members who were willing to keep the Lyceum flag flying, the immediate aftermath of the fire was a time of gloomy pessimism and despair. Yet, despite the difficulties, the thread of continuity persisted; even the apocalyptic fire did not destroy the organization.

In a paradoxical sense the destruction of the Lyceum's collections had a beneficial effect—not for the members, to be sure—but for the scheme to establish a natural history museum in New York. In the years since its establishment the Lyceum, by virtue of its unique position as the sole organization in the city for natural history, had effectively prevented any independent initiative towards the creation of a museum. Since, before 1866, the Lyceum was known to be perpetually on the look-out for a fire-proof building in which to house its collections, any separate initiative to create a museum would have been viewed as redundant and would never have received financial support from the city's patriciate. Suddenly, however, the Lyceum was no longer the principal protagonist in the drama; its surviving members were concerned only with keeping the organization intact and had no resources, morale, or spirit for the task of creating a museum.

The movement to establish a museum of natural history in New York was led by a small group of wealthy bankers, lawyers, and merchants who, because of their connections to the city's patriciate, were able to raise considerable sums for the new endeavor. A second group of advocates for a museum included the Commissioners of Central Park who, despite the earlier rebuff from the state legislature, still dreamed of the day when the Park would include not only a natural history museum but also a zoo and a major art museum. A third group consisted of leading members of the Lyceum of Natural History who, aware that they could no longer claim leadership in the scientific domain, were still anxious to promote science in New York City.

Representatives of the various groups first met formally on 30 December 1868. Those present included the financier, J. Pierpont Morgan; a wealthy glass importer, Theodore Roosevelt; the president of the New York Chamber of Commerce, Morris K. Jesup: and the banker, Levi P. Morton. Several prominent members of the Lyceum of Natural History attended the founding meeting of the American Museum of Natural History. These included: William A. Haines, the vice-president of the Lyceum who, when not involved in his dry-goods business, pursued an avocational interest in conchology; Robert L. Stuart who, as owner of the city's largest sugar refining business, had made a considerable fortune and was a patron of the Lyceum and a perennial contributor to the Lyceum's publication fund; and John David Wolfe, a wealthy hardware merchant, who generously supported the work of the Lyceum.[1]

The founders of the American Museum of Natural History were distinguished not only by their large fortunes but also by their concern to promote the intellectual and physical welfare of less fortunate citizens. Their shared concept of *noblesse oblige* found expression not only in the support of charitable institutions such as the New York Hospital, the Working Women's Protective Association, and the New York Association for Improving the Condition of the Poor, but also in less direct meliorist ventures that aimed to raise the cultural, moral, and physical condition of New Yorkers. In this sense the construction of Central Park in the middle of the nineteenth century and the establishment of two major museums, the American Museum of Natural History and the Metropolitan Museum of Art, as integral parts of the Park, reflected an aspiration to create an environment in the city that would offset the effects of industrialization. At a time when tens of thousands of immigrants were crowding into miserable tenements, the appeal of a park to improve conditions of public health was irresistible, even if it had little practical application.[2]

---

[1] John Foord, *The Life and Public Services of Andrew Haswell Green* (New York: Doubleday, Page & Co., 1913), 205. For the founding of the American Museum of Natural History, see William Adams Brown, *Morris Ketchum Jesup: A Character Sketch* (New York: Charles Scribner's Sons, 1910), 136–151; Geoffrey Hellman, *Bankers, Bones & Beetles: The First Century of the American Museum of Natural History* (Garden City, NY: Natural History Press, 1968), 9–23.

[2] Thomas Bender, *Toward an Urban Vision: Ideas and Institutions in Nineteenth Century America* (1975; reprint, Baltimore: Johns Hopkins University Press, 1982), 175–177, 179–181.

In a more abstract sense the park had an educational function. Andrew Haswell Green, the Comptroller of the Park in 1868, envisaged that the spirit that animated the construction of Central Park would "place our City in the same rank in the field of literature and art that she occupies in the affairs of commerce." A writer for the *New-York Times* predicted that if a zoological garden, art museum, and natural history museum were organized as components of the new park then "the visitor riding along its rustic roadways, or strolling in its quiet, woody places, will become a peripatetic philosopher in spite of himself. On every side the works of nature, animate and inanimate, and the choicest creations of art, will induce contemplation."[3]

The small group that met in December 1868 to plan a new museum had, however, chosen an inauspicious moment since the Park Commissioners, who were eager to promote the plan, had recently failed to secure the necessary financial support from the state legislature. There was every reason to believe, however, that where public support had fallen short the private initiative of wealthy citizens would continue the job to completion. In a letter intended to effect a symbiosis of public and private endeavor the original group of nineteen philanthropists notified the Park Commissioners that "having long desired that a great Museum of Natural History should be established in the Central Park, and having now the opportunity of securing a rare and very valuable collection as the nucleus of such [a] Museum, the undersigned wish to enquire if you are disposed to provide for its reception and development."[4]

The nucleus of the new museum consisted of a collection "at present equal about four and one-quarter tons in bulk" gathered by Albert Bickmore on an extended trip through the Dutch East Indies in 1866. While the group of nineteen founders provided the stamp of approval for the new museum as well as a large part of its initial funding, Bickmore provided the overall organization. A graduate of Dartmouth College, Bickmore had studied with Louis Agassiz at Harvard College, receiving a second undergraduate degree in 1864. As an assistant to Agassiz, Bickmore had witnessed the unprecedented achievement of the Harvard scientist in winning sufficient support both from individual patrons and the state legislature to establish the Museum of Comparative Zoology.

[3] "Zoological Gardens," *New-York Times*, 18 July 1868. For a cogent analysis of the meaning and significance of Central Park in the context of urbanization see Ian R. Stewart, "Central Park, 1851–1871: Urbanization and Environmental Planning in New York City" (Ph.D. diss., Cornell University, 1973), 348–359.

[4] John Michael Kennedy, "Philanthropy and Science in New York City: The American Museum of Natural History, 1868–1968" (Ph.D. diss., Yale University, 1968), 13.

Bickmore's association with Agassiz was crucial for the establishment of the American Museum of Natural History; in his appeals for support for the American Museum, Bickmore used the same strategy—a reliance on private funding with public support—that had proved so felicitous for Agassiz.[5]

The example of the Museum of Comparative Zoology had an additional value for the supporters of the American Museum since it could be used to great effect to demonstrate that the state of New York was falling behind its northern neighbor in science. Agassiz's museum at Harvard began with a legacy of fifty thousand dollars from Francis Calley Gray, a prominent member of the Boston Society of Natural History. In September 1857 Agassiz received the offer of a prestigious appointment as professor of paleontology at the Muséum National d'Histoire Naturelle in Paris; Harvard, however, reaffirmed its support for the Museum of Comparative Zoology and Agassiz remained in the United States. By April 1859 his efforts had been crowned with success; the Massachusetts legislature promised additional funds for the museum and, with some help from prominent members of the Boston patriciate, Agassiz eventually raised an additional seventy thousand dollars.[6]

Agassiz's success in creating the Museum of Comparative Zoology did not go unremarked in New York City. Most commentators agreed that the "Museum had already done much to advance science. . . . it had added to the honor of the country, and had placed America in such a position that instead of being a tributary to European museums, some of the finest and rarest specimens which scientific men desire to have preserved are constantly received at the museum at Cambridge." More telling for a New York audience was the lamentable failure of the efforts in the city to establish a museum; after P. T. Barnum's American Museum had burned down in July 1865, there had been an abortive attempt one year later by John Banvard to build a museum on Broadway under the sponsorship of the Grand Lodge of Free and Accepted Masons—this project quickly succumbed to poor management. The failure of New York's scientific and cultural societies to endow a respectable museum was a source of considerable mortification to the city elite which, having turned New York into a commercial and financial metropolis, now regretted the previous indifference towards cultural enrichment: "in respect of this sort of thing, our City is, and always has been, a marvel of poverty. Compared with any one of the hundred larger cities of Europe,

[5] "Collections for a Museum in New-York," *New-York Times*, 21 May 1866.

[6] Edward Lurie, *Louis Agassiz: A Life in Science* (Chicago: University of Chicago Press, 1960), 218–234.

we are beneath contempt. In no department of natural history or scientific study is there anything open to the public worthy of notice."[7]

The spur of civic pride, the initiative of a small group of wealthy citizens, the guidance and counsel of the Lyceum of Natural History, and the enthusiastic cooperation of the Park Commissioners coalesced in a cultural campaign that exceeded in scope and vision all precedents in New York. Andrew H. Green, who, a decade earlier, had worried about the cost of adding a museum to the proposed park, now envisaged not only a natural history museum but also a zoo, a botanical garden, and a paleozoic museum. The latter project was undoubtedly the most adventurous scheme connected with the construction of Central Park; it also proved to be the most controversial for, at a meeting of the Lyceum of Natural History in 1871, the paleozoic museum became a point of contention between the scientific community and the Tweed Ring that then dominated New York political life.[8]

In 1853, as part of the Crystal Palace exhibition in London, Benjamin Waterhouse Hawkins, a painter and sculptor, had constructed several dinosaurs at the behest of Richard Owen. Fifteen years later Hawkins migrated to the United States and, after a brief residence in Philadelphia, Hawkins moved to New York to accept a commission from Andrew H. Green to reconstitute the "phenomena of the ancient epochs of this continent." Such a project, Green speculated, would have especial value for the new park in New York since it would, at one and the same time, serve both to educate and to entertain. Hawkins, in his reply to Green's offer, linked the proposed exhibition of the dinosaurs to recent discoveries in geology and gave a promise that, if he were given adequate support from the park administration, the project would have a value not only for the general public but also for the cause of science: "the interest in the remains of ancient animal life which geology has revealed within the last half century, is world-wide and almost romantic in its influence upon the imagination. . . . there can hardly be a question as to the advantage of

[7] "Legislative Visit to Professor Agassiz's Museum," *Evening Post* (New York), 2 May 1868; A. H. Saxon, *P. T. Barnum: The Legend and the Man* (New York: Columbia University Press, 1989), 108; "Laying the Corner-stone of the New-York Museum—Masonic Ceremonies," *New-York Times*, 29 August 1866; Editorial, "A Museum Without Humbug," *New-York Times*, 18 March 1868.

[8] The following account of the paleozoic museum is based on Edwin H. Colbert and Katharine Beneker, "The Paleozoic Museum in Central Park, or the Museum that Never Was," *Curator* 2(1959): 137–150; Adrian J. Desmond, "Central Park's Fragile Dinosaurs," *Natural History* 83(October 1974): 64–71; Richard C. Ryder, "Dusting Off America's First Dinosaur," *American Heritage* 39(March 1988): 68–73.

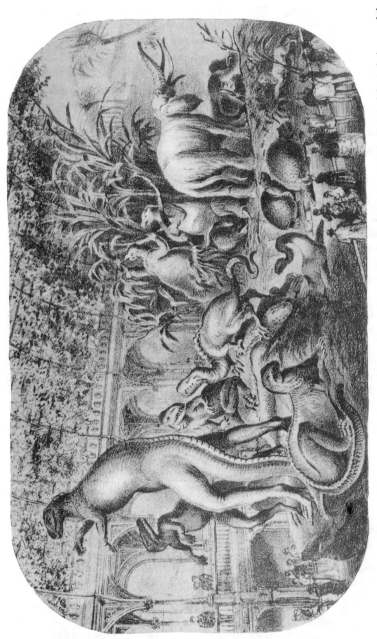

13. THE PALEOZOIC MUSEUM. This engraving (which first appeared in the *Thirteenth Annual Report of the Board of Commissioners of the Central Park* (New York, 1870), facing page 28) shows a variety of extinct animals from various geological periods. The proposed paleozoic museum was to be enclosed by an arch of foliage; unfortunately the models for the animals shown here were destroyed in 1871. (*Courtesy of the New York Public Library.*)

representing those remains clothed in the forms which science now ventures to define."[9]

Hawkins's plans for the paleozoic museum in Central Park included the construction of two groups of dinosaur; in the first division he included examples of *Hadrosaurus*, a dinosaur discovered in 1858 in marl beds in New Jersey by Joseph Leidy, professor of anatomy at Penn. The first division also included examples of the predator *Laelaps* as well as the marine species, *Elasmosaurus* and *Masasaurus*. In the second division, corresponding to the tertiary period, Hawkins intended to place ten specimens of such species as *Megatherium* and *Megalonyx*. In short, the whole enterprise, which also included the construction of a large iron-framed glass building at the southern edge of Central Park, was an extremely ambitious and costly undertaking.[10]

As the plans for the extension of the park and for the construction of the various museums were unfolding during 1870, the political context rapidly changed. Until 1870 Central Park had been one of the few projects that lay outside the control of William Marcy Tweed. As a consequence the park was untouched by the corruption and graft that were endemic to New York in the years following the Civil War. In 1870, however, Tweed persuaded the state legislature to pass a series of supplementary clauses to the city charter; one of the consequences of this maneuver was the subordination of the previously independent Board of Commissioners to the Department of Public Parks. Andrew Haswell Green, who had formerly administered the park project in an efficient, honest, and competent manner, was now answerable to one of Tweed's most loyal accomplices, Peter (Brains) Sweeney.

As everyone soon realized, this change spelt disaster for the general administration and management of Central Park. The *New-York Times*, in an editorial on the future of the park, grimly prophesied that the "expense of keeping up the Park would probably be quadrupled. Large numbers of the stipendiaries of the Ring would be quartered on it at immense salaries, to fill offices created for their benefit." The draining of the treasury, according to the editor of the *Times*, was to be expected; the greater calamity would be the rapid physical destruction of the park as the Tweed henchmen turned it into a playground for their own licentious amusements:

[9] Green to Hawkins, 2 May 1868; Hawkins to Green, 9 May 1868; quoted in "The Central Park," *New-York Times*, 8 August 1868.

[10] Colbert and Beneker, "Paleozoic Museum," 144–146; Douglas J. Preston, *Dinosaurs in the Attic: An Excursion into the American Museum of Natural History* (New York: St. Martin's Press, 1986), 10–11; *Thirteenth Annual Report of the Board of Commissioners of the Central Park* (New York, 1870), 28–29.

to realize thoroughly what the desolation of the scene would be, we must
imagine a force of thieves and rowdies and ruffians wearing the uniform
of the Police . . . skylarking with other rowdies of an upper grade, who,
having been longer in office, would be racing on the avenues with trotting
wagons. . . . We must farther imagine the little restaurant near the Terrace
turned into a common groggery and 'political head-quarters,' and peopled,
as well as the adjacent bowers and arbors, on fine evenings, by a select company such as now assemble at Florence's in Houston-street, and gash each
other with knives and glass bottles. . . . Fancy, too, the fate of the animals,
of which there is now a large and respectable collection; what quantities
of cheap garbage would be given them to eat; how fast they would die, and
what a salary some bespangled rascal would draw for 'taking care of them,'
even after they had dwindled down to one old goat.[11]

This apocalyptic vision did not, fortunately, come to pass largely on
account of the steady growth in 1871 of a reform movement organized to
oust Tweed and his cronies; the pilfering of the city treasury amounted
to many millions of dollars and, as it became clear that Tweed intended
to remain in office at least until the next election, the banks refused credit
to the city. As a consequence, in September 1871, the wages of all city
employees (including the police) were stopped and City Hall was be-
sieged daily by thousands of laborers demanding their pay. On 15 September the unity of the Tweed Ring cracked: the Comptroller, Richard
Connolly, was thrown to the wolves by his companions in crime and Connolly, in order to save his own skin, began to spill details of the corruption to the press.[12]

The campaign to oust Tweed was primarily based on the unprecedented theft from the city treasury. It was given added momentum, however, by an episode in the first half of 1871 that dismayed and alarmed
the organizers of the American Museum of Natural History, a group that
included many of New York's bankers and financiers. In 1870, almost as
soon as Central Park had come under the authority of the Department
of Public Parks (and thus under the control of Tweed), Peter Sweeney,
the president of the Park Commission, had effectively brought all future
work on the park to a close by refusing to extend the contracts of Frederick Law Olmsted and Calvert Vaux. Even more serious was Sweeney's
simultaneous decision to stop the construction of the paleozoic museum.

Waterhouse Hawkins, as might be expected, was disconsolate at this

[11] Editorial, "The Central Park," New-York Times, 13 March 1870.
[12] Foord, Life and Public Services, 90–97. For an account of Tweed's downfall, see Dennis
Tilden Lynch, "Boss" Tweed: The Story of a Grim Generation (New York: Boni & Liveright,
1927), 370–384.

unexpected turn of events. After laboring on the project for two years and with many of the animals completed, Hawkins now found himself suddenly out of a job. Influential members of New York's scientific community shared Hawkins's dismay since, if the paleozoic museum were to be abandoned, it seemed possible that the natural history museum, which relied in great part on concessions granted by the previous city administration, would also meet an untimely end. As a consequence of their shared alarm, leaders of the Lyceum of Natural History met with Hawkins to offer him a public platform from which he could provide members of the press with an account of the destructive effect of Tweed's management of Central Park.

The Lyceum organized the occasion well for, on 6 March 1871, when Hawkins was scheduled to appear with his charges against Tweed, the audience included not only journalists from the city press but also many prominent individuals who resented Tweed's summary abrogation of the park construction projects. Hawkins used the occasion not only to record the history of the museum but also to sound a warning and a call to arms against the depredations of the Tweed Ring: "the whole scheme of popular education which he had been endeavoring to carry out was annulled. He trusted, however, only temporarily, and thought in time the good sense of the people would awaken." After John Strong Newberry, the president of the Lyceum, had concurred with Hawkins's final remarks by noting that the "present circumstance was of far too great importance to pass by lightly" the meeting took a dramatic turn when E. George Squier, an associate of Tweed, rose to challenge Hawkins's criticism. Squier's speech that evening was little more than an *argumentum ad hominem* against Hawkins. According to Squier, Hawkins's competence was limited to the study of books; he knew nothing about the management of Central Park; and, in any case, Hawkins was not even an American but "only an Englishman . . . his trying to get up a museum in this City without a corresponding scheme for dividing the profits, was an absurdity."

Sharp words from members of the Lyceum followed closely on Squier's remarks; Isidor Walz, the most outspoken member present, stated that "an appeal to the City Government for this purpose [of supporting a museum] would be like asking the Enemy of Mankind to assist in advancing the cause of religion." The final word came in a resolution of the Lyceum that offered Hawkins encouragement for the continuation of his work: "the Lyceum of Natural History in the City of New-York has learned with deep regret of the temporary suspension of the work of restoration of the forms of extinct animals. . . . *Resolved*, That this Lyceum considers the proposed Paleozoic Museum . . . as a valuable acquisition to the scientific treasures and resources of the City."[13]

The Tweed Ring, having heard an account of the Lyceum meeting from Squier, took Hawkins's strictures as a calculated threat; his public criticism, uttered before an audience of wealthy and influential New Yorkers, was one of the first public blows in the fight against corruption at City Hall. Tweed's reaction to the speech was dramatic; on 3 May a group of laborers, armed with heavy hammers and iron bars, invaded Hawkins's studio and smashed into pieces the dinosaurs that Hawkins had constructed during the previous two years.[14]

When word of the destruction of the paleozoic animals got out among the sponsors of the American Museum of Natural History, the reaction was one of indignant alarm. It was now evident that, if Tweed felt threatened, he would stop at nothing to silence criticism. In this case his action proved counter-productive for, apprehensive that the American Museum of Natural History might eventually suffer a similar fate, the patrician class that had supported the American Museum now gave tacit encouragement to the reform movement that, a few months later, was to bring down the Tweed Ring and result in Tweed's disgrace and imprisonment.

In fact, in the last year of his reign, Tweed—in anticipation of the financial benefits (for himself) that might be siphoned from the construction of the two museums—supported legislation that would enable the municipal authorities to erect two buildings adjacent to Central Park for the Metropolitan Museum of Art and the American Museum of Natural History. Later in the year, a request for thirty thousand dollars as an annual maintenance stipend also passed the state legislature. Finally, the Park Commissioners received authority to grant land to the two museums for new buildings: the Metropolitan Museum of Art obtained a parcel of land, then known as the Deer Park, that lay on Fifth Avenue between Eightieth and Eighty-fourth streets while the American Museum of Natural History received a site known as Manhattan Square on the opposite side of Central Park. Work on the new buildings began in the fall of 1872; less than two years later, the American Museum of Natural History was formally inaugurated at a ceremony in June 1874 at which Ulysses S. Grant, president of the United States, made a short congratulatory speech. Joseph Henry, secretary of the Smithsonian Institution, followed Grant and, in a series of pointed remarks, made the case for the Museum

[13] "Meeting of the Lyceum of Natural History," *New-York Times*, 7 March 1871.
[14] Desmond, "Central Park's Fragile Dinosaurs," 71; Ryder, "Dusting Off America's First Dinosaur," 71; Preston, *Dinosaurs in the Attic*, 12.

as a scientific research institution, a mission that was not universally shared by many of the Museum's trustees present.[15]

For the Lyceum of Natural History the successful establishment of the American Museum necessarily meant the displacement of the Lyceum from its dominant position over the culture of science in New York City. The Lyceum was no longer able to claim a leading role in the diffusion of science to the educated public; after the fire of 1866 and the creation of the American Museum a few years later, the Lyceum—it seemed to the members—was now suited for a more modest role in the institutional life of the city.

The changed nature of scientific activity in New York City after 1866 was a consequence not only of the establishment of the American Museum of Natural History but also of the expanding role of science in the curriculum at Columbia College. As the 1854 controversy over the appointment of Wolcott Gibbs had demonstrated, the Columbia trustees were, at best, indifferent to the inclusion of science in the curriculum. The contretemps over Gibbs was not entirely negative for Columbia, however, because it subsequently served to galvanize a small group within the board of trustees to press for reforms and, eventually, to achieve a renewed emphasis at Columbia upon pure and applied science and the introduction of graduate education. Since both these and other changes at Columbia were to have a profound effect upon the subsequent character of science in New York and since they served to define further the role and function of the Lyceum, it is worth our while to take a detailed look at the transformation of Columbia into a locus of science.

The first change, the move uptown to Forty-ninth Street, was quickly accomplished; by 1857 the college had moved into the building previously occupied by the New York Institution for the Instruction of the Deaf and Dumb. Subsequent changes at Columbia took considerably longer to effect. Thus, although the trustees announced the introduction of graduate courses in the fall of 1858 and the concomitant creation of three separate Schools of Jurisprudence, Science, and Letters, the plan largely failed because few students enrolled for the graduate courses and even fewer professors could be induced to teach such courses. Within twelve months the trustees had abandoned their abortive attempt to introduce graduate education. Subsequent changes at Columbia took con-

[15] Kennedy, "Philanthropy and Science," 56–58, 60–62, 63–64; Winifred E. Howe, *A History of the Metropolitan Museum of Art* (New York: Metropolitan Museum of Art, 1913), 138–140; Calvin Tomkins, *Merchants and Masterpieces: The Story of the Metropolitan Museum of Art* (New York: E. P. Dutton & Co., 1970), 39–41.

14. THOMAS EGLESTON (1832–1900). Egleston, who joined the New York Academy of Sciences in 1861, was the principal founder of the School of Mines at Columbia University. Egleston was elected vice-president of the Academy in 1875 and served on the finance committee of the Academy for many years. (*Courtesy of Columbiana, Columbia University.*)

siderably longer to effect even though a majority of the trustees shared a common goal that was remarkably explicit in its outline and structure. George Templeton Strong, one of Columbia's most energetic trustees, saw the principal obstacle to reform in the low quality of the university faculty: "we have got to build our 'University' out of queer, questionable material. . . . It's an undertaking about which judicious men should not be sanguine."[16]

The inauguration of graduate education at Columbia, however, was not entirely fruitless for Theodore Dwight—hired in 1858 to teach in the ill-fated School of Jurisprudence—decided to continue his association with Columbia. Thus, when the School of Jurisprudence met its end, Dwight organized a School of Law which, although administratively independent of Columbia, was, at least in a formal sense, part of the university. Columbia was fortunate to have discovered the young law professor for, in three years, Dwight enrolled more students in his law school than any other in the country; his success laid the foundation for later eminence.[17]

At the same time as Dwight was creating the Columbia Law School, the medical faculty at the College of Physicians and Surgeons which had, throughout its history, been an entirely independent entity, was suggesting to the Columbia trustees the propriety of merger. The eventual association took place in June 1860 and, although the connection was purely formal (since the faculty of Physicians and Surgeons remained in control of every aspect of the medical college), it served both institutions well. Columbia had reason to be pleased, for its old rival, New York University, could no longer claim dominance in the field of medical education in the city while the professoriate at Physicians and Surgeons, alarmed at the growing success of the NYU Medical School and anxious to escape from the control of the Regents of the University of the State of New York, could find reassurance in the link with one of the country's oldest and most prestigious colleges.[18]

The most significant advance for Columbia during this period came in 1863 when Thomas Egleston, a recent graduate of the École des Mines

[16] John Fulton, *Memoirs of Frederick A. P. Barnard* (New York, 1896), 332–333; "Columbia College," *New-York Times*, 22 October 1858; Frederick Paul Keppel, *Columbia* (New York: Oxford University Press, 1914), 9; Allan Nevins and Milton Halsey Thomas, eds., *The Diary of George Templeton Strong*, 4 vols. (New York: MacMillan Co., 1952), vol. 2, *The Turbulent Fifties*, 387.

[17] Keppel, *Columbia*, 9.

[18] Keppel, *Columbia*, 9; John Shrady, ed., *The College of Physicians and Surgeons: A History*, 2 vols. (New York: Lewis Publishing Co., n.d. [1903]), 1: 110–111; John C. Dalton, *History of the College of Physicians and Surgeons* (New York, 1887), 102–106.

in Paris, approached the Columbia trustees with a proposal to establish a mining school. His request was unusual—there were only six schools of applied science in the country at the time and none taught mining engineering—but the trustees, encouraged by their recent success in gaining both a law school and a medical faculty, agreed to Egleston's proposal with one important qualification: Columbia would not make any financial contribution. As the trustees put it: "if you can start your School of Mines without asking us for any money, and if you are willing to take the professorship without a salary, and if you can find some other fellows to do the same, [then] if you can find any empty rooms in our building at 49th Street you may take possession of them."[19]

The successful establishment during the next decade of the School of Mines at Columbia was a consequence of Egleston's enthusiasm, the trustees' (limited) generosity, and the appointment, in 1864, of a new president at Columbia. Frederick A. P. Barnard possessed an expert's knowledge of science and a professional's acquaintance with higher education; in both senses he was the ideal choice for Columbia as it struggled to establish itself as a research university. As a young man, Barnard had first taught at the New York Institution for the Instruction of the Deaf and Dumb; during his residence in New York Barnard had developed an avocational interest in natural science and in a few years he soon possessed an enviable reputation as a savant. A chance meeting with Basil Manly, the president of the University of Alabama, led to an appointment as professor of mathematics and natural philosophy at Alabama where Barnard remained until 1854. At Alabama and during a later tenure at the University of Mississippi, Barnard wrote many pungent articles on the deplorable state of collegiate education in the United States. Barnard's contention—that the majority of American universities offered an impractical education and were, as a consequence, held in disdain by the rest of the world—was a controversial theme; his strictures on American colleges, originally published in the *Mobile Register*, were reprinted in book form and subsequently won Barnard a wide notoriety in educational circles.[20]

Contemporaneously with his growing eminence as an educational theorist, Barnard was also earning a reputation as a scientist. While he held the chair of mathematics and natural philosophy at the University of Mis-

[19] Keppel, *Columbia*, 10; Charles Frederick Chandler, "Inauguration of Chandler Lectureship," *School of Mines Quarterly* 35(1914): 316–317.
[20] Fulton, *Memoirs*, 76, 83–85, 143, 194.

sissippi, Barnard served on several committees of the American Association for the Advancement of Science, most notably, the committee appointed in 1857 to inquire into the organization of the United States Coast Survey. When the chairman of the committee, John Kintzing Kane, died in February 1858, Barnard took responsibility for directing the work of the committee; as a consequence, when the final report appeared in November 1858, Barnard won widespread praise for the report's breadth of vision and perspicuity of analysis. More significantly Barnard won important friends and supporters through his AAAS work; Alexander Dallas Bache, director of the Coast Survey, for example, was the most influential man of science in the United States and, under Bache's patronage, Barnard rose rapidly to national prominence within the American scientific community. Barnard's subsequent election to the presidency of the AAAS in 1861 was, however, quickly rendered irrelevant by the outbreak of the Civil War. Since he supported the Union, the hostilities between North and South put Barnard in an untenable position; as a consequence he left Mississippi in June 1861 shortly before the battle of Bull Run for a temporary position in Washington City.[21]

For the trustees of Columbia College, Barnard was an obvious choice to succeed Charles King as president of Columbia. Barnard was an energetic administrator, a prominent scientist, and an eminent educator. For Columbia, which had spent the past four decades in a state of drift and decline and which was, moreover, now threatened by the rise of City College and NYU, Barnard seemed the perfect choice for the triple task of expanding the college, introducing science into the Columbia curriculum, and developing the professional schools of law, medicine, and engineering. Barnard had a reputation as an innovator; John Burgess, the professor of political science at Columbia, remembered that he had "never met in any man, old or young, such an enthusiasm for new things, such a spirit for progress and improvement. In fact . . . I thought him, at times, too progressive."[22]

Barnard, on his appointment in 1864, soon pushed his vision of a future Columbia rapidly forward. His plans for the university, his appraisal of the rival colleges in New York, and his estimation of the obstacles that stood in his way are all clearly limned in a long letter written by Barnard to William A. McVickar, professor of theology, a few years after he, Bar-

[21] Horace Coon, *Columbia: Colossus on the Hudson* (New York: E. P. Dutton & Co., 1947), 78–79; Fulton, *Memoirs*, 261.
[22] John W. Burgess, *Reminiscences of an American Scholar: The Beginnings of Columbia University* (New York: Columbia University Press, 1934), 174.

15. FREDERICK A.P. BARNARD (1809–1889). After graduating from Yale in 1828, Barnard held a succession of posts in a variety of educational institutions, most notably, the chair of mathematics and natural history at the University of Alabama from 1837 to 1854. A subsequent appointment as chancellor of the University of Mississippi ended at the outbreak of the Civil War. Barnard was chosen to head Columbia University in 1864; he immediately entered upon a plan to transform Columbia from a small liberal arts college into a thriving research university with graduate and professional schools, a plan that was fully realized by one of Barnard's successors, Nicholas Murray Butler. (*Courtesy of Columbiana, Columbia University.*)

nard, had moved to New York. The goal, according to Barnard, was to transform Columbia from a small liberal-arts college into a university with professional schools for post-graduate instruction. Columbia had made great gains through the recent acquisition of schools of medicine, law, and engineering; these additions, however, were in a feeble condition and, moreover, they constituted only a small part of Barnard's vision for Columbia:

> its Schools of Law and of Mines saying nothing of the School of Medicine which belongs to it only nominally—represent but feebly what a University should be. The school of Mines must be developed into a Polytechnic School, where all Sciences may be taught as applied to the arts. The School of Law must become a school of political and governmental Science generally, instead of being confined, as it is almost wholly now, to the teaching of municipal law . . . besides these, we must have Schools of Philosophy, of Philology, of Theoretic & Practical Astronomy, of Natural History in its various departments, of Commerce, of Social science, of Pedagogy, of History—in short,—not to attempt to make the list exhaustive,—of whatever subjects of human Knowledge are capable of being presented in systematic form.

Barnard outlined his plan of action for the realization of this ambitious and impressive scheme on numerous occasions, most notably in his inaugural address and in his annual report for 1865. On these public occasions Barnard presented the outward appearance of optimism and self-confidence; in more private moments, however, he expressed considerable self-doubt: in 1869, five years after his arrival at Columbia, Barnard confessed that he was "much less sanguine as to the future of the college at present than I was in the beginning." The principal difficulty facing Columbia was its small endowment which was, in turn, an expression of a deeper malaise, the apathy toward the college not only of the citizens of New York but also of the alumni. By contrast to Harvard College which received enormous sums from Bostonians who had never been connected with Harvard in any way, Columbia received almost nothing from the New York patricians: "the first and capital difficulty in the way of the development of the college into a true university, is to be found in the lukewarmness toward it of the great body of its alumni, and the still greater indifference with which it is regarded by the wealthy commercial class who undervalue liberal education everywhere and the educated class who have received their culture in other institutions. . . . five years of effort and of observation have sufficed to show me that nothing substantial can be hoped from these sources in our day."

Barnard's jeremiad was underscored by the perception that, while Columbia College faced an uncertain future, City College had "aspirations to be regarded as the chief representative of the higher education in the city." While both Columbia and NYU could rely only on a "precarious private liberality," City College, as Barnard glumly noted, was

> supported out of the public taxes, and it is only necessary that it should seem capable of being in one way or another made useful to the oligarchs who impose our taxes . . . in order that the appropriations in its favor shall reach any amount demanded. . . . It is now about four years since an eminent gentleman of New York, formerly a member of the city Board of Education, to whom I was stating my then sanguine anticipations of the future of Columbia College, suddenly chilled me by remarking "You will have a competitor in this race which you will find it hard to beat. This new college of the city of New York is going to have a purse without any bottom."[23]

It is interesting, given the lachrymose tenor of Barnard's letter to McVickar, to note that, only twelve years later, a veritable flood of bequests and contributions began to pour down on Columbia from wealthy New Yorkers who had little or no connection with the college. In 1876, when John Burgess, the new professor of political science, first arrived at the gates of Columbia, he experienced a "deep discouragement. . . . I found the institution to consist of a small old-fashioned college, or rather school, for teaching Latin, Greek, and mathematics and a little metaphysics, and a very little science." Only twenty-five years later, Columbia was indisputably a member of the small, select group of major research universities in the United States; it had, at various times around the turn of the century, the largest faculty and the greatest number of graduate students and it spent more on education for each student than any other American university. Last but not least, Columbia had a well-deserved reputation, by 1900, as the center of academic scientific research in the United States.[24]

The foundations of Columbia's eminence in science were laid in the very first years of Barnard's tenure as president. In 1863 Thomas Egleston's innovation, the School of Mines, received guarded support from the Columbia trustees; it was not clear to anyone that the mining school, in a location far removed from any actual mines, would attract many students. Yet in a few years Egleston had won to his cause not only

[23] Frederick A. P. Barnard to William A. McVickar, 24 November 1869, John McVickar Papers, General Theological Seminary.
[24] Burgess, *Reminiscences*, 160; Roger L. Geiger, *To Advance Knowledge: The Growth of American Research Universities, 1900–1940* (New York: Oxford University Press, 1986), 12.

the largest enrollment in any division of the university but also a stellar faculty that was to enhance greatly Columbia's reputation.

The School of Mines opened its doors to the first incoming class on 15 November 1864. Much to everyone's surprise and gratification, twenty-four students showed up on the first day. As Charles Frederick Chandler, the new professor of chemistry, remembered those early days, it was as much as the faculty could do to keep up with the flood of prospective students: "we . . . sent out for a plumber and a carpenter to put up more tables and increase the accommodations. The next day more pupils came, and the following days we had more carpenters and more students alternately until there were 47 students the first Winter."[25]

Nobody was ever sure why the School of Mines, from the very beginning, was such a runaway success. In any case, the School continued to flourish under the most improbable circumstances. In the first year, having run up a debt of ten thousand dollars, the faculty of three was in a perilous situation. Quite evidently, such a substantial sum of money was not going to be remitted from tuition fees. Fortunately for Egleston, Chandler, and Francis L. Vinton, the professor of engineering, one of Columbia's wealthier trustees, hearing of the straits of the School of Mines, not only paid off the debt but also donated an additional four thousand dollars to the School.

Each educational innovation in New York during the previous forty years had had consequences to a greater or lesser degree for the city's scientific community. In this respect the School of Mines was no exception for not only did it impart cohesion to the scientific faculty at Columbia but it also provided additional opportunities for scientific employment. After the first year of operations the School of Mines quickly expanded; most notably professors teaching science at Columbia College soon joined the faculty at the School of Mines. Thus, during the second year, John Howard Van Amringe taught mathematics in both departments, William G. Peck taught surveying, and Ogden Rood became professor of physics at the mining school.

The final addition to the faculty in the early years was John Strong Newberry who became professor of geology and paleontology; apparently he was very popular with the students, one of whom remembered his professor as "an extremely handsome man. He had a long, brown beard, and my memory is that he wore a brown, velvet coat to match it in color." Newberry was a great catch for Columbia: in 1867, only one year after he had joined the faculty, he was elected to the presidency of the

[25] Chandler, "Inauguration," 317–318.

16. CHARLES FREDERICK CHANDLER (1836–1925). Chandler, who received a PhD in chemistry from the University of Göttingen in 1857, taught chemistry simultaneously at three different institutions (Columbia School of Mines, New York College of Pharmacy, and the College of Physicians and Surgeons). Chandler also served as president of the Board of Health and worked as a consultant to many chemical companies in the New York area; in 1876 he was instrumental in founding the American Chemical Society. Chandler was elected a member of the New York Academy of Sciences in 1865. (*Courtesy of Columbiana, Columbia University.*)

American Association for the Advancement of Science and, in 1868, he became president of the Lyceum of Natural History, a position that he held until his death twenty-four years later.[26]

During the next decade, however, it was another Lyceum member, Charles Frederick Chandler, who made the greatest impact on scientific life in New York City. Chandler had taught for several years at Union College in Schenectady and, during his tenure at Union, he had equipped the department of chemistry with a complete analytical laboratory, a library, reading-room, and an extensive mineral cabinet. Chandler was also known as a brilliant teacher who inspired his students at Union to establish a chemical society that met on Friday evenings to debate the latest advances in scientific knowledge.[27]

John Burgess recalled that, among the faculty at the School of Mines, Chandler soon became the organizer and leader: "Egleston, a man of considerable wealth and social standing and of French education, was the real originator of the school, but Chandler was a man of stronger will and more aggressive character and soon took the lead in its development. . . . He seemed never to find enough to do. . . . He was a ready talker and speaker and very persuasive. With such qualities, it was inevitable that he should get his way about everything." Chandler's drive and determination so impressed the Columbia trustees that, at the end of the second year, they voted to appropriate $30,000 for a new building for the School of Mines on Fourth Avenue; Chandler became dean of the school shortly afterwards.[28]

Once Chandler had secured a firm institutional base at Columbia he began to apply his entrepreneurial skills in other directions. His reputation in New York spread: it was common knowledge that the extraordinary success of the School of Mines was largely due to Chandler's leadership. Moreover Chandler was renowned for his ability as a chemistry lecturer to fire his students with enthusiasm for his own favorite subject. Michael Pupin, who graduated from Columbia in 1883, remembered how Chandler had transformed chemistry for him into a "thrilling epic. . . . [Chandler] described the wandering of the carbon atoms from the carbon

[26] T. O'Conor Sloane to Thomas Thornton Read, 27 April 1936, Thomas Egleston File, Columbiana, Low Library, Columbia University; Herman Le Roy Fairchild, "A Memoir of Professor John Strong Newberry," *Transactions of the New York Academy of Sciences* 12(1893): 158. For a biographical sketch of Newberry that traces the significance of his work for New York science, see Douglas Sloan, "Science in New York City, 1867–1907," *Isis* 71(1980): 39–40, 42–44.

[27] Egbert K. Bacon, "A Precursor of the American Chemical Society—Chandler and the Society of Union College," *Chymia* 10(1965): 183–197.

[28] Burgess, *Reminiscences*, 172; Chandler, "Inauguration," 319–320.

dioxide of the atmosphere . . . into the arms of the longing chlorophil after bidding goodbye to their deserted oxygen partners. . . . Oxygen and carbon atoms no longer appeared to me like mere symbolic entities carrying on their backs, like state prisoners, a number, which told me nothing beyond the meaningless tale of their atomic weight. Chandler's epic revealed them to me as my most precious personal friends who toiled day and night in order to keep me alive."[29]

As an entrepreneur of science, Chandler was always looking to extend his influence beyond Columbia. In 1866 an opportunity arose to teach chemistry at the New York College of Pharmacy. Established in 1829, the College of Pharmacy had led a precarious existence and, thirty-seven years later, its activity was so vestigial that it required only a single room in the main NYU building on Washington Square to hold its classes. Chandler's appointment to teach chemistry at the College of Pharmacy instantly transformed the situation; the Columbia professor successfully urged his colleagues at the pharmaceutical college to canvass for financial support from the druggists and apothecaries in the city: "the pharmacists of New York . . . [must] come forward and support the college in its efforts to elevate the profession. New Yorkers are liberal and public spirited; they contribute to every possible object of public utility. No false modesty should hold our College back." The Chandler magic worked admirably; the campaign for support from the apothecaries was so successful that within a few years the college was able to move to more spacious quarters on Twenty-third Street. In recognition of his efforts, the trustees appointed Chandler president of the college and in 1905, after discussions with the university, Chandler was able to negotiate the integration of the College of Pharmacy as a constituent part of Columbia University.[30]

In 1872 Chandler received an appointment to the chair of chemistry at the College of Physicians and Surgeons. Since its establishment in 1807 the College of Physicians and Surgeons had always maintained an uneasy relationship with Columbia. In 1814 the faculty of Physicians and Surgeons, led by David Hosack, had been largely responsible for the dissolution of the Columbia Medical School; in 1860 the College of Physicians and Surgeons became a part of Columbia but the arrangement was

[29] Michael I. Pupin, "Chandler: The Teacher and the Chemist," *Columbia Alumni News*, 15 January 1926, 312.

[30] Robert Lourie Larson, "Charles Frederick Chandler: His Life and Work" (Ph.D. diss., Columbia University, 1950), 61; Marston Taylor Bogert, "Charles Frederick Chandler, 1836–1925," *Biographical Memoirs of the National Academy of Sciences* 14(1932): 149.

largely fictitious—the medical faculty exercised complete control over its own affairs.

For the trustees of Columbia College, who looked with great condescension at New York University, it was a source of considerable feeling that the NYU Medical School was a flourishing and prosperous institution while the College of Physicians and Surgeons was, as everyone knew, prepared to break the link with Columbia at a moment's notice. A principal goal of Frederick Barnard, therefore, was to cement the connection with the College of Physicians and Surgeons in order to save Columbia from the embarrassment that would result from the desertion of Physicians and Surgeons. In this regard Charles Frederick Chandler was to provide the perfect link. In 1872 Chandler was appointed adjunct professor of chemistry at Physicians and Surgeons; four years later Chandler became professor of medical jurisprudence. As a consequence of Chandler's presence the College of Physicians and Surgeons experienced a rapid increase in student enrollment; this precipitated an expansion and improvement of the facilities and in a short period Physicians and Surgeons was successfully challenging the NYU Medical School for medical leadership in the city. Most important of all, Chandler's presence on the faculty was the catalyst for the eventual incorporation of the College of Physicians and Surgeons as a constituent part of Columbia University.[31]

By 1876, therefore, Columbia was well on the way to future glory as a center of scientific research. It possessed, in the School of Mines, one of the most eminent scientific schools in the country; it had successfully obtained a creditable medical school; and, last but not least, it had a president who appreciated and supported the role of science in the curriculum. The growth of Columbia as a center of science was paralleled by the steady expansion of the American Museum of Natural History. For the Lyceum of Natural History the appearance, during the second half of the century, of these two institutions meant a change in function and role. In previous decades the Lyceum had intermittently aspired to serve the function of a museum; now, not only had that hope irretrievably disappeared but, with the rise of Columbia, it would seem that the Lyceum would have to abandon also its ambition of becoming a resource for scientific research.

These displacements of the Lyceum were a consequence of the local context: two institutions, particular to New York, had assumed functions

[31] Larson, "Charles Frederick Chandler," 63–65.

that might, under different circumstances, have remained with the Lyceum. For a contrast to the New York situation we need look only as far as Philadelphia where the Academy of Natural Sciences – an institution that closely resembled the Lyceum in the early decades of the nineteenth century – preserved its function as a museum and, in cooperation with the University of Pennsylvania, also evolved into a significant center of scientific research.

A third change in the character of the Lyceum was consequent on the changing intellectual configuration of science. That is, as scientific knowledge was becoming more extensive so, at the same time, certain areas of science were becoming more specialized. By the late nineteenth century science had clearly become a profession; it received support from the federal government, industry, and the universities. These changes, together with the appearance of the American Museum of Natural History and the rise of science at Columbia, forced upon the Lyceum the most radical transformation in its long history.

The alteration of the name in 1876 to the New York Academy of Sciences reflected the inescapable fact that the category of natural history no longer resembled a unified body of knowledge. The Lyceum members were not savants in the sense that Samuel Latham Mitchill, John Torrey, and James Ellsworth DeKay had understood the word; the Academy members of 1876 were scientists with a primary affiliation to a scientific discipline, whether it were biology, chemistry, physics, or geology. Concomitant with the appearance of disciplines – a process that took shape in American science in the second half of the century – was the dominance of specialization. Science after 1870 also became a career and a profession for many individuals; hence, during these decades, many disciplinary societies, staffed primarily by academic specialists, appeared not only in local contexts such as New York City but also in national and international settings.

These long-term trends all found their reflection in the structural changes that the New York Academy of Sciences carried out in the 1870s. The power to make decisions no longer rested, as it had in previous decades, with the weekly membership meetings but with the Council of the Academy, an organizational innovation that consisted of the officers of the Academy. A second change was the division of the Academy into specialist sections; the members of each section elected their own officers who were then answerable not only to the members of the section but also to the Council of the Academy.

There is no doubt that these moves by the Academy were appropriate for the changed context of American science. Indeed it would not be too great an exaggeration to say that, if the Academy had not undergone this series of transformations in name and structure, it would have been judged as irrelevant by the great majority of New York scientists and would subsequently have faded into oblivion.

No episode more clearly reveals the pressure exerted on the New York Academy of Sciences by the changed context of American science than the establishment of the American Chemical Society in 1876. The moving spirit behind the formation of the ACS was the ubiquitous Charles Frederick Chandler who, with his brother, William Chandler, a professor of chemistry at Lehigh University, had edited a journal, the *American Chemist*, since 1870. This journal served the primary purpose of unifying the disparate community of academic and industrial chemists into a cohesive group and, most important of all, of giving support to Chandler's goal of creating a national chemical society. The first step toward the realization of the latter aim came in 1874, when H. Carrington Bolton, a prominent member of the Lyceum of Natural History (as it was then called) proposed, in an article in the *American Chemist*, that a centennial gathering be held to commemorate the discovery of oxygen by Joseph Priestley; as Bolton put it in his article: "already the country resounds with preparations for a National Centennial in 1876. Why should not chemists meet to enjoy a social reunion in commemoration of events important alike to science and civilization?"[32]

Bolton and Chandler subsequently distributed a circular to prominent scientists around the country and, much to their gratification, they received a favorable response to the proposal from many leading academic and industrial chemists. The most pertinent reply came from Rachel L. Bodley, professor of chemistry at the Woman's Medical College of Pennsylvania, who suggested that the nation's chemists meet at Northumberland, Pennsylvania where Priestley had lived during his exile in the United States. As Bodley wrote in a letter to Charles Chandler: "I made a pilgrimage last August to the grave of Priestley . . . and was deeply impressed by the locality, its associations, and its charming surroundings; my proposition is, therefore, that the centennial gathering be around this

[32] H. Carrington Bolton, "Centennial of Chemistry, 1774–1874," *American Chemist* 4(1874): 362. For an analysis of the emergence of chemistry as a discipline in the final decades of the nineteenth century—a development that precipitated the formation of the American Chemical Society—see Arnold Thackray et al., *Chemistry in America, 1876–1976: Historical Indicators* (Boston: D. Reidel Publishing Co., 1985), 147–154.

grave, and that the meetings, other than the open-air one on the ceme-tery hill-top, be in the quaint little church built by Priestley."[33]

Both Charles Chandler and H. Carrington Bolton were leading mem-bers of the Section of Chemistry of the Lyceum of Natural History and, at the Section's meeting on 11 May 1874, they presented the plan to the membership, suggesting that if the Lyceum were to take the initiative in organizing the event and in giving approval of the plan, it would re-bound not only to the advantage of the chemical community but would also provide the Lyceum with much favorable publicity. There was no dis-sent. John Strong Newberry, president of the Lyceum and a colleague of Chandler and Bolton on the School of Mines faculty, was present that evening and indicated that he expected the Lyceum's other sections to fall in with this plan. Newberry appointed a committee of the Lyceum—led by Chandler and Bolton—to make the necessary arrangements and issue the formal call for the centennial meeting at Northumberland.[34]

Chandler, as the chairman of the Lyceum committee, was very much in charge of the celebration at Northumberland in the summer of 1874. It came as a great shock, therefore, that, when Persifor Frazer, a professor of chemistry at Penn, duly proposed the "formation of a chemical society which should date its origin from this centennial celebration," there was immediate dissent. The opposition was based on the supposition of the academic chemists present at the meeting that they were being pushed to join a movement that, notwithstanding Frazer's support for the pro-posal, was little more than a vehicle for Chandler's ambition. Chemists from New Haven, Cambridge, and Philadelphia were reluctant, more-over, to establish an organization that promised to be under the control of a coterie of scientists from New York City. Apprehensive that a formal vote against a national organization would put a decisive end to their plans, the Chandler forces beat a quick retreat; the motion was rapidly withdrawn and one of Chandler's accomplices from New York, H. Car-rington Bolton, in a short speech at the end of the meeting, created a di-versionary maneuver. Perceiving (as Bolton put it) that "the sense of the meeting was strongly against the advisability of such a new departure," he proposed in its stead a motion that the assembled chemists "co-operate with the American Association for the Advancement of Science

[33] Rachel L. Bodley to Charles F. Chandler, 1 May 1874, quoted in "1774—Centennial of Chemistry—1874," *American Chemist* 5(1874): 35.

[34] Larson, "Charles Frederick Chandler," 310–311. See also Samuel A. Goldschmidt, "The Priestley Centennial," in *A Half-Century of Chemistry in America, 1876–1926*, ed. Charles A. Browne (Philadelphia: American Chemical Society, 1926), 3.

at their next meeting, to the end of establishing a chemical section on a firmer basis."[35]

The leaders of the movement were not alone in their disappointment at this outcome; the editor of the *Daily Graphic* regarded the failure of the meeting to establish a permanent organization as a matter for deep regret: "if the chemists . . . had combined in certain definite proportions to accomplish what was really the obvious purpose of their merely mechanical mixture . . . the world would have had cause to rejoice in their synthesis. . . . Hitherto America has done but little for the science, each chemist being but an isolated molecule giving but little show of affinity for others, binary compounds of professor and assistant at some college being generally the most complex that were to be found." The Lyceum of Natural History also shared in the general disappointment; its support had accrued to Chandler in the expectation that his efforts would meet with success; after witnessing the rebuff to the proposal at Northumberland, however, the Lyceum became persuaded that the idea was hopelessly ambitious.[36]

Two years later, therefore, when Chandler revived his proposal, the membership of the New York Academy of Sciences firmly rejected it not because they were opposed to a national chemical society but because they feared that, if Chandler were to pursue his vision, the result would not be a national organization (since chemists in other parts of the country were opposed to the idea) but a local chemical society restricted in membership to the New York area. Needless to say, this possibility was anathema to the Academy because it would draw away resources and support from the chemical section of the New York Academy of Sciences. If other disciplines, moreover, were to follow Chandler's lead, the result could be disastrous for the Academy since its specialist sections would collapse for lack of support.

The threat to the New York Academy of Sciences in 1876, when Chandler made his second attempt at a chemical society, was correspondingly greater because it was organized in a more systematic manner. Chandler had made sure to canvass his local constituency beforehand and, as a consequence, he was able to report to the first organizing meeting of the American Chemical Society that approximately one hundred chemists worked in New York City of whom nearly half had "promised to join the proposed society." The ultimate aim of the second effort,

[35] "Proceedings of the Chemical Centennial at Northumberland," *American Chemist* 5(1874): 41.

[36] Editorial, *Daily Graphic* (New York), 6 August 1874.

as Chandler put it, was to "bring the chemists together in scientific and social intercourse, to secure rooms which should be open in the day and evening, and to establish there a library of reference and a chemical museum." Isidor Walz, a close associate of Chandler, seconded Chandler's introductory remarks by noting that the "want of a professional organization among chemists has been frequently deplored . . . sooner or later a chemical society must and would be formed to bring the members of our profession into closer personal relations, and to stimulate and concentrate original research."[37]

There seems to have been a certain amount of tergiversation in the intent of the founders over the scope of the new organization. Walz claimed that they aimed at a "national instead of a merely local society"; this, however, seems to have been merely a ruse to deflect growing opposition to the scheme from the New York Academy of Sciences. Only a few weeks previously—on 21 February 1876—the Academy had changed its name from the Lyceum of Natural History in order to "accurately express the scope of its deliberations and actions, inasmuch as many of the subjects discussed in its meetings more properly belong to the sciences of Chemistry, Physics, Technology, &c., which are not branches of Natural History." The Academy had also previously divided itself into four sections: biology; chemistry and technology; geology and mineralogy; and physics, astronomy, and mathematics. This structural change had had the desired effect for it accelerated the re-building process since the fire a decade earlier. The membership figures increased, meetings of the Academy witnessed greater attendance, and the papers read at section meetings improved in quality.[38]

Chandler, by virtue of careful preparation and an energetic mobilization of available resources, succeeded in creating the American Chemical Society despite the opposition of prominent members of the Academy. At the first meeting of the ACS held in the main building at New York University, Thomas Egleston expressed his skepticism on the possibility of successfully creating a chemical society. If his own experience with another professional society, the American Institute of Mining Engineers, were to provide a guide, then the ACS faced a formidable future. The AIME, with six hundred members and an annual income of $6000, was able to do little except publish its proceedings; there was scant reason to believe that the American Chemical Society, with barely fifty members and in competition, moreover, with an older organization, would even

[37] "The American Chemical Society," *American Chemist* 6(1876): 401.
[38] "American Chemical Society," 401; Herman Le Roy Fairchild, *A History of the New York Academy of Sciences* (New York, 1887), 127, 129, 131.

be able to survive. Egleston counseled patience: "at some future time, un-doubtedly, we ought to have a Chemical Society, but not now. . . . In union there is strength. Let the chemists join forces with the Chemical Section of the New York Academy of Sciences, till they shall be strong enough to cut loose and go ahead for themselves."

H. Carrington Bolton, another prominent member of the Academy, made a similar appeal to the assembled chemists. Bolton could claim a certain credibility in his appeal against forming the American Chemical Society for, two years earlier, he had been one of Chandler's accomplices in the debacle at Northumberland. Convinced that a second attempt was sure to succeed only in crippling the New York Academy of Sciences, Bolton urged his audience not to commit the fratricidal act: "[there is a] strong nucleus of chemists at the Academy of Sciences; it having thirty-eight resident Chemists among its members; eight of its officers and sixty corresponding members are chemists. It would be unfortunate to have a division of forces. . . . the present time [is] inopportune, though a Chemical Society at some future time is desirable."

Unfortunately for Bolton and Egleston their arguments failed to have the slightest effect. Charles Chandler, who was presiding that evening, quipped that it "would be desirable to hear from the other side also; it would almost seem as though we had met for the purpose of deciding not to organize a Chemical Society." Isidor Walz accounted for his silence by explaining that the discussion had been going on for some time in-formally among the proponents of the plan; they were sure it was going to be successful: "the chemists present had had the subject before them so long and had discussed it so thoroughly in private that a prolonged expression of views at this meeting was deemed unnecessary." Walz was a little impatient with the previous speakers and the discussion began to get a little ragged: "the new society would not only bring all chemists together and give the profession a recognized standing, but it would stim-ulate original research throughout the country. . . . This field had partly been occupied by societies that had no right to it, simply because we stood by and permitted it." Walz was followed by several other speakers until Charles Chandler, realizing that there was no significant opposition to his plan, outlined the constitutional structure of the proposed society and called for a vote. The motion passed easily—only Egleston, Bolton, and a third member of the Academy, Albert Leeds, raised their hands in dissent. Chandler was a little sorry that the meeting had witnessed some sharp remarks by some of the more intemperate members: Her-mann Endemann, for example, had claimed that the library of the New York Academy of Sciences was "not one useful to chemists; he had searched it and found hardly one work on chemical subjects." Chandler was anxious that the chemical section of the Academy not be irrevocably opposed to the new society; accordingly he printed the proceedings of the May meetings (which included a long talk by Bolton on "The Early Literature of Chemistry,") in full in the next number of the *American Chemist.*[39]

In subsequent years the American Chemical Society failed to develop an active membership outside the vicinity of New York City. In the early period the members occasionally ventured outside of New York; on one memorable occasion they took the ferry to Hoboken where Henry Morton, president of the Stevens Institute of Technology, demonstrated a "curious instrument which seemed to have some possibilities. This instrument was the telephone." On another occasion, shortly after the formation of the Society, the ACS hosted foreign chemists at Philadelphia who were visiting the centennial Exposition in Fairmount Park. Yet it soon became abundantly clear, most especially to chemists in other cities, that the American Chemical Society was very much a New York organization.[40]

Fortunately for the Academy the existence of the ACS seems to have had little effect on the fortunes of the Section of Chemistry of the Academy; indeed it may very well have strengthened the section since Chandler's society, in contradistinction to the section, was composed to a great extent of chemists working in industry. The Section of Chemistry, which found its membership among the academic community, was able, therefore, to co-exist peacefully with the American Chemical Society.

The establishment of the ACS in 1876 was not, by any means, an isolated event for, in the decades following the Civil War, a plethora of small, local, specialist societies appeared. These included the Linnaean Society of New York, the West Side Natural History Society, the New-York Microscopical Society, the Hulst Botanical Club of Brooklyn, the New York Mineralogical Club, the New York Mathematical Society, and the Bronx Society of Arts and Sciences.

The Torrey Botanical Club, one of the most important scientific organizations on the local scene, consisted of a group of botanists who first met together as early as 1858. The membership of the Torrey Botanical

---

[39] "American Chemical Society," 403–404; "New York Academy of Sciences: Chemical Section," *American Chemist* 6(1876): 407–412; H. Carrington Bolton, "Notes on the Early Literature of Chemistry," *American Chemist* 6(1876): 413–422.

[40] William H. Nichols, "The Organization of the American Chemical Society," in *Half-Century of Chemistry,* 15–16.

Club overlapped significantly with that of the New York Academy of Sciences and, in later years, both organizations worked together in close cooperation. As a consequence of its local importance and on account of its significance in the second half of the century, the Torrey Botanical Club is worth more than a passing mention. It serves admirably, moreover, as an exemplar of the type of scientific organization so common in the late nineteenth century; on one level, utterly obscure and ephemeral, but within its context, an organization that did a great deal to give cohesion to the scattered acolytes of natural history in New York in the Gilded Age.

In 1858 the nucleus of the embryonic Botanical Club of New York (as it was originally called) consisted of John Torrey, Timothy F. Allen, William H. Leggett, James Hogg, James Hyatt, and Daniel Cady Eaton. This small group met each Saturday during the summer to make field excursions to the swamps and hills of upper Manhattan, Staten Island, and Westchester County. During the rest of the year, when not engaged in discovery, the botanists would meet regularly at the herbarium at Columbia College where John Torrey, the leader of the group, would serve as the chairman and genial host, providing the discussants with "biscuits and cakes, and a cup of the most exquisite coffee ever tasted."[41]

Even in 1858, before the establishment of the School of Mines, Columbia College served as a resource for local groups of savants. Thus the Botanical Club of New York, through the influence of John Torrey, was able to use the Columbia College herbarium as a meeting-place; an alumnus of Columbia, John J. Cooke, donated one thousand dollars to the Botanical Club; and when John Strong Newberry began teaching at the School of Mines, he encouraged his students to visit the herbarium and to attend meetings of the Botanical Club. In this respect the connection between the Botanical Club and Columbia was especially felicitous for the later development of science in New York; Nathaniel Lord Britton, who was to win renown a few decades later as the president of the New York Academy of Sciences and the founder of the New York Botanical Garden, first developed an interest in science through membership in the Botanical Club. Arthur Hollick, a class-mate of Britton at the School of Mines, vividly recalled the occasion when he and Britton first met the members of the Botanical Club: "I shall never forget the first meeting I attended. I felt that I was under indictment for the crime of being a young man. There were no young botanists in those days. . . . No woman had

---

[41] Edward S. Burgess, "The Work of the Torrey Botanical Club," *Bulletin of the Torrey Botanical Club* 27(1900): 552, 555-556; James Hyatt, "Reminiscences of John Torrey," *Bulletin of the Torrey Botanical Club* 27(1900): 559.

17. JOHN TORREY (1796–1873). In 1853 Torrey relinquished his teaching duties at Columbia University to take up an appointment as assayer for the United States Mint in New York. Seven years later he donated his herbarium and library to Columbia in exchange for the use of a house located on the campus. Torrey spent the remainder of his life studying botany and serving as the informal leader of the Botanical Club of New York (later known as the Torrey Botanical Club). (*Courtesy of the New York Botanical Garden.*)

yet been elected to membership in the Club. Any such innovation would have been unthinkable at that time."[42]

For its first nine years the Botanical Club remained the most informal of organizations. In 1867 the Botanical Club sponsored a banquet at the Astor Hotel to commemorate the publication, almost fifty years earlier, of John Torrey's *Flora of New York*, the first publication to receive the imprint of the Lyceum of Natural History and, more significantly, the first catalogue of the plants growing in and around New York City. In a less formal sense the banquet at the Astor Hotel that night also paid homage to the only founding member of the Lyceum still alive; in tribute each dinner guest wore a sprig of *Torreya* in his button-hole. The dinner was also the occasion for the formal organization of the Botanical Club; the members elected John Torrey as chairman, Peter V. Le Roy as secretary, and Timothy F. Allen, a prominent local physician, as curator. Three years later the twenty-nine members voted to adopt a new name for the society in honor of their chairman, and in the same year, William Leggett began publishing the *Bulletin of the Torrey Botanical Club* in order to "form a medium of communication for all those interested in the Flora of this vicinity, and thus to bring together and fan into a flame the sparks of Botanical enthusiasm." The steady accretion of resources and status culminated in April 1873 when the state legislature passed an act of incorporation of the Torrey Botanical Club, an action that conferred few practical benefits except, as one wag put it, the "privilege of 'sueing and being sued'."[43]

The relationship between the New York Academy of Sciences and such organizations as the Torrey Botanical Club was generally harmonious. The Academy, despite its misgivings about the American Chemical Society, soon realized that, if anything, the establishment of specialist scientific societies tended to strengthen the Academy since members of, say, the Torrey Botanical Club often also joined the Academy. In a second sense, the various scientific groups in New York gave each other mutual support through shared leadership. Thus John Strong Newberry was president of the New York Academy of Sciences for almost three de-

---

[42] Hyatt, "Reminiscences," 560; Arthur Hollick, "Torrey Botanical Club Reminiscences," *Memoirs of the Torrey Botanical Club* 17(1917): 29–30. For an interpretation of the Torrey Botanical Club as a specialist community organization, see Sloan, "Science in New York City," 44–46.

[43] "The Torrey Festival," *American Naturalist* 2(1869): 41; "The Club," *Bulletin of the Torrey Botanical Club* 1(1870): 45; Hyatt, "Reminiscences," 559; Henry H. Rusby, "A Historical Sketch of the Development of Botany in New York City," *Torreya* 6(1906): 134; [William H. Leggett], "Prefatory," *Bulletin of the Torrey Botanical Club* 1(1870): 1; "Organization of the Club," *Bulletin of the Torrey Botanical Club* 4(1873): 27–28.

cades; during much of that time Newberry was also the president of the Torrey Botanical Club.

The desire for cooperation between the different scientific organizations in New York City occasionally went further; as a consequence the Academy established formal guidelines that codified the relationship with other groups. Thus in 1880 the New-York Microscopical Society, an organization established in July 1865 by a "number of scientific gentlemen," formally requested a "Union with the Academy." In response the Academy renounced any irredentist ambitions towards other scientific societies and advised the Microscopical Society that while individual members were free to join the Academy it was not possible to accommodate separate organizations.[44]

The discussions with the New-York Microscopical Society pre-dated the formation of a network of scientific groups that, known as the Scientific Alliance, formulated a cohesive policy for the many scientific groups in New York City. The formation of the Scientific Alliance in 1891 was consequent, however, on an event that gave impetus to the cause of science in New York and, at the same time, strikingly revealed the strengths and weaknesses of the various scientific groups in the city.

The meeting of the American Association for the Advancement of Science in New York in 1887 was significant in several respects. First and most obvious, it marked the first time that the AAAS had held its annual conference in New York. Second, it provided the scientific institutions in the city with an opportunity to display their increased influence and reputation to the national scientific community. Third, the AAAS meeting, conducted at times in a carnival atmosphere, went a long way towards the popularization of science among the general citizenry of the city. Fourth, it gave greater cohesion to the New York scientific community which, on account of the appearance of the many specialized organizations during the previous two decades, was almost kaleidoscopic in its variety. Last but not least, the 1887 AAAS meeting served to confirm the authority of the New York Academy of Sciences; the Academy, by successfully organizing the AAAS visit, proved that, despite the recent growth and appearance of science outside its borders, it was still able to provide effective leadership.

The New York Academy of Sciences had first invited the AAAS to meet in New York in 1884; in that year, as Alexis A. Julien, the vice-president of the Academy, remarked, the British Association for the Ad-

[44] "The Microscope," *New-York Times*, 7 July 1865; Minutes of the Council of the New York Academy of Sciences, 2 April 1880, NYAS.

vancement of Science would be meeting in Montreal and, as a consequence, the British savants might be persuaded to attend also the AAAS
meeting: "it is very desirable for the interests of Science in New York that
the annual Meeting of the American Association for 1884 should be held
here subsequent to the meeting in Montreal—thus securing the attendance of Scientific Gentlemen from Great Britain."[45]

To the disappointment of the Academy membership, the anticipated
coincidence of the BAAS and the AAAS did not take place. Three years
later, however, the Academy, in concert with the other scientific societies
in the city, invited the AAAS to New York a second time. On this occasion the Academy, cognizant of the immense amount of necessary organizational work, was careful to include as many individuals and groups
as possible. Thus on 31 March 1887 the Academy appointed a committee
of five leading members to "confer with other societies of this city and
the vicinity regarding the formation of a Local Committee to arrange for
the proposed meeting of the A.A.A.S." The Academy's initiative aimed
not only at securing the active involvement of the many scientific societies in the city but also at obtaining the imprimatur of New York's political and economic leadership. Herman Le Roy Fairchild, secretary of
the Academy, was the principal organizer of the local efforts; at his invitation "about 50 delegates from scientific and educational institutions
and societies" attended the first organizing meeting held at the Brunswick Hotel on 29 April. Fairchild had also made sure that the necessary
dignitaries were on hand to give the work an appropriate aura of importance; the local committee of arrangements included, *inter alios*, Abram
S. Hewitt, mayor of New York; Henry M. MacCracken, vice-chancellor of
New York University; and Morris K. Jesup, prominent philanthropist
and principal benefactor of the American Museum of Natural History.
Winifred Edgerton, one of the first women scientists to join the Academy,
was appointed to lead the "ladies section" of the local committee while
Frederick A. P. Barnard was persuaded to chair the committee of arrangements. Other tasks received equally eminent stewardship: the finance
committee, for example, included Seth Low, who, a few years later, was
to succeed Barnard as president of Columbia University; Joseph H.
Choate, one of New York's legendary bankers; and Andrew Haswell
Green, president of the Board of Commissioners of Central Park.[46]

[45] Minutes of the Council of the New York Academy of Sciences, 31 May 1883, NYAS.

[46] Minutes of the Council of the New York Academy of Sciences, 31 March 1887, NYAS;
"For the Scientists' Meeting," *New-York Times*, 30 April 1887; "To Welcome the Scientists,"
New-York Times, 18 May 1887. See also "Meeting of the American Association for the Ad-
vancement of Science, New York, 1887," *Scientific American*, 13 August 1887, 95, 100.

During the greater part of 1887 the activity of the New York Academy of Sciences became wholly centered around the preparations for the AAAS meeting. John Strong Newberry, who, as president of the Academy, took a leading role in the organizational work, was always aware of the wider significance for the city of the Association's visit. Thus, at one of the first meetings of the committee of arrangements, Newberry took especial care to motivate his colleagues by noting two important consequences of the AAAS meeting. In his introductory speech Newberry pointed out that there was the possibility of winning a greater cohesion for the city's scientific community; the AAAS conference could be "used for the bringing together of scientific men into something more compact and mutually helpful, something in short like a guild." His remark was the muted expression of an extended informal debate among leading members of the Academy that had begun several months previously; Newberry was careful not to be explicit but he was clearly offering to the assembled savants the hint that there should be an alliance among the city's various scientific institutions. The second consequence of the AAAS visit was the possibility of winning additional converts to the scientific cause; Newberry's ambition was to "popularize science by making the public aware of the number and intellectual weight of the local scientists."[47]

Newberry's campaign also had the (intentional) effect of alerting the city newspapers to the significance of the AAAS visit. The editor of the *New-York Times*, for example, found it deplorable that the Association had never previously held an annual meeting in New York. This lamentable state of affairs was about to be rectified but, as the *Times* darkly speculated, the *hauteur* of the AAAS was surely evidence of a sinister conspiracy: "[in past years] Philadelphia, Boston, even little Ann Arbor received and feasted the scientific and uplifted against this metropolis the proboscis of scorn. We fear it was this unkind spirit that caused the association to fix on August as the month for the next meeting. For then a failure would be most certain, and the dismal provincial prophet would be surest of a triumph." In the face of such unprincipled scheming the *Times* advised the New York Academy of Sciences to "make the August week the most interesting event in all the association's history. The scientific men are here in abundance to furnish the intellectual part, if they are approached properly. The city itself has twenty times the attractions of any other town in North America. . . . Let these bold bad scientists come."[48]

47 "To Welcome the Scientists," *New-York Times*, 18 May 1887.
48 Editorial, "A Feast of Reason," *New-York Times*, 18 May 1887. For a similar admonition

Despite this appeal, the local population remained curiously indifferent to the coming festival of science. For whatever reason – most scientists ascribed the materialism of the metropolis and a consequent disdain for the higher aspects of civilization – the coming of the AAAS did not arouse the anticipated degree of interest among the general population. As Chauncey Depew, a member of the New York Academy of Sciences, pointed out at an organizing meeting on 13 June, "there had been hardly any notice taken of it. New-York apparently did not know anything about it. If the meeting was to be in any of the outlying villages – Philadelphia, Boston, or St. Louis – it would be made a great occasion, while New-York was so big and so busy that it paid little attention to the matter." As a consequence of Depew's remarks, two more committees were formed, one for publicity and another for increasing the local membership of the Association. The one cheerful note of the meeting that day was an announcement that the ladies committee had already raised more than one thousand dollars.[49]

By the end of July the organizing committee had made substantial progress. Frederick Barnard had generously offered the use of the rooms at Columbia College for the AAAS during its stay in New York and Thomas L. James, treasurer of the local committee, was able to announce that the finance committee had raised almost four thousand dollars. Frederick W. Putnam, the national secretary of the AAAS, brought the challenging news that he expected over one thousand scientists to attend the meeting.[50]

The annual convention of the American Association also provided the occasion for the gathering of other scientific organizations. The International Congress of Geologists, for example, had a sizable number of North American members; this group met a few days before the start of the AAAS proceedings not only to prepare reports that "would reflect the opinions of American geologists" but also to prepare a lobbying effort

to the New York scientists, see Editorial, "American Science Association," *Harper's Weekly*, 13 August 1887, 582.

[49] "New-York's Opportunity: Mr. Depew Thinks it is to Encourage the Scientists," *New-York Times*, 14 June 1887.

[50] "Plans of the Scientists," *New-York Times*, 19 June 1887; "A Scientific Centre: New-York's Opportunity to Prove Herself Such," *New-York Times*, 1 July 1887; "The Advancement of Science," *New-York Times*, 28 July 1887; "Ready for the Scientists: Combining Pleasure and Profit," *New-York Tribune*, 8 August 1887; "Science to be Advanced: The First Meeting to be Held To-day," *New-York Tribune*, 10 August 1887. See also "Advancement of Science: The Coming Meeting at Columbia College," *Evening Post* (New York), 8 August 1887.

18. THE MEETING OF THE AAAS IN NEW YORK, 10–16 AUGUST 1887. This illustration of the New York meeting of the American Association for the Advancement of Science first appeared in *Scientific American*, 13 August 1887, 95. (*Courtesy of Columbia University Libraries.*)

to win the election of John Wesley Powell, the head of the United States Geological Survey, to the presidency of the AAAS.[51]

On the opening day of the AAAS meeting, Frederick Barnard gave the welcoming address to the scientists who assembled in the library at Columbia at 10:30 A.M. on Wednesday, 10 August. As a founding member of the National Academy of Sciences in 1867 and a former president of the American Association for the Advancement of Science, Barnard was ideally suited for the role of genial host. Consequently the room was packed—one observer noted that the "library of Columbia College was crowded, and in some parts unpleasantly so"—but Barnard soon put his audience at ease with a speech that sounded the themes of the forthcoming meeting. The president of Columbia exhorted his audience to take full advantage of the city's resources for science and to visit "her libraries, her scientific collections, her museums of art and natural history . . . her theatres, her churches, her menageries—the one in Central Park, the other, more interesting, perhaps, in Wall Street—everything, in short, that civilization has created at this its highest point of culmination upon the Western Continent."

Barnard's jibe at the New York Stock Exchange brought a ripple of appreciative laughter from his audience. Barnard won an even greater degree of appreciation when he praised the scientists as "those whose labors have done honor to our common humanity." Barnard, as he warmed to his theme, went even further; the history of the AAAS was a story of "achievements more honorable than those of the soldier, and more lastingly beneficent than were those of the philanthropic statesmen." Barnard's encomiums were sincerely meant; indeed the success of the Association seemed, to his audience at least, to provide compelling evidence that, by contrast to the situation only forty years earlier, science had won a place for itself within American society that was in full accord with its merits.[52]

For many of the participants the highlight of the conference took place the following day. At the first meeting of the Physics Section of the AAAS held in Hamilton Hall on the Columbia campus, Albert A. Michelson, a professor at the Case School of Applied Science in Cleveland, and Edward W. Morley, a professor at Western Reserve University, reported

[51] "Geologists at Spring Lake: Considering Papers to be Presented before the Society for the Advancement of Science," *New-York Tribune*, 10 August 1887.

[52] "Men of Science at Work: Harmony in Action, but Diversity in Thought," *New-York Tribune*, 11 August 1887. For synopses of the talks delivered before the various sections by the vice-presidents on the afternoon of the opening day, see "The American Association for the Advancement of Science," *Scientific American*, 20 August 1887, 112.

their results obtained, only a month previously, from an experiment to detect the luminiferous ether. In the late nineteenth century physicists were unanimous in their belief that light waves were transmitted through an ether. To test this hypothesis Michelson and Morley had constructed an elaborate apparatus in the basement of the Case School; it consisted of a platform floating on mercury (to eliminate any extraneous vibrations) on top of which Michelson attached a light source, several mirrors to reflect the beam of light, and a finely calibrated telescope to record interference fringes. The two scientists believed that there was an ether; consequently the time taken by a beam of light transmitted in the direction of the orbital motion of the earth and reflected back to the source would be greater than the time taken by a beam of light transmitted at right angles and reflected back to the same source. Since light traveled in waves, then if the ether were present, the time taken by the two beams of light would differ (because of the drag imposed by the ether) and an observer would witness a series of interference fringes as a consequence of the different times taken by the light over equal distances.[53]

Since Michelson and Morley had taken particular care to ensure the accuracy and precision of their experiment, it came as a great surprise — after they first performed the experiment in July 1887 — to find that there was no difference in the times taken by the two beams of light. In other words, the absence of an interference fringe meant that the light travelling in the direction of the earth's orbital rotation travelled at the same velocity as the light travelling in a direction perpendicular to the earth's orbital motion; in sum, the luminiferous ether had no measurable effect on the light waves.

For the physicists who heard this news at the AAAS meeting on 11 August 1887 the results of the Michelson-Morley experiment seemed altogether too implausible to credit; the existence of the luminiferous ether was so entrenched in their minds that the experiment was not taken at face value. To many members of the Physics Section the report by Michelson and Morley — the first report of the experiment before a scientific audience anywhere — was explicable only if the readings were in-

---

[53] On the significance of the Michelson-Morley experiment for relativity studies, see Loyd S. Swenson Jr., "The Michelson-Morley-Miller Experiments before and after 1905," *Journal for the History of Astronomy* 1(1970): 56–78; idem., *Genesis of Relativity: Einstein in Context*, Studies in the History of Science no. 5 (New York: Burt Franklin & Co., 1979), 59–92. For an important article that presents the heterodox view that there was little direct link between the Michelson-Morley experiment and Einstein's subsequent work on relativity theory, see Gerald Holton, "Einstein, Michelson, and the 'Crucial' Experiment," *Isis* 60(1969): 133–197.

correct or if the scientists had omitted to take some unknown factor into consideration.

The Michelson-Morley experiment remained a conundrum for several years until Albert Einstein wrote his first paper on special relativity in 1905; Einstein's theory helped to resolve the question through the hypothesis that the speed of light is a constant and is independent of the observer. In 1887 the Michelson-Morley experiment was viewed as an irritating anomaly that neither proved nor disproved the existence of the luminiferous ether.

Given the significance of the Michelson-Morley experiment for twentieth century physics, it is ironic that the second presentation that day by the two scientists made the greater impact. In a paper entitled "A Method for Making the Wave Length of Sodium Light the Actual and Practical Standard of Length" Michelson and Morley demonstrated that, by a calculation of the number of interference fringes in a measured space, an "unvarying standard" of length could be obtained. The demonstration was so clear and intellectually compelling that, as one observer reported, it took the "audience by storm." One prominent scientist in attendance that day, William Augustus Rogers, president of the American Microscopical Society and a professor of physics at Colby University, had been working on a similar problem; Rogers was heard to exclaim at the meeting that the demonstration by Michelson and Morley had been so impressive that it had gone "to the bottom of his heart." More important for the two Cleveland scientists, the Section on Physics was so moved by the beauty of the demonstration that it immediately "voted to recommend to the council to appropriate money to continue this investigation and ultimately to produce a standard unit of length which should be known as the American Association unit."[54]

The meeting of the American Association for the Advancement of Science was the occasion not only of theoretical advances in science but also of institutional shifts. Thus in 1887 the principal concern of American botanists was the paucity of support from the federal government for botany. A telling example of this phenomenon was the refusal of the federal government to endow the United States National Herbarium with the income necessary to meet its increasing needs. At the AAAS convention members of Section F (biology) met with the members of the Torrey Botanical Club to press for action from the national government; George Vasey, a representative of the United States Department of Agri-

[54] "Science in Many Forms: Papers Read Before the Association," New-York Tribune, 12 August 1887. See also "Advancement of Science," Scientific American, 27 August 1887, 128.

culture, urged the assembled botanists to begin a lobbying campaign for the national herbarium: "an expression from you relative to the importance of extending the work of the Botanical Division will be useful in securing such help as is needed from Congress."[55]

The New York meeting of the AAAS, therefore, provided an occasion for political lobbying as well as for the exchange of ideas and information. A third function of the meeting was the display to a national audience of the achievements of the local scientific institutions. On the evening of 12 August, for example, the Torrey Botanical Club held a reception for the Botanical Section of the AAAS in the library of Columbia College; on the following Monday, the Brooklyn Entomological Society, the Staten Island Natural Science Association, and the Torrey Botanical Club jointly sponsored an excursion for the AAAS scientists to Sandy Hook to "look into the alleged flora and fauna of the New-Jersey Coast." Later that same day, the New York Academy of Sciences organized a lecture by Henry Drummond, the legendary explorer of Africa; four hundred people crowded into the library to hear Drummond's "graceful descriptions of African scenery and witty touches of African life."[56]

Drummond's talk proved to be a fitting climax to the week's events. The Association met for one more day to conclude some official business; the members passed resolutions calling on the federal government to establish a Bureau of Standards, to appoint a permanent Superintendent of the United States Coast Survey, and to reduce the "tariff on scientific books and apparatus." The Association also decided—despite bids from San Francisco and Toronto—to meet the following year in Cleveland. John Wesley Powell was the choice of the delegates for the presidency of the AAAS for the coming year.[57]

The success of the 1887 meeting was an indication to many that science had become an indispensable element of the nation's material progress. In a review of the meeting, the *New-York Tribune* lauded the AAAS members as representatives of the "forces which have created a new world . . . the advance of science has wrought such revolutions that the world of

[55] "Proceedings of the Botanical Club of the A.A.A.S.," *Bulletin of the Torrey Botanical Club* 14(1887): 203, 204.

[56] "A Holiday for Scientists: To Leave their Papers for One Day," *New-York Tribune*, 13 August 1887; "Advancement of Science: Papers on a Variety of Subjects," *Evening Post* (New York), 12 August 1887; "The Scientists Kept Busy: Many Important Papers Read," *New-York Tribune*, 16 August 1887; "Proceedings," *Bulletin of the Torrey Botanical Club* 14(1887): 107–108. See also "Advancement of Science: Production of Electricity from Fuel," *Evening Post* (New York), 15 August 1887.

[57] "Advancement of Science: The Closing Day of the Society's Session," *Evening Post* (New York), 16 August 1887.

1837 not only no longer exists, but is almost completely forgotten. . . . The part of science in all our labors is recognized as it never was in old times."[58]

For the members of the New York Academy of Sciences the meeting had come off splendidly; their organizational efforts bore eloquent witness to the advances made since the dark days of 1866. More significantly the AAAS meeting had given strength to the thought that the Academy could play a leading role in the scientific life of New York through the creation of a network of local institutions; cooperation between the Academy and other scientific groups in New York City had proved very efficacious in the preparations for the AAAS visit. Would not a more permanent and stable alliance between the many New York groups produce equally beneficial results?

[58] Editorial, "Science and Industries," New-York Tribune, 14 August 1887.

4

Consolidation and Cooperation
1887–1907

THE NEW YORK ACADEMY OF SCIENCES, in the aftermath of the AAAS meeting, was able to speak for the scientific community in New York City with greater authority; the small specialist societies, like the Torrey Botanical Club and the Linnaean Society of New York, looked increasingly to the Council of the Academy for leadership and advice. In October 1887, for example, the New York Mineralogical Club approached the Academy with a request to "become the mineralogical Section of the Academy." This proposal, coming less than two months after the conclusion of the AAAS conference, confirmed the Academy's stature as the leading scientific society in the city; nevertheless, the Council of the Academy exercised a due degree of caution and followed the regular procedure of appointing a committee of the Academy to "confer with the committee of the Club." One month later the Academy committee, which consisted of Daniel S. Martin, Alexis A. Julien, and Nathaniel Lord Britton, reported that, after meeting with officers of the Mineralogical Club, both sides had concurred that the Academy "establish a separate 'Section' of mineralogy." Once this step had been taken the New York Mineralogical Club would effectively disband and the entire membership would join the Academy.[1]

By March of the following year, after long discussions on the matter, the Council of the New York Academy of Sciences was ready to enact its part of the agreement. At a meeting of the Council on 1 March 1888 it was resolved that the "Council shall be . . . empowered, subject to the approval of the Academy . . . to organize any such section as an auxiliary society, and to provide regulation for its government, meetings and ex-

---

[1] Minutes of the Council of the New York Academy of Sciences, 13 October 1887, 3 November 1887, NYAS. See also Douglas Sloan, "Science in New York City, 1867–1907," *Isis* 71(1980): 47.

penses." A small minority within the New York Mineralogical Club, however, balked at ceding authority over its affairs in such a decisive manner. The advantages of affiliation to the Academy for the tiny coterie of mineralogists in New York City—most notably, a greater degree of publicity for its meetings and an enhanced opportunity of publishing articles on mineralogy in the *Annals* and *Transactions* of the Academy—were not so great as to surrender autonomy in so complete a fashion.[2]

Accordingly, in the next four weeks, another compromise between the Academy and the Mineralogical Club was hammered out. Under this second protocol the Academy was to organize a "special section of Mineralogy—the Mineralogical Club would attend the meetings of such section, and there present its matter desirable for publication, the club being mentioned in the announcement cards and in the publications." By this stratagem all parties were able to agree on an acceptable compromise: the Academy would be strengthened by an influx of new members, the city's community of mineralogists would receive a greater degree of publicity, and the minority that wished to retain a certain autonomy would have the chance to preserve the Mineralogical Club even if its continued existence were dependent on the strong link with the Academy.[3]

The negotiations between the two organizations in 1888 were related both to the changing structure of science and to the altered status of science in a context of urban expansion. During the final decades of the nineteenth century both Columbia University and the American Museum of Natural History had emerged as leading centers of scientific research and education. Other cultural and educational institutions that had been established after the Civil War were now consolidating and, as a consequence, were commanding the attention and support of the city's educated class. The diversification and growth of cultural institutions were fueled by the increasing prosperity of the city: the urban context, as a crucible of financial, economic, and industrial expansion, provided increased support for cultural, literary, and artistic endeavors.

Such changes threatened to overwhelm the small scientific clubs that had habitually appealed to a limited constituency for financial support. Even the New York Academy of Sciences, with its long history and its influential membership, was finding it an increasingly difficult task—on account of the proliferation of cultural institutions in the Gilded Age—to command the attention of the city press and the financial support of the patriciate. One solution, for the small specialist societies, was to seek a limited degree of security by affiliating with the Academy. In addition to

[2] Minutes of the Council of the New York Academy of Sciences, 1 March 1888, NYAS.
[3] Minutes of the Council of the New York Academy of Science, 29 March 1888, NYAS.

the affiliation of the Mineralogical Club in March 1888, there had been an attempt by the Linnaean Society at the end of 1887 to work out a slightly different arrangement; the officers of the Academy had reacted favorably and had even encouraged the Linnaean Society to request a "union of the two societies for mutual helpfulness and advantage" but the deal was never consummated.[4]

It was not until the end of 1890 that a more comprehensive solution was broached within the New York Academy of Sciences. In December of that year, Nathaniel Lord Britton, the librarian of the Academy, gave a report on the condition of the Academy and its relationship to the local specialist societies. Britton, who was also professor of botany at Columbia and a leading member of the Torrey Botanical Club, was in an excellent position to evaluate the situation of science in New York City, to suggest a strategy for the Academy to follow, and to win the cooperation of his fellow-members. In his remarks at the Academy meeting on 22 December 1890, Britton was keen to dispel the illusion, cherished by a section of the old guard, that the Academy could somehow combine the many scientific clubs into a "single organization with subdivisions. . . . [this] would be futile, and it would be . . . evidently antagonistic to the process of the origination. That possibility has been repeatedly discussed, and if there were any chance of carrying it into effect, it is certain that some effort would have been made to carry it out."

By contrast to the belief of a small minority that the Academy could return to the glorious past when it exercised a solitary hegemony over scientific life in New York, Britton warned his audience that, if anything, the process of specialization was likely to accelerate in coming decades: "the epoch of Societies devoted to General Science is evidently past. The specialization and growth of the numerous departments of Science has necessitated the development of special societies for its presentation, and this process is sure to be continued perhaps with greater vigor than ever before." In the opinion of Britton this diversity was more a sign of strength than of weakness and, if properly organized in an appropriate federation of societies, could result in great advantages for science and the scientific community; the creation of a formal alliance by the various groups would confer immediate benefits: "the membership of the organizations would, it is believed, soon be doubled."

In a more immediate sense, Britton held out the promise of a "monthly Bulletin of lectures, meetings, exhibitions and excursions . . . [to] be printed at small expense, each society contributing pro rata to its membership, and distributed to every member of every organization. . . . This would effect a very considerable saving in expenditure for printing and postage, for these Bulletins could serve as notices for the meetings." Britton was also optimistic that the city newspapers, which were not giving science the publicity that it deserved, would pay more attention to the activities of the various societies if they presented a united front: "a systematic attack in the Press would surely be successful in obtaining notices of everything done or proposed."[5]

Britton, when he gave his report to the Academy on the afternoon of 22 December, was only thirty-one years old; his youth was apparently no inhibition to ambition for, at the same time as he was proposing the creation of an alliance of the various scientific societies, he was also organizing a campaign for the creation of a botanical garden in New York. For the next forty years Britton was indubitably the leading individual in New York science; for much of that period he led the New York Academy of Sciences to undertake the most significant scientific project in its history, the Puerto Rico survey, and, at the same time, he provided leadership and direction to the successful establishment of the New York Botanical Garden.

Britton's leadership of the Academy was closely related to his simultaneous creation of the New York Botanical Garden; indeed the former cannot be successfully analyzed without a consideration of the latter. The early history of the Botanical Garden, moreover, serves admirably to illustrate how the pattern of private and public support for a scientific institution resulted—just as it had twenty years earlier with the American Museum of Natural History—in a synergy of success.

The original idea for a botanical garden in New York can be traced back to 1886 when Henry Hurd Rusby, a leading member of the Torrey Botanical Club, returned from a journey to South America with a large collection of Bolivian plants. Rusby, together with his close friend Britton, examined the collection at the herbarium at Columbia but, largely on account of an absence of comparative material from South America at the Columbia herbarium, the two botanists made little progress in analyzing the Bolivian specimens. Not until 1888, when Britton and his wife, Elizabeth Knight Britton, took the Bolivia collection with them on a visit to the Royal Botanic Gardens at Kew in England, could any progress be

[5] Nathaniel L. Britton, [Communication on the Alliance of Scientific Societies], in Minutes of the Council of the New York Academy of Sciences, 22 December 1890, NYAS.

made on the plants; their visit to Kew had the effect of revealing to the Brittons that the facilities for botany in New York were nugatory by comparison with those in London. Thus on their return to the United States the two Brittons began a systematic campaign for the establishment of a botanic garden.[6]

The first task was to persuade the Torrey Botanical Club to lend its support to the campaign. Elizabeth Knight Britton described the Kew gardens at a meeting of the Club on 24 October 1888; at a subsequent meeting a committee was appointed to prepare an appeal to the public for the creation of a New York garden. This committee, which included, in addition to Nathaniel Britton, such stalwarts of science as John Strong Newberry, president of the New York Academy of Sciences, and Addison Brown, president of the Torrey Botanical Club, aimed to establish a subscription fund, to win the support of the Department of Public Parks, and to garner publicity for the proposed garden by placing articles in the city newspapers.[7]

Fortunately for the members of the Torrey Botanical Club, the editors of the *New York Herald* were quickly convinced of the value of the proposed garden and, in a series of articles that appeared in November 1888, the *Herald* attracted considerable publicity to the scheme. The arguments in favor of the garden were strikingly similar to those utilized by the founders of the American Museum of Natural History. Civic pride was one strong incentive; as a reporter for the *Herald* pointed out: "we are still far behind many comparatively insignificant European cities. . . . New York city has signally failed to have for any length of time a horticultural society at all worthy of comparison with the horticultural societies of Philadelphia and Boston. For that reason, if for no other, when the subject of New York city having a botanical garden . . . is proposed, every one interested in botany or horticulture will most heartily acquiesce." National pride was also a factor for, while European royalty had endowed gardens at St. Petersburg, Paris, Brussels, Frankfurt, and Berlin, the republican government of the United States sponsored only one garden; this establishment at Washington, D.C., was reputedly a "'swindle on the public' . . . simply useful in supplying the Senators, Congressmen and big politicians with flowers at the expense of the taxpayers."[8]

[6] Nathaniel L. Britton, "History of the New York Botanical Garden," 1, Typescript, Nathaniel Lord Britton Papers, NYBG; Henry A. Gleason, "The Scientific Work of Nathaniel Lord Britton," *Proceedings of the American Philosophical Society* 104(1960): 217.

[7] Britton, "History," 1.

[8] "Our Botanical Weakness: Park Commissioners Favor the Herald's Educational Sug-

19. NATHANIEL LORD BRITTON (1859–1934). After graduating from the School of Mines at Columbia University in 1879, Britton worked as an assistant geologist in the Geological Survey of New Jersey. In 1886 Britton was appointed Instructor in Geology and Botany at Columbia; ten years later, after rising in the ranks to become professor of botany, Britton left Columbia to accept an appointment as the first director of the New York Botanical Garden. Britton was an active member of many New York scientific societies; he joined the New York Academy of Sciences in 1880 and was elected president of the Academy in 1906. Throughout most of his early life he was the principal organizer and leader of the Torrey Botanical Club. (*Courtesy of the New York Botanical Garden.*)

Most commentators believed that the garden in New York should be as independent of the municipal government as possible; yet this stipulation—obviously motivated by the intent to avoid corruption and bureaucratic red tape—would make the project less certain of success. The city's cooperation was necessary if, as most experts agreed, the garden were to be part of Central Park; if the garden were to be located elsewhere, in the Bronx or in Brooklyn, substantial sums of money would be necessary to buy up a sufficient amount of land. It was possible that the garden might be created under the aegis of the state legislature, but that seemed a hazardous procedure that would not necessarily obviate a future danger of corruption.

A second issue was the question of control. It seemed unlikely that the municipal authorities would provide financial support and then cede legal control of the garden to private groups, yet everyone allowed that the participation of the Torrey Botanical Club in the maintenance and administration of the garden would have a salubrious influence. Also, since the botanical garden was promoted primarily as an educational venture then it was surely desirable that the city's colleges, most obviously Columbia, New York University, and City College, have representatives on the garden's board of directors.[9]

Various interest groups quickly coalesced around the plan. The academic community at Columbia, commercial seedsmen and horticulturalists, the Department of Public Parks, and, last but not least, the scientific societies—most obviously the Torrey Botanical Club and the Linnaean Society of New York—all declared an interest in the project. Given the numerous advocates of the plan and given that a delicate balance would have to be maintained between, on the one hand, the public authorities and, on the other, the private institutions, it was evident to all that a great deal of perseverance, determination, energy, and resourcefulness would be necessary for the success of the enterprise. It is in this sense, therefore, that the ability of Nathaniel Lord Britton is so strikingly revealed, for the Columbia professor combined an extraordinary capacity for organizational and administrative detail with a breadth of vision that was always several steps ahead of his colleagues. These two qualities—the es-

gestion," *New York Herald*, 27 November 1888; "A Great Garden Needed: New York Should Have an Artistic Floral Study Ground," *New York Herald*, 26 November 1888.

[9] A comprehensive discussion of the debate over the garden can be found in the *New York Herald* articles. See especially "A Great Garden Needed," *New York Herald*, 26 November 1888; "Our Botanical Weakness," *New York Herald*, 27 November 1888; Editorial, "What New York Ought to Have," *New York Herald*, 27 November 1888; "Nichols on Botany," *New York Herald*, 2 December 1888.

sence of leadership—were concentrated to perfection in the slender, almost diminutive, frame of Nathaniel Britton.

As soon as he had obtained the support of the Torrey Botanical Club, Britton approached the municipal authorities to ask that the city donate land; Britton, as part of his request, agreed to cede partial control of the project to the Department of Public Parks. A few months later, having obtained a promise of support from the mayor, Britton approached the state legislature for its support of the project. An act of incorporation of the New York Botanical Garden was sent to the state Assembly on 6 March 1891 and on 28 April—having obtained the consent of the House and the Senate—the governor of New York signed the legislative bill.

In the two years between the time of the original proposal before the Torrey Botanical Club and the signing of the act of incorporation, Britton had won to his side a wide array of supporters. Needless to say, every section of New York's scientific community—including the professoriate at Columbia and the research staff of the American Museum of Natural History—enthusiastically supported the measure. Britton had also won strong backing from the small group of wealthy philanthropists who were then contributing large sums of money to Columbia and the American Museum. This group included Seth Low, Cornelius Vanderbilt, Morris K. Jesup, J. Pierpont Morgan, Andrew Carnegie, William E. Dodge, and William C. Schermerhorn. Since the state legislature had stipulated, in amendments to the act of incorporation, that it would donate 250 acres of Bronx Park only if $250,000 were raised from private sources, the support of the philanthropists was crucial to the endeavor. Over the next three years Britton, with the help of a resourceful finance committee, canvassed those acquaintances who had previously expressed their support. Morgan, Carnegie, Vanderbilt, and John D. Rockefeller each gave $25,000; Dodge and Schermerhorn each donated $10,000; while Samuel Sloan, George J. Gould, Helen M. Gould, and William Rockefeller each contributed $5,000. The subscription drive was a phenomenal success and, as a consequence, the Commissioner of Public Parks not only presented 250 acres of land but also persuaded the City Board of Estimate to provide half a million dollars for the construction of the main buildings.[10]

Britton resigned his chair of botany at Columbia in 1896 to devote himself full-time to the organization of the New York Botanical Garden; in that year a topographical survey of the land was completed, a border screen of trees was planted around the perimeter, and a temporary railway was built for the transportation of the large quantities of earth

[10] Britton, "History," 1–4.

and rock necessary for the landscaping of the garden. In the next few years a comprehensive plan of construction was put into effect; this included the "system of driveways and paths, water supply, drainage, planting, the museum building, the first range of public greenhouses . . . and minor structures." At the same time the herbarium was organized, and the planting of the fruticetum, arboretum, and the pinetum was begun. Columbia University generously agreed to donate its "herbarium and botanical library" and Britton promised to deliver a regular series of lectures on botany. Last but not least, a publication and research program was initiated; subscribers to the building fund learned about the scientific research performed in the new laboratory through the *Journal* and the *Bulletin of the New York Botanical Garden.*[11]

Since Britton, during the same period, was also organizing the Scientific Alliance of New York, his achievements at the Botanical Garden seem even more remarkable. In 1890, when he was beginning to gather support for the garden, Britton was also involved, as a member of the Council of the New York Academy of Sciences, in pushing forward his plan for a federation of scientific societies. In his proposal of December 1890 Britton had suggested that a representative from each specialist society be appointed to a committee of the Council of the Academy. Having canvassed his idea among the Academy leadership beforehand, Britton was simultaneously able to put forward names of individuals who combined leadership in a specialist society with membership in the Council of the Academy. John K. Rees, professor of geodesy and astronomy at Columbia, agreed to represent the New York Mathematical Society; Daniel S. Martin, professor of geology at the Rutgers Female College and a former vice-president of the New York Academy of Sciences, was the delegate of the New York Mineralogical Club; John A. Allen was a representative for the Linnaean Society of New York; H. Carrington Bolton, who had resolved his differences with Charles Chandler several years previously, was, as a leading member of the American Chemical Society, willing to represent the ACS on the committee; and Charles F. Cox was the delegate of the New-York Microscopical Society. Nathaniel Britton served on the committee as a representative of the Torrey Botanical Club while Oliver P. Hubbard, as vice-president of the New York Academy of Sciences since 1885, was ideally suited to represent that organization.[12]

[11] Gleason, "Scientific Work," 217–218; Britton, "History," 4–5, 7; "The New York Botanical Garden," *Scientific American*, 21 March 1896, 183.

[12] Nathaniel L. Britton, [Communication on an Alliance of Scientific Societies], in Minutes of the Council of the New York Academy of Sciences, 22 December 1890, NYAS.

The list of representatives from the various societies clearly shows the overlapping connections between the officers of the Academy, the professoriate at Columbia and the scientific staff of the American Museum. While each specialist society may have been composed of laymen with little or no professional training for whom science was an avocation, at the level of leadership of such organizations as the Mineralogical Club, the Microscopical Society, and the Torrey Botanical Club, the officers of each group had strong academic affiliations. Since, moreover, each representative on the committee was also a leading member of the New York Academy of Sciences, the dominant role of the Academy in the affairs of the Alliance was evident from the beginning.

It came as no surprise, therefore, when, at its meeting of 26 February 1891, the Council of the Academy expressed its support of Britton's initiative and nominated Charles F. Cox and Britton to serve as the two permanent representatives of the Academy on the Council of the Scientific Alliance. At the first meeting of the Scientific Alliance on 11 March, representatives were present from the Torrey Botanical Club, the Microscopical Society, the Linnaean Society, the Mineralogical Club, the New York Mathematical Society, and the New York Academy of Sciences. Britton served as secretary for the meeting and, under his guidance, the delegates agreed to form a "permanent organization to be composed of the President and two other members of each Society." The immediate goals were suitably modest and included the "preparation of an annual Directory giving the name and address of each member of each society . . . [and] the preparation of a periodical Bulletin, to give the time and place of meeting of each society." At the end of the meeting a general discussion ensued on such topics as the "holding of periodical joint meetings . . . [and] the arrangement of courses of scientific lectures," but no further decisions were taken.[13]

For the next few months Britton spent much of his time consolidating the initial work of the Alliance. He was keenly aware that, if the Alliance remained limited to the six founding societies, it would fail to become a representative organization that could speak with authority to the press and the general public on scientific matters. As a consequence, Britton devoted a great deal of effort in the early period to persuading other scientific societies in New York City to join the Alliance. By April 1891 neither the local section of the American Chemical Society nor the New York branch of the Archaeological Institute of America had replied to

[13] Minutes of the Council of the New York Academy of Sciences, 26 February 1891, NYAS; "Conference of Representatives of the Scientific Associations," Minutes of the Council of the Scientific Alliance, 11 March 1891, NYAS.

Britton's formal letter of invitation; members of the Council learned that "both organizations still have the matter under consideration." Unfortunately the American Geographical Society, which had about twelve hundred members at the time, declined an invitation to join the Alliance; since the admission of the Geographical Society would have approximately doubled the individual membership of the Alliance, this decision was a deep disappointment for Britton. His feelings were assuaged to a certain degree, however, by a proposal from the Brooklyn Institute of Arts and Sciences for a series of joint lectures with the Scientific Alliance.[14]

Britton's plan to expand the Alliance was complemented by the appearance in the fall of 1891 of the first number of a monthly *Bulletin*. Since it aimed to list both the organizational and educational meetings of each constituent society and because it was to be mailed to each member, the *Bulletin* served admirably to save the costs of mailing and printing that were incurred when each society performed this essential task of notification. In November 1891 the *Bulletin* proved its worth; the annual meetings of the National Academy of Sciences and the American Ornithologists' Union took place in New York during that month and both organizations received prominent coverage in the *Bulletin of the Scientific Alliance*.[15]

This necessary organizational work served, for Britton, as preparation for the essential task of unification and cohesion. A great deal would be possible, for example, when the various societies could act and speak in unison on matters of concern to the scientific community. Britton was also keenly aware of the munificent financial support that both Columbia and the American Museum were receiving from the small group of wealthy New York philanthropists. In order to win the backing of such men as Cornelius Vanderbilt, Andrew Carnegie, and John D. Rockefeller, the officers of the Scientific Alliance launched an appeal for a building fund. A campaign for a new building to house the Scientific Alliance would, most obviously, be a great material asset for the various scientific groups. The New York Academy of Sciences, the Torrey Botanical Club, and the Mathematical Society all presently met in rooms in Hamilton Hall on the Columbia campus; the Linnaean Society used a room pro-

---

[14] "Conference of Representatives of the Scientific Alliance," Minutes of the Council of the Scientific Alliance, 23 April 1891; "Meeting of the Joint Commission," Minutes of the Council of the Scientific Alliance, 23 April 1891, NYAS.

[15] Minutes of the Council of the Scientific Alliance, 28 September 1891, 23 October 1891, NYAS. See also "The Scientific Alliance: A Union for Announcements Perfected," *Evening Post* (New York), 10 November 1891.

vided by the American Museum of Natural History; and the Microscopical Society held meetings at the private home of a member on Madison Avenue. With their own building the scientific groups would be able to combine their libraries and collections; this, in turn, would render the Scientific Alliance a more attractive proposition for those scientific societies that had not yet joined. Finally, as Britton fully realized, the campaign for a new building would provide the Alliance with a tangible ambition that would be both worthwhile and eminently desirable; as a consequence, it would serve to inspire not only the members of the individual groups but also (Britton hoped) the wealthy philanthropists who would now have a material reason for donating large sums of welcome cash.

In the campaign for the latter, Britton was acutely aware, however, of a danger of the perceived irrelevance of the activities of the various societies. While Columbia University, the American Museum of Natural History, and even the New York Botanical Garden could make grandiose claims about the vital importance of educating the citizenry, the Scientific Alliance was occasionally hard-pressed to justify its reason for being. Mineralogy, mathematics, and microscopy were all perfectly good ways to spend one's leisure hours but, as Britton appreciated, that fact was not going to be sufficient reason for generous donations. Accordingly, in the publicity campaign launched in the fall of 1891, the officers of the Scientific Alliance were careful to stress the "importance of science to the industrial and commercial world. . . . the propriety of its having a home of its own and a recognized centre will be appreciated in a city that has proven so lavish in its gifts to museums, hospitals, and philanthropic institutions."[16]

Britton, after his recent journey to England, had returned to New York with the ambition of creating an American equivalent of Burlington House in London which, at the time, served as the headquarters not only of the Royal Academy of Art and the Royal Society but also of a host of specialist organizations including the Linnaean, Chemical, Geological, and Astronomical societies. If Britton could successfully realize this cherished dream, it would not be long, he believed, before New York would rival and perhaps surpass the capitals of Europe as centers of scientific excellence.

Britton's publicity campaign for the Scientific Alliance was generally successful. During the next year the plan received intermittent notices

[16] "The Scientific Alliance: Efforts to Obtain a Central Club-House," *Evening Post* (New York), 1 November 1891.

in all of the city's major newspapers. The *Evening Post* remarked that the "citizens of New York have been very generous in giving" and queried its readers why science "still remains homeless, and at the present late hour is asking to be received into the comfort of a worthy habitation." The *New-York Tribune* reported copiously on the "steps . . . [being] taken by the different scientific societies in this city to unite in erecting a handsome headquarters in which all these societies may have their own separate set of rooms for meetings, lectures or private discussions," while the *New-York Times* expressed the hope that the "day was not far distant when the Scientific Alliance would be housed as handsomely and advantageously as were the artists and the musicians and their congeners of the great metropolis."[17]

Among the scientific community in the United States few publications were as influential as the weekly magazine, *Science*. In his reports on the building campaign, the editor of *Science* was careful to adumbrate the many reasons why wealth should come to the aid of science: "music and other fine arts and various charities have recently received munificent assistance. . . . it seems reasonable to think that the man, or men, will soon be found with sufficient appreciation of scientific research, for both its educational and its practical value, to place it in a position as solid and substantial as that now likely to be occupied by the fine arts and by organized benevolence."[18]

The Scientific Alliance, in the initial stages of the effort to find sponsors of the building fund, scored an early success in persuading Seth Low to serve on the subscription committee. Low's public endorsement of the building campaign was a vote of confidence from the one man who, more than any other individual in the city, epitomized the union of culture, wealth, and patronage. Low, formerly the mayor of Brooklyn, was, in 1892, president of Columbia and, on account of his political and social connections, had been largely instrumental in winning sizable donations to the university from the New York patriciate. The leadership of the Scientific Alliance was well aware of Low's campaign for Columbia; Low's effort involved not only a shift in educational policy towards advanced research but also a cultivation of the city's patriciate in

---

[17] "A Home for Science in New York," *Evening Post* (New York), 14 November 1892; "A Building for Scientists: Societies Unite for the Purpose," *New-York Tribune*, 31 July 1892, sec. 2; "As a Scientific Centre: The Metropolis Could Serve Well in that Capacity," *New-York Times*, 16 November 1892.

[18] "The Scientific Alliance," *Science*, 11 March 1892, 142.

the expectation that the millionaires of Manhattan would identify their interest with that of the university.[19]

At his inauguration in February 1890 as Columbia's twelfth president, Low decisively marked out the path he intended Columbia to follow during his tenure. At a speech before the alumni, for example, Low expressed his belief that Columbia could prosper only if it became an integral part of the city; there was a necessary dependence of the college on the development of the city and (he hoped) there would be a future dependence of the city on Columbia. "The real world," the new president intoned, "is not to be found in books. . . . There is a variety to life in this city, a vitality about it and withal a sense of power, which, to my thought, are of inestimable value to the student whose desire it is to become a well-rounded man." Although (in the presence of powerful local politicians) Low refrained from being specific, he pointed out in his speech that New York had problems "in their gravest forms . . . an education in New York is likely to be of especial value to any man who wishes to be of service in meeting the great problems with which our cities confront the country."

The kernel of his speech, however, concerned his plans for the type of education to be had at Columbia. The aim was, as before, to "develop the cultivated man, the educated gentleman." Yet, at the same time, Columbia—with its medical school, law school, and the School of Mines—was ideally equipped to train men who wished to enter the professions; this part of the educational program would continue as before. The new ingredient of the Columbia education, an ingredient that Low intended to install as rapidly as possible, was the promotion of original research in law, philosophy, and science. Columbia, according to the new president, "aims to do systematically more and more of the original work which belongs especially to our conception of the university. . . . She looks assuredly for the day when European students shall come to New York and Columbia, where now our American youth go to Oxford and Paris and Berlin."[20]

The realization of Low's ambition to develop Columbia as a research

[19] For an account of Low's political influence, see Steven C. Swett, "The Test of a Reformer: A Study of Seth Low, New York City Mayor, 1902–1903," New-York Historical Society Quarterly 44(1960): 5–41.

[20] "President Low Installed at Columbia," Critic, 8 February 1890, 69–70; see also "A New Move in Columbia College," Nation, 8 May 1890, 370. Low's vision of Columbia as a research university reflected broader changes influencing American higher education. These included the transfer from the German university system of an ideal of non-utilitarian learning. See Laurence R. Veysey, The Emergence of the American University (Chicago: University of Chicago Press, 1965), 125–133.

university was contingent, however, on a successful campaign to per-suade New York's monied elite to increase their donations to the univer-sity; in the years following his inauguration, Low proved his value to Co-lumbia by winning, to an unprecedented degree, the necessary financial support. In 1895, when the Columbia trustees decided to move the uni-versity to the countryside about two miles north of the former location on Forty-ninth Street, Low himself donated one million dollars for the construction of a new library. The Low Library, as it was called, was one part of a classical triad which also included, to the south, the Cathedral of St. John the Divine, and to the north, the gargantuan tomb of Ulysses S. Grant. Many observers likened the university's new situation on a hill to the Acropolis and all agreed with one (foolishly) optimistic writer who pointed out a further advantage: "the heights of Morningside are forever removed from the noise and din of a city's traffic."[21]

In the first six years of Low's tenure as president, Columbia raised over five million dollars. The new site on Morningside Heights was purchased with donations of one hundred thousand dollars each from Cornelius Vanderbilt, J. Pierpont Morgan, and William C. Schermerhorn; Samuel P. Avery donated $150,000 for "architecture and allied arts," Daniel B. Fayer-weather left Columbia $308,000 in his will, Charles M. DaCosta contrib-uted $100,000 for zoology, George W. Vanderbilt gave $150,000 to pur-chase the land for Teachers College, and Joseph Pulitzer donated $350,000 for a scholarship fund. In 1896 the Havemeyer family contrib-uted $450,000 for a chemistry building, while William C. Schermerhorn gave a similar amount for a "building for natural sciences." Since most of the contributions went for specific purposes and often for the construc-tion of a building, the Columbia campus rapidly expanded; however, since the university was not able to provide concomitant funding for the maintenance and teaching staff, the continued donations became a source of difficulty for the university; as Seth Low's successor, Nicholas Murray Butler, complained: "those who make gifts to . . . [Columbia] really put upon the university the new obligation of acting without com-pensation as their own trustees or executors for the purpose of carrying out some plan or purpose of their own."[22]

[21] Nicholas Murray Butler, "Columbia University and the City of New York," *Harper's Weekly*, 16 May 1896, 485. See also "Columbia's Dedication," *Critic*, 9 May 1896, 328.

[22] The gifts to Columbia through 1913 are listed in Frederick Paul Keppel, *Columbia* (New York: Oxford University Press, 1914), 280–286; Roger L. Geiger, *To Advance Knowledge: The Growth of American Research Universities, 1900–1940* (New York: Oxford University Press, 1986), 52. For the changes at Columbia during Seth Low's tenure, see Horace Coon, *Co-lumbia: Colossus on the Hudson* (New York: E. P. Dutton & Co., 1947), 88–92. For a cogent

Naturally enough, the officers of the Scientific Alliance regarded Seth Low's support of the building fund as an auspicious sign. For his own part, Low looked with especial favor on the Alliance for, although he was no scientist, he regarded the promotion of science in the city as a worthy cause that would benefit New York and, by extension, Columbia University. Low, moreover, pursued science as an intellectual avocation; he had been a member of the New York Academy of Sciences for several years and, shortly before his appointment at Columbia, Low had served as vice-president of the Academy.[23]

As part of the effort to find sponsors of the building fund, the Scientific Alliance, in the fall of 1892, held a large public meeting at the American Museum of Natural History. The keynote speaker, Seth Low, took as his subject the goal of making the "city a great scientific center, in the sense that the city shall become a positive power in the world of scientific thought and action." The most felicitous comparison, according to Low, was between science and business. Just as the Chamber of Commerce served the financial community as the "common meeting ground of every business," so the Scientific Alliance could, if given an adequate amount of support, serve as the "agency which the city has long needed to develop to the utmost its scientific activities in the direction of pure science." If the Scientific Alliance—the first attempt to give cohesion to the scientific cause—succeeded, science in New York City, Low predicted, would win a stronger and more powerful voice.

Nothing could be more persuasive, in Low's opinion, than the example of the Brooklyn Institute of Arts and Sciences. This organization, established in 1824, encompassed all areas of knowledge and, so successful had it been in attracting the attention and support of the literate class of the city that the Brooklyn Institute now had the resources to maintain a "successful seaside laboratory of Biology at Glen Cove." The Scientific Alliance should set its ambition on the same plane and should not rest until it had awakened "a veritable enthusiasm for the encouragement of scientific research. . . . This city will surely be a nobler and a better place to dwell in, the more it can draw to itself . . . the men who question nature for its secrets and reveal them for the service and advancement of mankind."[24]

analysis of the role of private philanthropy in supporting American colleges in the Gilded Age, see Daniel A. Wren, "American Business Philanthropy and Higher Education in the Nineteenth Century," *Business History Review* 57(1983): 321–346.

[23] Minutes of the Council of the New York Academy of Sciences, 29 January 1890, NYAS.

[24] Seth Low, "Advantages to New York City of the Alliance of the Scientific Societies," in *Addresses Delivered at the First Joint Meeting* (New York, 1893), 5–9.

A frequent jeremiad of scientists in late nineteenth century America was the lack of appreciation for pure science; while technology, in the guise of applied science, was putatively fueling the industrial revolution in the United States, scientific research with no apparent immediate application received little notice. Thus Simon Newcomb, professor of mathematics at the Naval Observatory in Washington, D.C., in an essay commissioned by the *North American Review* to mark the progress of theoretical science since 1776, candidly acknowledged the dismal state of intellectual life in the United States by contrast with its condition in Europe. Newcomb had no single explanation for the invidious comparison: on the one hand he suggested that in America "the analytical power which traces the laws of nature . . . [has been] partially replaced by the inventive genius which has taken the lead in giving the world steam-navigation, the telegraph, and the sewing-machine," while on the other hand, Newcomb ascribed part of the problem to a "want of public recognition and appreciation." He was unequivocal, however, in blaming the low level of the exact sciences on the lack of support from the federal and state governments: "on the Continent the learned societies are under the immediate patronage of their respective governments. . . . In this country we are aware of but a single State which has thus taken upon itself the patronage of science, and it will probably surprise many readers to hear that this is Wisconsin."[25]

Over the next two decades Newcomb's complaint found a repeated echo within the scientific community. Henry Rowland, a professor of physics at Johns Hopkins University, in his 1883 address as vice-president of Section B (physics) of the American Association for the Advancement of Science, urged his colleagues not only to promote theoretical science as energetically as possible but also to propagate the notion that their calling was the highest ideal towards which humanity could aspire: "we are tired of seeing our countrymen take their science from abroad . . . we are tired of seeing our professors degrading their chairs by the pursuit of applied science. . . . We wish for something higher and nobler in this country of mediocrity." In his speech before the physicists of the AAAS on the future of American science Rowland leavened his pessimism with occasional bursts of extravagant optimism—"the land which science promises us in the future . . . shall . . . flow with milk and honey"—but, above all else, he gave forceful expression to the need of the scientific community to carve a place for itself within the higher echelons of the social structure. The level of scientific research within the United States, Row-

[25] Simon Newcomb, "Abstract Science in America, 1776–1876," *North American Review* 122(1876): 97, 111, 118.

land maintained, could only be raised to a status comparable with European science if American scientists received funding from a central source and, moreover, if that funding were channeled to those few institutions capable of directing original research. In other words, Rowland was calling for a termination of the democratic spirit within the American scientific community, a spirit that was consequent on the republican ideals of 1776. Not a few members of his audience must have felt uncomfortable with the tone of Rowland's remarks; his sarcastic contempt for the avocational scientist in America was forcefully expressed: "there are very many local societies dignified by high-sounding names, each having its local celebrity, to whom the privilege of describing some crab with an extra claw, which he found in his morning ramble, is inestimable."[26]

If any members of the Scientific Alliance had been present that day they would have recognized Rowland's speech for what it was: a direct attack upon their science, their reputation, and their institutions. Yet it should not be supposed that, while the elite of the scientific community was preparing *its* campaign for control of future funding from public and private sources, that the local societies, whose members were overwhelmingly avocational scientists, were not cognizant of the need to argue their case, to preserve the character of American science as equalitarian, democratic, and non-exclusive, and to maintain a viable niche within the scientific community for the dilettante.

Thus, at the public meeting of the Scientific Alliance held at the American Museum of Natural History in 1892, Addison Brown, president of the Torrey Botanical Club, sounded a similar set of themes to those expressed by Rowland but to a different purpose. In a survey of American science, Brown repeatedly affirmed the poor position of science in the United States by comparison to its situation in Europe. While it was self-evident, he claimed, that technology was fundamentally dependent on advances in pure science, this relationship did not receive the attention that it deserved and the scientists who performed original research never attracted the support that society, which derived so much benefit from their labors, owed them: "research in pure science can never be made a self-supporting pursuit . . . nearly all the great advances . . . have been achieved by men who . . . have been supported through institutions or endowments. . . . Government appointments, professorial chairs, or

---

[26] Henry Augustus Rowland, "A Plea for Pure Science," *Proceedings of the American Association for the Advancement of Science* 32(1883): 108, 122, 123. The interpretation of Rowland's speech as "best-science elitism" is lucidly expressed in Daniel Kevles, *The Physicists: The History of a Scientific Community in Modern America* (New York: Vantage Books, 1979), 43-44.

salaried positions in scientific institutions of some kind, have been and must continue to be, our chief dependence."[27]

Unfortunately the actual situation—whether in government service or university appointments—was utterly dismal. While a handful of federal bureaux and government agencies—most notably, John Wesley Powell's United States Geological Survey—did provide employment for scientists, such positions were always under siege from members of Congress who could rarely resist a demagogic attack on the apparent frivolity of pure science. In 1885, for example, Hilary Abner Herbert, a Congressman from Alabama, queried the funding by the federal government of the Geological Survey and, in particular, demanded to know how research in paleontology (one of the activities of the Survey) was supposed to contribute towards the better administration of the country. Powell was able to fend off this attack but the episode clearly illustrates the tenuous nature of federal science in the nineteenth century.[28]

In the universities the situation was not much better. Brown, in his speech before the Scientific Alliance in 1892, pointedly reminded his audience that the three major scholarship endowments for scientific research at American universities had all been contributed by an Irishman—in 1885 John Tyndall, the professor of natural philosophy at the Royal Institution, who had realized a profit of thirteen thousand dollars from a lecture tour in the United States, had magnanimously given the proceeds of his tour to endow scholarships at three major colleges: Columbia, Penn, and Harvard. Scientific research in the university context was essentially nugatory since most of the professoriate was too busy teaching; as a consequence few American scientists could hope to keep pace with their European counterparts. By contrast to the United States, in Germany, for example, there were "from 800 to 1000 persons of high scientific attainments, supported by the government in the universities, who are regularly and systematically engaged in the discovery of new scientific truth."

For Brown, who was by inclination and avocation a botanist, the most shocking example of American poverty revealed itself, in embarrassing clarity, by the state of affairs at the biological laboratory at Naples—the "most thoroughly equipped, and . . . the most advantageous for study of any in the world"—where research tables were available for an annual fee of five hundred dollars. In the twenty years since its establishment Germany had paid for thirteen tables each year; Italy, for eight; Austria,

[27] Addison Brown, "Need of Endowment for Scientific Research and Publication," in *Addresses Delivered*, 22–23.

[28] Kevles, *The Physicists*, 55; A. Hunter Dupree, *Science in the Federal Government: A History of Policies and Activities* (1957; reprint, Johns Hopkins University Press, 1986), 222–224.

Spain, Britain, and Russia, for three each; Switzerland, Belgium, and Holland, for one. American students, by comparison, had been able to study at the station only through the good-will of other nations.[29]

Brown's speech at the meeting of the Scientific Alliance focused on the contrast between pure and applied science simply because the New York societies, in intellectual terms at least, were decidedly in the camp of the pure sciences. Of the seven organizations that constituted the Scientific Alliance, only the American Chemical Society, which had recently joined the Alliance, could claim to have any practical relevance; the remaining six groups promoted such sciences as mineralogy, botany, mathematics, microscopy, zoology, physics, and astronomy. Addison Brown could express the hope, in the coda of his talk before the Scientific Alliance, that "when . . . the people at large shall come to see that the cause of scientific advance and the discovery of all new truth are in the deepest sense their cause, responses will, I believe, come to every urgent need," but more canny observers believed that the struggle of the Scientific Alliance for the financial support of the "people" was to be arduous and protracted.[30]

Thus, in 1892 Nathaniel Lord Britton, whose fund-raising for the New York Botanical Garden was proceeding apace, was sufficiently convinced that while the wealthy elite of New York society was prepared to support the Botanical Garden, it was not, at present, willing to undertake a similar effort for a second scientific project—the Scientific Alliance—in the same year. Britton was undaunted, however, by his perception of the reluctance of the patriciate to support the Scientific Alliance. His propaganda campaign on behalf of the Scientific Alliance during 1892 served a double purpose: not only did it keep the Alliance in the eye of the public as a worthy cause to support at a later date but it also enabled Britton to push the Alliance forward as a possible candidate for the funds controlled by the Tilden Trust.

Samuel Jones Tilden, a leading member of the bar in New York City, had first come to public attention as a prominent figure in the reform movement that ousted the Tweed Ring; Tilden parlayed his reputation as a legal expert on political matters into the Democratic nomination for governor of New York state and after serving at Albany for two years, he was nominated by the Democratic Party as the candidate for the presidential election of 1876. Tilden's defeat that year did little to injure his reputation in his native state and, on his return to New York City, Tilden re-

---

[29] Brown, "Need of Endowment," in *Addresses Delivered*, 18, 23.
[30] Brown, "Need of Endowment," in *Addresses Delivered*, 41.

sumed his highly successful and profitable career as a lawyer. Tilden was not only a lawyer and politician but also a bibliophile who had amassed, at the time of his death in 1886, a library of fifteen thousand volumes exclusive of his law library. In his will Tilden directed that, of his fortune, one million dollars was to be distributed among his next-of-kin (one sister, two nephews, and four nieces) while the residuary estate—five million dollars—was to constitute the Tilden Trust for the "establishment and maintenance of a Free Library and Reading Room in the City of New York."[31]

Given his reputation as one of the most brilliant legal minds of his generation, it is ironic that Tilden was unable to draw up a will that was sufficiently foolproof against the depredations of his sister, nephews, and nieces; these ingrates contested the will and broke its principal clause and, as a consequence of the judgement of the Court of Appeals, the entire residuary estate was given to the next-of-kin. Partly on account of the subsequent uproar in the New York newspapers that the city had been robbed of its opportunity to gain a library that could compare with those recently established in Boston and Chicago and partly on account of the troubled conscience of Tilden's granddaughter (who had inherited the share bequeathed to Tilden's sister) the Tilden Trust did eventually recoup two and one half million dollars. Unfortunately, as most knowledgeable observers pointed out, this was insufficient to enable the trustees both to finance the construction of a new building and to provide an endowment for the purchase and maintenance of a circulating and reference collection. As the editor of the *World* pointed out, the Tilden Trust could now provide the city with "merely . . . an addition to its small public libraries, and not the munificently endowed and fully equipped institution which was contemplated in the original bequest."[32]

Nathaniel Lord Britton had been following the controversy with increasing interest; as the details unfolded in the last few months of 1891, Britton suddenly realized that an opportunity had opened up for the Scientific Alliance. While the city possessed a variety of libraries that catered to many different tastes, it did not, as yet, possess a respectable scientific library. The New-York Historical Society, the Mercantile Library, Columbia University, the Astor Library, and the Lenox Library all possessed

[31] Harry Miller Lydenberg, *History of the New York Public Library: Astor, Lenox and Tilden Foundations* (1923; reprint, Boston: Gregg Press, 1972), 129; Phyllis Dain, *The New York Public Library: A History of its Founding and Early Years* (New York: New York Public Library, 1972), 36–37.

[32] Dain, *New York Public Library*, 39–42; Editorial, "The Tilden Will Decision," *The World* (New York), 9 December 1891.

sizable collections; none of them, however, had any significant holdings in science. If, however, the Scientific Alliance were to persuade the Tilden trustees to unite their efforts with that of the Alliance, then it would surely be possible to create a scientific library that would have few rivals.

Britton's sudden anticipation that there was a possibility of using the Tilden bequest to create a scientific library was eminently feasible. In the thirty-fifth section of his will, Tilden had expressly empowered the trustees to "promote . . . scientific and educational objects." An even more auspicious mark of favor for Britton's plans was the inclusion of Andrew Haswell Green as one of the three Tilden trustees; ever since the time when he had fought the Tweed Ring over the control of Central Park, Green had been closely associated with the leadership of the Lyceum of Natural History when they had jointly deplored the destruction of the paleozoic museum. It was, in addition, increasingly apparent that the Tilden trustees were unable to decide how to spend the bequest. The great desideratum—a reference and circulating library to dwarf all others—now seemed out of reach and the trustees, uncomfortably aware of the risk of public censure if they continued merely to invest the bequest in bonds, were anxious to reach a decision.[33]

As a consequence, the trustees began making discreet inquiries among the New York clerisy on the prospects of creating a library. In the early part of 1892, an intermediary for the Tilden Trust, Nathaniel D. C. Hodges, the editor of *Science*, approached Charles F. Cox, president of the Scientific Alliance, stating that he (Hodges) represented "a Board of Trustees which controlled a sum of money not less than $1.000.000. which sum it was planned to devote to the foundation of a Library." Hodges kept his cards close to his chest and although Cox undoubtedly guessed that Hodges was representing the Tilden Trust, Cox felt constrained to report to a subsequent meeting of the Council of the Scientific Alliance that Hodges "desired information respecting the Scientific Alliance and its works and needs, with a view of aiding the parties whom he represents to determine on the most desirable method of disposing of the whole or a part of this fund, several other interests being also considered."[34]

As soon as the search by the trustees for a suitable purpose for the bequest became public knowledge a variety of cultural institutions in New York City advertised their willingness to make good use of the

[33] Lydenberg, *History*, 130; John Foord, *The Life and Public Services of Andrew Haswell Green* (New York: Doubleday, Page & Co., 1913), 208–209.
[34] Minutes of the Council of the Scientific Alliance, 23 March 1892, NYAS.

money. Seth Low, president of Columbia University, proposed that if the Tilden trustees were to construct a library building on the Columbia campus and give $40,000 annually for the purchase of books, Columbia would add its own collection and open it to the public as a reference library. Henry M. MacCracken, chancellor of New York University, suggested that the Tilden Trust fund the construction of two libraries, one at the campus at Washington Square and the other at the university's new campus in the Bronx. MacCracken pointed out that, since Tilden had been an alumnus of New York University, his scheme would honor Tilden in the most appropriate possible manner.[35]

Neither Columbia nor NYU were eventually successful in their attempts to appropriate the Tilden bequest—both were private universities and there was an obvious contradiction in establishing a public library under private control. Negotiations with the Scientific Alliance, however, continued—at a meeting of the Council in May 1892, Charles Cox was able to report that a "very satisfactory interview had been held by Dr. Britton, Professor Trowbridge and himself, with the members of the Tilden Trust. . . . they had presented the needs and aims of the Alliance to the Trustees of the fund, and had been most cordially received."[36]

Not until the fall, however, did negotiations between the Tilden Trust and the Scientific Alliance resume; in September 1892 the Council of the Scientific Alliance, in a letter to the trustees, presented detailed plans for a scientific library. By suggesting, in the first section of the letter to the trustees, that the bequest be used to provide, in addition to a scientific library, "suitable accommodations for the associated societies composing the Scientific Alliance," the Council overplayed its hand; with the exception of Andrew Green, the trustees needed to know not what the Tilden Trust could do for the Scientific Alliance but what the Scientific Alliance could do for the Tilden Trust. Britton, who composed the appeal to the Trust, uncharacteristically alienated his potential sponsors by demanding, furthermore, that the "quarters of the Societies should consist of a separate room or apartment for each, and should include a photographic chamber and chemical, microscopical and other laboratories appropriate to their several needs. These accommodations should be secured to the Societies permanently, free of rent or other expense." In exchange for this munificence the societies of the Scientific Alliance were willing to give an annual series of lectures, to exhibit their collections of scientific specimens in a museum in the building, and to donate their

[35] Dain, New York Public Library, 50.
[36] Minutes of the Council of the Scientific Alliance, 19 May 1892, NYAS.

own libraries which would also include the "books and serial publications obtained by them in exchanges with other societies."

In response to a statement by one of the Tilden trustees, John Bigelow, that the Trust was also considering a proposal to the municipal authorities for support for a library, Britton, in his letter of September 1892, pointed out that a joint appeal with the Scientific Alliance would make this route more palatable to public opinion. If the Tilden Trust were to approach the city alone this might "meet with opposition on political and personal grounds, based upon the theory that city money was asked for the erection of a colossal monument to a single individual." If, however, the Alliance were part of the plea for municipal funds, then the rationale for the request to the city could be for the "encouragement of Science and the elevation of New York City to the position of a great scientific centre . . . much of the opposition would be changed to favor . . . the connection of the Scientific Alliance with the enterprise would be an element of considerable strength."[37]

Despite the enthusiastic support of Andrew Haswell Green and an eloquent speech by H. Carrington Bolton at the public meeting of the Alliance in November 1892 entitled "A Plea for a Library of Science in New York City," any sentiment in favor of a scientific library that existed outside of the ranks of the Scientific Alliance steadily eroded as momentum gradually built elsewhere for a central reference collection combined with a branch system of circulating libraries. In January 1893 the attention of the trustees was attracted to a scheme proposed by the Tammany mayor, Thomas Gilroy, to dismantle City Hall and, since it was one of the city's architectural treasures, to reconstruct it on the site then occupied by the reservoir facing Fifth Avenue on Forty-second Street. This elaborate plan, which included the construction of a new City Hall on the former site of the old City Hall, was widely interpreted as a byzantine plot whereby the new Tammany administration could siphon off sizable sums of money from building contracts. As a ploy to win the support of the Tilden trustees, Gilroy proposed that once the old City Hall had been removed to Forty-second Street, it would be available for use as a library.[38]

Andrew Haswell Green remained a steadfast opponent of Gilroy's proposal and, almost alone among the Tilden trustees, he remained an advocate of the Scientific Alliance. In January 1893 Charles F. Cox reported to Britton that Green, in a private conversation with Cox, had expressed

[37] Council of the Scientific Alliance to Trustees of the Tilden Trust, [19] September 1892, Box 2, Records of the Scientific Alliance, Nathaniel Lord Britton Papers, NYBG.
[38] Dain, New York Public Library, 53–54.

"himself very decidedly in favor of devoting the whole fund to Science, substantially in the way that we have proposed." In the next few months, as the various protagonists jostled for position in the continuing drama over the removal of City Hall, Green proved to be a source of much useful inside information for the Scientific Alliance. In May, when a secondary scheme was being hatched by the ever resourceful Seth Low towards the unification of the Tilden Trust with Columbia for the construction of a "public Hall in the centre of the city when Columbia moves to its new site," Green warned Charles Cox of the plan, suggested that the "Scientific Alliance should be included," and even had a discreet discussion with Charles Frederick Chandler, professor of chemistry at Columbia, to the effect that the Alliance should become a player in the drama between the university and the Tilden Trust.[39]

Unfortunately for Cox, Britton, and the Scientific Alliance, the procrastination of the Tilden trustees (who had not reached a decision more than three years after their original appointment) suddenly ended in the spring of 1894 when a chance conversation between Lewis Cass Ledyard, a Tilden trustee, and John L. Cadwalader, a trustee of the Astor Library, led to discussions between the two sets of trustees on the union of the Tilden Trust and the Astor Library. The latter, established in 1848 by a bequest of $400,000 from the merchant and landowner, John Jacob Astor, operated as a private reference library open on a restricted basis to the public. By 1894, when the Tilden trustees were still searching for a suitable way to spend their endowment, the Astor Library contained over a quarter of a million volumes but, since the Astor family never supported it to an extent commensurate with its needs, the Astor Library was increasingly in financial straits.[40]

By the end of 1894 a third partner, the Lenox Library, had become involved in the discussions between the Tilden Trust and the Astor Library. The Lenox Library, endowed by the bibliomaniac James Lenox in 1870, contained twenty thousand rare books, including the first Gutenberg Bible brought to the United States, and a spectacular collection of valuable manuscripts and portraits. Understandably perhaps, James Lenox

[39] Charles F. Cox to Nathaniel Lord Britton, 5 January 1893, 2 May 1893, Nathaniel Lord Britton Papers, NYBG. See also Britton to Andrew Haswell Green, 7 December 1892, Nathaniel Lord Britton Papers, NYBG; Foord, Life and Public Services, 213–214. For a consideration of Green's often pivotal role in the affairs of the city's cultural institutions, see David C. Hammack, Power and Society: Greater New York at the Turn of the Century (1982; reprint, New York: Columbia University Press, 1987), 189–191.

[40] Dain, New York Public Library, 58; on the Astor Library, see ibid., 3–9. See also Laurence Hutton, "The New York Public Library—Astor, Lenox, and Tilden Foundations," Harper's Weekly, 23 March 1895, 273–274.

was cautious in his admission policies and on account of the numerous
restrictions, use of the Lenox Library had been virtually impossible for
all but a dedicated minority who had the time and patience to endure
a rigorous examination.

By 1894, however, the trustees of the Lenox Library had relaxed their
standards of admission; the new policy of the trustees was reflected in
the ready reception they extended to the invitation of the Tilden and
Astor trustees to participate in the discussions on merger. These discussions moved rapidly forward and in the early part of 1895, the trustees
of each institution formally agreed to establish a new library which—with
an eye to avoiding any invidious distinctions between the three parties—
was to be called The New York Public Library, Astor, Lenox and Tilden
Foundations. A successful appeal to the municipal authorities resulted,
first, in the donation of the plot of land occupied by the defunct reservoir
adjacent to Bryant Park and second, in an agreement that the city would
provide a suitably majestic building for the new library.[41]

The negotiations between the Astor, Lenox, and Tilden trustees never
included any of the other cultural institutions in the city. Seth Low was
the most persistent suitor; at least until the end of 1894 he remained
hopeful that the Tilden Trust would construct a new library on the Columbia campus. The Scientific Alliance, despite the enthusiastic support
of Andrew Haswell Green, also failed to climb onto the Astor-Lenox-
Tilden bandwagon and, once the momentum for the merger had gained
speed, there was little possibility that the Alliance would be invited to
participate. The final configuration that resulted in the creation of the
New York Public Library reflected the complementary aspects of the
three parties: the Tilden Trust promised a substantial amount of money,
the Astor Library was able to offer one of the largest collections of general
books in the country, and the Lenox Library came forward with an unrivalled treasure-trove of rare books and manuscripts. The constituent societies of the Scientific Alliance could offer only about twenty thousand
books on science; this collection was never a strong enough inducement
for the majority of Tilden trustees to extend an invitation to the Alliance.

For the members of the New York Academy of Sciences the failure of
the negotiations with the Tilden Trust signalled a break with the past.
While the Scientific Alliance had considerable value as a federation of the

[41] "The Triple Library: Astor Will Consolidate with Tilden and Lenox," *The Press* (New
York), 14 March 1895; "Libraries Will Unite: Astor Trustees Ratify the Proposition," *The Sun*
(New York), 14 March 1895; "Libraries Agree to Consolidate: Legislation is to Follow," *New
York Herald*, 14 March 1895.

city's scientific societies, it was apparent that the Academy—if it were to maintain its unique position on the cultural map of New York—had to develop its own activities in a way that would appeal both to the membership and to the general public. The Academy was no longer a center of scientific research, and its educational mission had seemingly disappeared with the 1866 fire; yet, despite its reduced role in the world of science, the Academy still possessed an experienced and energetic leadership. It was, moreover, an institution that encompassed a wide variety of scientific disciplines; in addition, the Academy commanded the allegiance of a sizable membership that ranged from college professors to interested laymen.

The Academy had intermittently presented popular lectures on science for several years. These lectures were well-received by the public; as a consequence, Henry Fairfield Osborn, the vice-president of the Academy, suggested to his fellow-members in 1894 that the organization's appeal to the scientific community would be enhanced by "a series of addresses on scientific subjects, of a more advanced character than the popular lectures." Osborn's suggestion was not adopted *in extenso* but, in a modified form, served as the stimulus for an annual series of scientific exhibitions that aimed to display science as a research activity. To this end, prominent members of the Academy, together with their colleagues at the American Museum, Columbia, City College, and NYU, were invited to construct exhibits that would illustrate the most recent theories and discoveries. It was anticipated by the Academy leadership that the general public would thus obtain a sense of the advancement of science through research. The exhibitions would also have, it was hoped, a second purpose of advertising to a wider audience the practical benefits of the work performed by the various institutions. Science was becoming increasingly specialized, arcane, and even recondite; members of the Academy looked to the annual exhibitions as a means to bridge the gap between public perception and private knowledge.[42]

In 1894 the Academy, drawing on the energy and enthusiasm of its members, held its first annual exhibition of scientific progress. It was not a success. Insufficient preparation caused the exhibition to pass unnoticed in the city's newspapers and attendance was disappointingly small. Not even *Science*, which was now edited by James McKeen Cattell, a leading member of the Academy, carried a report on the exhibition.

By the following year, the lessons of this initial attempt had been well learnt by the officers of the Academy. For the second display of scientific

---

[42] Minutes of the Council of the New York Academy of Sciences, 1 June 1894, NYAS.

exhibits—held in the building of the American Fine Arts Society on Fifty-seventh Street—no effort was spared to ensure a spectacular success. From the first, the support of the patriciate was ensured: an honorary committee was formed of ten prominent New Yorkers including Seth Low, Morris Jesup, J. Pierpont Morgan, William C. Schermerhorn, Samuel Sloan, Charles P. Daly, and Abram S. Hewitt. The members of this illustrious group had few demands placed on their time; their presence at the opening reception was sufficient to act as a cynosure for those New Yorkers who wished to rub elbows with the magnates of finance and big business.

Particular care had been taken with arrangements for the press; the silence of the newspapers the previous year had not been forgotten—precautions were necessary to make sure it was not repeated. The exhibit in 1895 formally opened with an evening reception on Wednesday, 13 March; during the afternoon of that same day, "there was a private review for the representatives of the press" when the journalists were escorted around the exhibition by the officers of the Academy.[43]

No-one could have claimed that the Academy lacked ambition: the reporter from the *New York Herald* counted a total of sixteen different departments. In the Vanderbilt Gallery, the visitors could inspect exhibits illustrating the latest advances in anatomy, biology, botany, geology, mineralogy, paleontology, and zoology; each department was attended by an expert on his particular subject. Henry Fairfield Osborn, who was not only vice-president of the New York Academy of Sciences but also head of the department of mammalian paleontology at the American Museum, was in charge of the paleontological display; here the visitor could see illustrations depicting the "evolution of various prehistoric animals into their modern types. . . . Placed side by side were the skeletons of the ancestral four-toed horse and the modern horse. The former measured 3 1/3 hands high, while the latter measured 15 1/2 hands. The interval in time which separates these types is roughly estimated at 2,000,000 years." In the anatomy section, there were "any number of things in bottles" and moving further along, visitors could see at the zoology department the "chimpanzee Chico, whose lifelike appearance illustrates the possibilities of the newer taxidermy. . . . Chico attracted many visitors, and the taxidermist who mounted him, J. Rowley, Jr., of the American Museum of Natural History, was proud of the attention he received."[44]

[43] "Interesting Exhibits: Shown at the Second Exposition of the Academy of Sciences," *The Press* (New York), 14 March 1895.

[44] "Fine Exhibits in the Sciences: Attractions at the Second Annual Reception of the New York Academy," *New York Herald*, 14 March 1895; "Recent Progress in Science: Suc-

In the Middle Gallery there were exhibits of bacteriology, photography, physiology, and experimental psychology. The reporter from the *Sun* expressed satisfaction on inspecting "Dr. T. M. Cheesman's bacteriology booth" where he saw a "specimen of diptheria anti-toxin and the corresponding toxin. There were also bacteria of every sort in abundance, and with names in inverse proportion to their sizes."[45]

The photography exhibit caught the eye of almost all the Academy's guests. Color photography had recently been invented, and many specimens of the genre were to be seen lining the walls of the gallery. The technical process seemed rather wearisome and excessively time-consuming yet the results were a complete novelty: "the negatives are made on specially prepared plates corresponding to the three primal colors, red, yellow, and blue. When the red plate is exposed a screen is placed before the camera to shut out the green and yellow constituents, and the same process is observed with the other two. In making the reproduction an imprint is taken mechanically from the red plate with red ink, and the blue print and yellow print are superposed in the same way."[46]

Finally, in the South Gallery, booths were set up displaying work in astronomy, chemistry, electricity, mechanics, and physics. For the majority of the scientifically educated public, conscious of the intellectual advances that had recently been made in the physical sciences, this final section received the greatest acclaim. Francis Bacon Crocker, chairman of the department of electrical engineering at Columbia, was only too pleased to demonstrate the "machines for producing alternating currents of various frequencies, for multiplex telegraphy and other purposes [and] . . . a new type of unipolar dynamo, now in course of development." The reporter from the *Sun*, ever on the look-out for the quixotic, remarked on the curious feat in the electrical department of "making disinfectants out of sea water. . . . The disinfectant, made on the spot, was sprayed upon a glass slide fairly alive with microbes while the observer looked through a microscope and saw them stop short and shrivel up almost as quickly as if they had been suddenly frozen in."[47]

All in all, the members of the Academy felt great relief and satisfaction that their second exhibition had proved such a hit both with the public

---

cessful Exhibition by the New-York Academy," *New-York Times*, 14 March 1895; "Fin de Siecle Science: An Up-to-date Exhibition in Fifty-seventh Street," *The Sun* (New York), 14 March 1895. See also "Exhibit of the N.Y. Academy of Sciences," *New-York Tribune*, 14 March 1895.

[45] "Fin de Siecle Science," *The Sun* (New York), 14 March 1895.

[46] "Fin de Siecle Science," *The Sun* (New York), 14 March 1895.

[47] "Fine Exhibits in the Sciences," *New York Herald*, 14 March 1895; "Fin de Siecle Science," *The Sun* (New York), 14 March 1895.

and the city's newspapers. Not the least of the Academy's triumph was its success in attracting the cooperation of the faculties of Columbia, City College, New York University, and the Stevens Institute of Technology. The scientists who participated in the annual exhibitions were not slow to appreciate that the benefits of favorable publicity did not accrue to the Academy alone. Everyone acknowledged that the munificence of the wealthy financiers had benefitted both Columbia and the American Museum to an extraordinary degree; in addition it was also evident that some scientific disciplines had profited while others had been neglected. The success of Charles Frederick Chandler, for example, in persuading the Havemeyer family to give $450,000 for the construction of a new chemistry building at Columbia in memory of Frederick Christian Havemeyer had been contingent on Chandler's ability to sell chemistry as a socially useful and beneficial scientific discipline. Not every scientist could expect to emulate Chandler but, at a time when the New York patricians were giving a new meaning to the concept of *noblesse oblige*, it was essential to promote knowledge in order to win the necessary financial support. Thus, as the Academy exhibitions increased in size and popularity, so they served the scientific community as an intellectual marketplace where the scientists could display their wares to the best advantage.

In subsequent years, a troop of scientists jumped onto the Academy's bandwagon. In anticipation of its increased popularity, the Academy's third exhibition, held in 1896, moved to the American Museum of Natural History. Once again, it was a grand success; the Academy received a gratifyingly large attendance despite the move so far from the center of the city. The electrical department, which was displaying the effect of X-rays, received the greatest number of visitors: "the apparatus for making Röntgen Rays was shown. . . . One of Edison's photoscopes, made like an old-fashioned stereoscope without any lenses in the top, and with a layer of tungstate of calcium sprinkled on black paper on the bottom, was provided, and many young women looked at the skeletons of their own hands without alarm." In the evening the "halls were crowded with throngs of persons who went to see the exhibits"; they were also able to attend a talk by John James Stevenson who presented a "survey of recent scientific work." The most popular event, however, proved to be a lecture by Michael I. Pupin on Roentgen rays; Pupin took the opportunity to show his listeners the effects of wearing Edison's X-ray spectacles which, according to the reporter from the *New-York Times*, was the most entertaining event of the whole exhibition.[48]

48 "Things New in Science: The Third Exhibit made by the New-York Academy," *New-*

The Academy's fourth exhibition, held at the American Museum of
Natural History in April 1897, attracted an even more extensive and favorable publicity for the small core of scientists who had spent much energy
and effort in mobilizing and coordinating a wide variety of scientific displays. Not only had the Academy managed to spread the proceedings
over a total of four days, it had also scored somewhat of a coup by getting
Nicola Tesla to give a lecture on the "Roentgen and Lenard rays" on the
evening of 6 April. Tesla was quite a catch for the Academy; among scientific circles he was known as somewhat of a recluse, secretive about
his work and taciturn about his findings. As the reporter for the *New York
Times* observed: "it is only once in two or three years that Nicola Tesla,
the electrician, can be persuaded to give a lecture. . . . he carefully refrains . . . from letting his fellow-electricians know what he is driving at
in his experiments."[49]
As a consequence—and in anticipation of a good show—a large crowd
gathered that evening outside the auditorium of the American Museum.
When the doors were flung open and everybody filed in, the expectant
audience could see Tesla—dressed, as always for his lectures, in formal
evening wear and standing almost seven feet tall (he wore thick cork
soles as protection against mishaps)—behind an "array of high-pressure,
rapid-vibration instruments." Unfortunately, Tesla was not one to make
allowances and in his speech that evening—delivered in "decidedly
broken English"—he persisted "in using technical words, many of them
coined by himself." As a consequence, the "electricians who went to hear
him speak before the academy in hope that he would reveal something
of the nature of his investigations were disappointed. They failed to discover what he is 'driving at.' Tesla made apparently free use of his wonderful high-power instruments for producing rapid vibration, but beyond suggesting their value in scientific experiments, and remarking that
their practical value would be made apparent to everybody before long,
he kept his own counsel."[50]
For the Academy, the closing lecture was an anti-climax. Fortunately

York Times, 27 March 1896. See also Edmund Otis Hovey, "The Annual Reception of the New
York Academy of Sciences, March 26," *Scientific American*, 11 April 1896, 230.

[49] "A Crowd to Hear Tesla: The Academy of Science Exhibition This Year Draws Well,"
New York Times, 7 April 1897; "Tesla Keeps his Secrets: Refrains from Gratifying the Curiosity
of Electricians about his Experiments," *New York Times*, 9 April 1897.

[50] "A Crowd to Hear Tesla," *New York Times*, 7 April 1897; "Tesla Keeps his Secrets," *New
York Times*, 9 April 1897. See also "The Fourth Annual Reception of the New York Academy
of Sciences," *Electrical World*, 10 April 1897, 470. For a description of Tesla at the podium
see Margaret Cheney, *Tesla: Man Out of Time* (Englewood Cliffs, NJ: Prentice-Hall, 1981), 51.

the blame for this disappointment could be conveniently dumped on the notoriously eccentric Tesla without reflecting any opprobium on his sponsors. Richard E. Dodge, the secretary of the Academy and one of the principal organizers of the exhibition, crowed that "not only was it the most successful exhibition of the Society in point of scientific display and attendance, but people who went were not actuated by mere curiosity. They asked questions about all that they saw, and asked them with an intelligent understanding." Dodge's judgement was surely accurate; on Wednesday, 7 April, the attendance had peaked at an estimated four thousand—no mean accomplishment for an organization which—only a few years previously—had been in a state of drift and decline.[51]

The success of the Academy was dependent on the enthusiasm and organizing abilities of a small coterie of young scientists who clearly perceived that the expanding role of science within late nineteenth-century American society had portentous implications. No-one could fail to appreciate that the success of the Academy's exhibitions heralded the dawning of a new era. It was not simply that science had become fashionable for a greatly enlarged audience but, because the exhibitions expressly aimed to display the most advanced theoretical and experimental research, it was rather that science had acquired a deeper meaning and significance for a wider circle.

Much of the appeal of science in the Progressive Era relied on its putative ability to solve both material and social problems; it did not, perhaps, lead to utopia but it was certainly an essential ingredient in the construction of a more equitable, prosperous, and enlightened future. Science was thus attractive not merely in its own right but for its social implications; additionally, for the elite of New York, it served as a cultural resource and, concomitantly, a mark of civic accomplishment. As a token of cultural achievement, science was no different from art, music, or literature; indeed, because of its added dimension of utilitarian promise, science could be perceived as especially valuable.

The Academy scientists who had worked so diligently to ensure the success of the exhibitions were by no means oblivious to the added significance of science as a cultural activity. Nor were they insensitive to their relatively precarious situations as scientists. The Academy itself was never a source of financial reward; its activities were uniformly run on a voluntary basis. At Columbia University science as a research activity had only established a foot-hold in the face of much apathy and even hos-

[51] "A Crowd to Hear Tesla," New York Times, 7 April 1897. See also "New York Academy of Sciences: Annual Exhibition and Reception," Scientific American, 17 April 1897, 246.

tility from a majority of the trustees; it had been a struggle to attain recognition that advanced research at Columbia was a worthwhile activity. Even at the American Museum of Natural History, there was opposition to the idea that research was worthwhile; a strong group within the Museum believed that its purpose would be better served through popular displays to a diffuse audience.

Within this context of equivocal support for advanced scientific research, the Academy exhibitions served the research scientists in a fundamental way. By attracting a large public audience and a favorable press for explicitly advanced science, the research scientists demonstrated an appreciation, understanding, and support of their work among an educated public. For precisely this reason the Academy group invited such a speaker as Nicola Tesla; the talk may have been incomprehensible for many, but the fact that the auditorium was packed to capacity was proof that advanced research was appreciated for reasons other than pure utilitarianism.

During the years when the New York Academy of Sciences was holding its successful annual exhibitions, the Scientific Alliance, meanwhile, seemed to be on the verge of collapse. Thus, in the early part of 1897, Frank N. Cole, the secretary of the American Mathematical Society and professor of mathematics at Columbia, notified the Alliance that the mathematicians had decided to "withdraw from membership in the Scientific Alliance at the end of the present year." The failure of the Alliance to effect a partnership with the Tilden trustees had prompted a movement within the AMS against affiliation; a more proximate cause was the continuing high cost of printing the annual Directory and the monthly Bulletin. The Mathematical Society derived little benefit from notification to its members of the meetings on natural history sponsored by the other organizations in the Alliance and if there were little likelihood of winning a new building for the Alliance, there seemed no reason for the AMS to continue its affiliation.[52]

For the remaining societies the departure of the AMS, just at the moment when the Alliance was re-grouping its forces for a second appeal

[52] Frank N. Cole to [Nathaniel Lord Britton], n.d. [May 1897] in Minutes of the Council of the Scientific Alliance, 20 May 1897, NYAS. The American Mathematical Society grew out of a predecessor organization, the New York Mathematical Society, founded in 1888, that "was at first not much more than a small mathematical club meeting periodically at Columbia College." Emory McClintock, "The Past and Future of the Society," *Bulletin of the American Mathematical Society* 1(1895): 85. See also Thomas S. Fiske, "Mathematical Progress in America," *Science*, 10 February 1905, 209–215.

to the wealthy, was a public relations disaster that would effectively end the Alliance's credibility as a cohesive organization. As a consequence, Britton held several long talks with leading members of the American Mathematical Society, most of whom were professors at Columbia, with the result that the Society formally reconsidered its original decision. The members again debated the question and in June 1897 informed the Scientific Alliance that they would "retain the membership of the Society" at least until the end of 1898.[53]

Britton's appeal to the AMS not to secede from the Alliance possessed especial urgency since, during the greater part of 1897, the Council of the Alliance had again begun to consider seriously the prospect of a building campaign. The building committee, which, in addition to Britton and Charles F. Cox, included William McMurtrie and E. G. Love, reported in December 1897 that, after extensive consultations with three prominent New York architects, a comprehensive plan had been adopted for a "building which will occupy four city lots . . . giving one hundred feet frontage on each street. . . . The first floor plan provides for two rentable offices or stores from which it may be possible to obtain sufficient income, in connection with rentals of the lecture-halls etc. to pay the operating expenses of the building." Inside the building, the architects had proposed, on the first floor, a "large auditorium . . . calculated to seat one thousand persons" and on the second floor there would be a "clubroom . . . a place of general rendezvous and social intercourse for the members of the Societies." The plan was nothing if not ambitious for the architects had also included three more stories which would contain space for laboratories, meeting-rooms, and a library.

The whole project was estimated to cost half a million dollars; the apparent stimulus to the Alliance's ambition was the belief that the "general financial condition of the country was beginning to improve." More specifically, the committee of the Alliance pointed to the "revival of public spirit and local pride manifested by many generous gifts and other practical aids bestowed upon various benevolent and educational enterprises by the citizens of New York."[54]

While the plans of the Alliance for its own building might, in retrospect, have seemed hopelessly ambitious, to the members of the Council in 1897 the project was, if anything, conservative. The Alliance had the backing of several influential members of the city aristocracy—at a banquet in March 1898 sponsored by the Alliance as part of its campaign for

[53] Minutes of the Council of the Scientific Alliance, 14 June 1897, NYAS.
[54] Minutes of the Council of the Scientific Alliance, 10 March 1898, 19 May 1898, NYAS.

a new building the dais was occupied by such notables as Morris K. Jesup, the principal benefactor of the American Museum of Natural History; Seth Low and William E. Dodge, two of Columbia's most generous supporters; and Andrew Haswell Green, one of the city's most powerful political figures who had steadfastly promoted the cause of science in New York City for over two decades. Green, who had apparently not relinquished the notion of including the Alliance in an arrangement with the New York Public Library, was, as he reported to the leaders of the Alliance, cautiously exploring the possibility of obtaining land on the north side of Bryant Park for the new building of the scientific societies. Last but not least, a series of laudatory articles had appeared in the *Evening Post* and the *New York Tribune*.[55]

Unfortunately the formula that had worked so well for the American Museum of Natural History and the New York Botanical Garden never succeeded for the Scientific Alliance despite the best efforts of Nathaniel Britton and Charles F. Cox. In the appeal for funds from private sources the Alliance was never able to secure a simultaneous guarantee of support from the municipal authorities. Both the American Museum and the NYBG had been able to use the tangible offers of land and money from City Hall to convince private donors to add their financial backing; the Alliance, which had never won encouragement from the city, was consequently unable to secure the necessary funds to construct a building.

During the four-year period following the launch of the building campaign a few small battles were won but the war was eventually lost. In 1901 Abram S. Hewitt, William E. Dodge, Andrew Carnegie, and Samuel Sloan all agreed to serve on an honorary committee that endorsed the building fund and, in that same year, a few major contributions — including $25,000 from J. Pierpont Morgan, $10,000 each from William K. Vanderbilt and Esther Hermann, and $5000 from William C. Schermerhorn — did help raise the eventual total to almost fifty thousand dollars. In the interim, however, the American Mathematical Society decided to withdraw permanently from the Alliance; a second defeat came in October 1902 when the New York section of the American Chemical Society — claiming that "the Section was not receiving a direct benefit from the Alliance commensurate with its annual assessment for the expenses of the Council" — also decided to leave the Alliance.[56]

The secession of the ACS dealt a fatal blow to the building campaign; no donations were recorded in subsequent months and in 1906 the cam-

[55] Minutes of the Council of the Scientific Alliance, 10 March 1898, 19 May 1898, NYAS.

[56] Minutes of the Council of the Scientific Alliance, 19 January 1899, 18 May 1899, 28 February 1901, 16 May 1901, 31 October 1901, 16 October 1902, NYAS.

paign formally ended when Herman C. Bumpus, the new director of the American Museum of Natural History, offered the use of office-space for the Alliance "essentially without cost." Bumpus's generosity was not entirely altruistic; since his arrival at the AMNH he had been intent on refocussing the activities of the Museum away from scientific research and towards public education. Bumpus had already persuaded the New York Academy of Sciences, the Linnaean Society, and the New York Mineralogical Club to use rooms in the American Museum for public meetings; the physical presence of the constituent societies of the Alliance at the museum would provide his educational program with the benefits of gratuitous exhibitions and lectures by the scientific organizations in the city. Bumpus, with an eye to the increased popularity of the museum among the general public, could thus offer the Alliance not only the necessary space but also "lanterns and other service required . . . at a nominal charge."[57]

With the move of the various societies into rooms at the American Museum, the building campaign was obviously redundant. To some delegates on the Council of the Scientific Alliance the new arrangement also suggested a re-definition of the relationship between the various groups. Abraham Dutcher, a representative of the Linnaean Society, felt that the formal meetings of the Council, which required a great deal of pre-arrangement to suit the schedules of the various delegates, had become increasingly superfluous. Early in 1906, therefore, he suggested the "desirability of effecting a closer relationship of the special scientific Societies . . . with the parent Society, the New York Academy of Sciences, suggesting an organization by means of which these Societies . . . should become in some way sections of the New York Academy of Sciences."[58]

To the surprise of almost everyone, this radical proposal found almost unanimous assent; by 11 April 1906, when the delegates of each society again convened, Dutcher's suggestion, albeit modified, had won a consensus. The various groups (which now also included both the New York Entomological Society and the Brooklyn Entomological Society) were to

[57] Minutes of the Council of the Scientific Alliance, 24 January 1906, NYAS. On the shift of the American Museum of Natural History towards public education, see Herman C. Bumpus, "A Great American Museum," World's Work 15(1908): 10027–10036; Everett Wallace Smith, "Natural Science for the Every-day Man," Outlook, 23 May 1908, 183–191. An overview of the comparative development of the educational role of American museums can be found in Sally Gregory Kohlstedt, "International Exchange and National Style: A View of Natural History Museums in the United States, 1850–1900," in Scientific Colonialism: A Cross-Cultural Comparison, ed. Nathan Reingold and Marc Rothenberg (Washington, D.C.: Smithsonian Institution Press, 1987), 167–190.
[58] Minutes of the Council of the Scientific Alliance, 24 January 1906, NYAS.

become, not sections, but "affiliated Societies" which would maintain a considerable amount of autonomy over their own affairs. The agreement between the various groups served to strengthen the New York Academy of Sciences since each affiliated society had the "right to delegate one of its members to the Council of the Academy"; in addition, the individual members of each affiliated society were encouraged to "become members of the Academy by paying the Academy's Annual Fee." The Academy, for its part, was expected to "encourage the work of Societies affiliated with it by furnishing means for paying distinguished lecturers, [and] by awarding grants to aid scientific investigation by their members." Since the Academy had also to mail "notices of all meetings . . . to all members . . . without charge to any affiliated Society" an impartial observer might conclude that the affiliated societies had struck a very favorable bargain. The Academy, however, became the recipient of the funds of the Scientific Alliance; these included the endowment of the Newberry Fund as well as that part of the building fund designated by the donors, after the campaign had ended, for purposes other than the construction of the building. Most notably these funds included the contribution of ten thousand dollars donated to the Alliance by Esther Hermann in memory of her husband; this money was, in 1906, converted into an endowment for the Hermann Fund for scientific research.[59]

The Scientific Alliance remained in existence until April 1907; by that date the necessary formalities for merger with the New York Academy of Sciences were complete and all legal considerations had been taken into account. Charles F. Cox, who had served in a double capacity as president of the Council of the Alliance and as one of the representatives of the New York Academy of Sciences, was, in a nostalgic retrospective, able to conclude in his final remarks on the sixteen years since the creation of the Alliance, that although the building campaign had not succeeded, "all the other objects sought had been attained."[60]

The New York Academy of Sciences was the principal beneficiary. The affiliation of the specialist societies resulted in a substantial increase in membership and the transfer of the funds from the Alliance provided the Academy with the means to sponsor research in a variety of disciplines. Since the Academy now possessed substantial funds for research, it became an arbitrator with the power to pass judgement on the value of new projects in natural history. Most significant, however, was that part of the protocol that stipulated that at least one representative of each special-

[59] Minutes of the Council of the Scientific Alliance, 11 April 1906, NYAS.
[60] Minutes of the Council of the Scientific Alliance, 18 April 1907, NYAS.

ist group be a member of the Council of the Academy; this codicil had the effect of winning the allegiance of the city's scientific leadership to the Academy and, in the early decades of the twentieth century, when the Academy undertook the most important project in its history, the allegiance of the scientific elite was all-important in the future success of the Puerto Rico survey.

5

The Puerto Rico Survey
1907–1934

IN THE FIRST DECADE of the twentieth century, the New York Academy of Sciences possessed four sections: geology and mineralogy; biology; anthropology and psychology; and astronomy, physics, and chemistry. These sections, which attracted numerous scientists who were not otherwise closely involved with the Academy, provided the organization with a structure that enabled the membership to organize a comprehensive survey of Puerto Rico and the Virgin Islands. The strength of the sections in the early decades of the twentieth century was contingent on the links between the Academy, Columbia University, and the American Museum of Natural History; the vitality of a section was generally proportional to the participation of the scientific staff at Columbia and the American Museum.

No discipline exemplified this relationship better than biology. The creation of the department of zoology at Columbia and the division of mammalian paleontology at the American Museum of Natural History eventually resulted in a section of biology at the Academy that served as a forum for discussion on such important issues as heredity, embryology, sex-determination, and evolution.

In 1891 Charles M. DaCosta, a graduate of Columbia and a member of the board of trustees, donated $100,000 for the endowment of a chair in zoology. Columbia had long been aware that, despite the success of the School of Mines, the university was falling behind as other colleges— most notably, Cornell and Johns Hopkins—were steadily expanding research work in botany and zoology. As a consequence, with the assistance of Da Costa's donation, a new department of zoology was included in the creation at Columbia in 1892 of a Faculty of Pure Science. In conjunction with the American Museum of Natural History, which was

20. HENRY FAIRFIELD OSBORN (1857–1935). In 1890, when this photograph was taken,
Osborn was professor of comparative anatomy at Princeton University. The following year
he moved to New York to become professor of biology at Columbia University and curator
of mammalian paleontology at the American Museum of Natural History. Osborn, who
was elected president of the New York Academy of Sciences in 1898, later served as president of the American Museum and was principally responsible for the development of the
museum into an internationally pre-eminent research institution. (*Courtesy of the American
Museum of Natural History.*)

searching for a capable scientist and administrator to head a new division of mammalian paleontology, Seth Low invited Henry Fairfield Osborn, a young faculty member at Princeton University, to head the new department of zoology.[1]

It is doubtful that Low could have made a better choice. At the age of twenty, while still an undergraduate at Princeton, Osborn had initiated an expedition to Colorado to collect fossil fishes, plants, and mammals from the Eocene formation. From that moment on, Osborn dedicated his education to the study of those ancillary scientific disciplines necessary for the pursuit of paleontology. In 1878 he studied anatomy and histology at the College of Physicians and Surgeons at New York and, in the following year, Osborn traveled to Britain where he studied embryology with Francis Balfour at Cambridge University and comparative anatomy with T. H. Huxley at the Royal College of Science. On his return to the United States, Osborn obtained a fellowship at Princeton where he remained for twelve years, serving in his final year as professor of comparative anatomy. For Osborn the transfer to Columbia in 1891 was particularly auspicious since it coincided with the physical removal of the university from Forty-ninth Street to a location in the countryside two miles north of the city. As part of the new building program on Morningside Heights, William C. Schermerhorn had provided a generous donation for the construction of a new building for the natural sciences. As a consequence, Henry Fairfield Osborn, as chairman of the department of zoology, was able to plan the new laboratories, the library, and the administrative offices to suit his program of research and study. In addition, Osborn, using his joint position at the museum (where he was curator of paleontology) and the university, was able to recruit a galaxy of promising young scholars to work under his guidance at Columbia. At such universities as Harvard and Penn, biology failed to develop independently of medicine; at Columbia, however, because the medical school (on account of its quasi-autonomous status) was only minimally involved with the introduction of science into the college curriculum, the department of zoology flourished.[2]

Osborn quickly established the intellectual pattern that his new depart-

[1] Henry Fairfield Osborn, "Zoology at Columbia," *Columbia University Bulletin* no. 17 (June 1897): 17–18; Henry E. Crampton, "A History of the Department of Zoology of Columbia University," *Bios* 21(1950): 221–222.

[2] William K. Gregory, "Henry Fairfield Osborn, 1857–1935," *Biographical Memoirs of the National Academy of Sciences* 19(1938): 57–60, 67, 69; Philip J. Pauly, "The Appearance of Academic Biology in Late Nineteenth-Century America," *Journal of the History of Biology* 17(1984): 387–389.

ment was to follow in future years. In a series of lectures at the College of Physicians and Surgeons in the early part of 1892, Osborn gave a comprehensive survey of research work on problems of evolution and heredity. These included the competing claims of the Lamarckian and Weismannian schools of heredity theory, the relationship between the body cells and germ cells, the phenomenon of cell division and the distribution of chromatin to the tissues, and the nature of fertilization.[3]

Most important of all for his zoological and paleontological work at Columbia, Osborn attracted a large group of graduate students and research assistants who were to develop into a cadre with great influence in later years. Edmund B. Wilson, professor of biology at Bryn Mawr College, came to Osborn's new department not long after it opened; Bashford Dean, formerly an instructor at the School of Mines, also joined the department of zoology; and Oliver S. Strong was awarded a research fellowship to study with Osborn at Columbia. During the next five years Osborn worked strenuously to consolidate his base at Columbia and to strengthen the links between the university and the American Museum of Natural History. As soon as the funds permitted the teaching staff at Columbia was augmented: Henry E. Crampton, who served as a research assistant from 1893 to 1895, became a Fellow in 1896; Gary N. Calkins, one of Osborn's first graduate students, was appointed a tutor in 1894; and Nathan R. Harrington was an assistant at Columbia from 1895 to 1897.[4]

In addition to his work at Columbia and the American Museum of Natural History, Osborn, not long after his arrival in New York in 1891, became a leading member of the New York Academy of Sciences. Under Osborn's leadership, the Section of Biology, which, in 1890, had been the weakest of the Academy's four sections, quickly became the most active department; in recognition of his energy and enthusiasm, Osborn was elected vice-president of the Academy in 1894. At the time the zoology department at Columbia and the division of mammalian paleontology at the museum were both inchoate; for Osborn and his co-workers, therefore, the Section of Biology at the New York Academy of Sciences was important because it could serve the purpose of a research seminar for the discussion of new ideas and concepts. The section attracted both knowledgeable laymen and the faculty of such institutions as NYU and City College—as a consequence, it served Osborn as a forum for discus-

[3] Gregory, "Henry Fairfield Osborn," 67–68.

[4] Henry E. Crampton, *The Department of Zoology of Columbia University, 1892–1942* (New York: Columbia University Press, 1942), 11–14.

sion and, in later years, he could use the section to introduce his graduate students and research assistants to the wider world of science.

His election as vice-president of the Academy had little effect on Osborn's involvement with the Section of Biology; his interest in its affairs never slackened and, as a consequence, it developed into one of the liveliest centers of debate and discussion on biological questions in New York. Much of this debate reflected Osborn's research interests as well as those issues that were of consuming importance for biology at the time. Thus, one of the most crucial questions for biologists at the turn of the century centered around the mechanisms of evolution as a phys-iological process. In 1896, for example, Arnold Graf, in a talk before the Section of Biology entitled "The Problem of the Transmission of Ac-quired Characters," propounded the view that acquired characters, adopted as a response to ecological conditions, were transmitted to suc-ceeding generations of the organism. Interestingly enough, Graf cited the fossil record as evidence for his belief and, in particular, the "evolu-tion of the chambered shell in a series of fossil Cephalopods." In his re-marks on Graf's paper, Osborn also adduced evidence from the fossil record when he pointed out the difference between "*ontogenic* and *phyl-ogenic* variation. . . . the change in the forms of the skeletons of the ver-tebrates first appears in ontogeny and subsequently in phylogeny. During the enormously long period of time in which habits induced on-togenic variations it is possible for natural selection to work very slowly and gradually upon predispositions to useful correlated variations, and thus what are primarily *ontogenic variations* become slowly apparent as *phylogenic variations* or congenital characters of the race."[5]

Osborn, whose specialty was vertebrate paleontology, determined the focus of the Section of Biology on the fossil record in discussions of evo-lutionary theory. In 1898, when Osborn was elected president of the New York Academy of Sciences, the Section of Biology was fully controlled by Osborn's colleagues in the division of vertebrate paleontology at the American Museum. From 1900 onwards, however, discussions on evolu-tionary theory became increasingly focused less on the philosophical as-pects of Darwin's theory and more on the mechanism by which evolution worked at the cytological level.[6]

[5] Minutes of the Section of Biology, 9 March 1896, in Minutes of the New York Academy of Sciences, 1896, NYAS.

[6] The connection between paleontology and biology was unique to Osborn. In most academic centers in the United States, paleontology was subsumed under geology. See Ronald Rainger, "Vertebrate Paleontology as Biology: Henry Fairfield Osborn and the Amer-ican Museum of Natural History," in *The American Development of Biology*, ed. Ronald

21. EDMUND BEECHER WILSON (1856–1939). Wilson received his PhD in biology from Johns Hopkins University in 1881. After studying in Europe, he taught at the Massachusetts Institute of Technology and Bryn Mawr College before receiving an appointment at Columbia University in 1891 as professor of biology. During his years in New York City Wilson was a stalwart member of the New York Academy of Sciences; he was a leading member of the Section of Biology and was elected president of the Academy in 1904. (*Courtesy of Columbiana, Columbia University.*)

Edmund Beecher Wilson, one of Osborn's closest colleagues at Columbia, was the principal force behind this shift in the activity of the section. Wilson, after receiving his doctorate from Johns Hopkins University in 1881, had spent a year in Europe studying biology at research centers at Cambridge and Leipzig and at the zoological station at Naples. On his return to the United States he taught for a brief time at Williams College, the Massachusetts Institute of Technology, and Bryn Mawr College before accepting an offer in 1891 from Osborn to join the faculty at Columbia. Wilson, who became chair of the Section of Biology at the New York Academy of Sciences in 1897, was primarily interested in experimental embryology and, in particular, the process of differentiation of the individual organism. During the first decade of the twentieth century, Wilson's experimental approach was gradually subsumed by his more speculative research on the relationship of Mendelism to cytology, the problem of sex determination, and the structure, function, and organization of the cell.[7]

Eventually Wilson came to have an influence on the work of the section that was comparable to that exerted by Henry Fairfield Osborn; as a consequence the debate on heredity and evolution within the section was influenced by two contrasting methodologies: Osborn used evidence from the fossil record while Wilson employed his own research in cytology. As a consequence, attendees at the section meetings participated in a series of lively debates that covered the question of evolution in the most comprehensive manner possible. Thus, at a meeting of the Section on 9 May 1898, Wilson delivered a lecture on the structure of protoplasm in the eggs of echinoderms while Osborn, who immediately followed Wilson, talked about the research at the American Museum of Natural History on a "huge herbivorous Dinosaur, bringing out in particular . . . the peculiarly avian structure of the posterior cervical and the anterior dorsal vertebrae." In subsequent years Osborn and Wilson continued to play leading roles both in the development of the Section of Biology and within the leadership group of the Academy. Osborn was elected president of the Academy for a second time in 1899 while Wilson was elected a councilor of the Academy in 1903, an honor that served as

---

Rainger, Keith R. Benson, and Jane Maienschein (Philadelphia: University of Pennsylvania Press, 1988), 219–230.

[7] Thomas Hunt Morgan, "Obituary: Edmund Beecher Wilson, 1856–1939," *Science*, 24 March 1939, 258–259. For a comprehensive biography, see Thomas Hunt Morgan, "Edmund Beecher Wilson, 1856–1939," *Biographical Memoirs of the National Academy of Sciences* 21(1940): 315–342.

22. THOMAS HUNT MORGAN (1866–1945). Morgan, shown here in the "fly room" at Columbia, received a PhD from Johns Hopkins University in 1890; he later taught at Bryn Mawr College (1891–1904), Columbia (1904–1928), and the California Institute of Technology (1928–1945). At Columbia, Morgan led a research team that, by tracing hereditary patterns in the fruit fly *Drosophila melanogaster*, demonstrated, *inter alia*, that genes were linearly arranged in specific positions on the chromosome. For his work at Columbia Morgan received the Nobel Prize in 1933; he was president of the American Society of Naturalists (1909), the American Association for the Advancement of Science (1930), and the National Academy of Sciences (1927–1931). (*Courtesy of Columbiana, Columbia University.*)

a prelude to his election to the presidency of the Academy during the following year.[8]

In 1904, Wilson, who had recently been appointed chairman of the zoology department at Columbia, invited Thomas Hunt Morgan, an expert in the physiology of the embryo, to the chair of experimental zoology at the university. Morgan, who had received his doctorate at Johns Hopkins, had initially focused his attention on the morphology of marine invertebrates, most notably on the embryology of *Pycnogonida*. In subsequent years he adopted an experimental approach to the study of the early development of the embryo with a particular emphasis on the eggs of sea urchins, mollusks, and teleost fishes. The addition of Morgan to the Columbia faculty, therefore, reinforced the approach adopted by Wilson, that of an emphasis on processes of development; Morgan's subsequent work on the problem of sex determination was a continuation of the research on the questions of heredity and evolution. Morgan, in his later studies of *Drosophila melanogaster*, was to earn the Columbia department an international reputation as a center of sophisticated and complex research that combined the Mendelian laws of genetics within a context of the physiology of the embryo.[9]

Shortly after his arrival in New York, Morgan joined the New York Academy of Sciences; his election in May 1904 served to place the Section of Biology firmly in control of the faculty of the zoology department at Columbia. This event was not, however, an unmitigated blessing for, as the research at Columbia became ever more specialized, the section officers discovered that the lay membership, which had previously given valuable support to the Academy, was drifting away as section meetings became steadily more incomprehensible. Thus, in December 1907, Morgan presented a lecture on experiments performed at Columbia on the eggs of *cumingia*; this experiment, which demonstrated that a centrifugal force had a negligible effect on the "cleavage pattern, the size of the cells, and their tempo of division" despite the artificial movement of the visible substances of the egg, was highly technical; it represented the acme of Morgan's work on the embryo at this stage, and, as a consequence, was readily understood only by the faculty and graduate stu-

---

[8] Minutes of the Section of Biology, 9 May 1898, in Minutes of the New York Academy of Sciences, May 1898, NYAS.

[9] Crampton, *Department of Zoology*, 25. The definitive study of Morgan's intellectual development during this period is Garland Allen, *Thomas Hunt Morgan: The Man and his Science* (Princeton, NJ: Princeton University Press, 1978), 84–106.

dents in the audience but not by the laymen with little or no background in the subject.[10]

In subsequent years Wilson and Morgan pursued research on the Mendelian theory of dominance and recessiveness, the chromosome theory of heredity, and the mutation theory recently advanced by Hugo de Vries; as a consequence the section meetings became hopelessly complex. Both scientists attempted to give the occasional popularized version of the Columbia research—in April 1908, for example, Wilson gave a lecture illustrated with slides on the "Types of Sexual Differences of the Chromosomes"—but by 1912 it was evident that even those talks presented in a more accessible manner were failing to hold the interest of the section's constituency. As a consequence the officers of the section, in a special report delivered in November 1912, frankly confessed that the traditional constituency of the Academy—laymen with little or no specialized training—had deserted the section: "technical papers . . . are often presented but . . . those who have come hoping to be entertained with popular science are mystified and disappointed while the man who has taken the trouble to prepare a carefully written paper is mortified and feels that he has bored the audience."[11]

In short, the Section of Biology was caught on the horns of a dilemma; as science became increasingly more technical and specialized and as the section was progressively dominated by the Columbia faculty, so the section steadily lost the support of the Academy's traditional constituency. At the same time, as the critical mass of research scientists at the university reached a point where the faculty could profitably discuss the latest theories to a large and appreciative audience of professors and graduate students, so the previous value of the section as an ersatz research seminar gradually declined.

By contrast, the Section of Geology and Mineralogy managed to appeal simultaneously to the Columbia professoriate and the Academy laymen and, as a result, was the most successful section during the first two decades of the twentieth century. Unlike other scientific disciplines at the time, geology was not highly technical and complex: interested laymen could thus participate fully in the discussions and, on many occasions, even gave competent and significant presentations to the section

[10] Minutes of the New York Academy of Sciences, 2 May 1904, NYAS; Minutes of the Section of Biology, 9 December 1907, NYAS.

[11] Minutes of the Section of Biology, 13 April 1908, NYAS; Report of the Committee on the Condition of the Section, 4 November 1912, in Minutes of the Section of Biology, 1912, NYAS.

audiences. The study of geology did not require expensive laboratory equipment; unlike physics and biology, both of which demanded the resources and support of major research institutions, geology was accessible to all who were willing to study rock formations that, in many cases, were only a few miles outside New York City. Finally, there were the building projects then financed by the municipal authorities. Around the turn of the century the city was engaged in the construction of several tunnels and bridges that linked Manhattan to New Jersey and Brooklyn; these various projects enabled geologists to obtain an immediately accessible picture of the rock formations of the island.

The Section of Geology and Mineralogy included not only the professoriate and the laymen; at several periods its leadership consisted of civil engineers who were employed on the various bridge and tunnel projects. Most notably there was James Furman Kemp, a graduate of Amherst College who had continued his studies at the School of Mines at Columbia before becoming, in 1886, an instructor in geology at Cornell University. In 1891 Kemp was appointed professor of geology at Columbia and, not long after his arrival in New York City, Kemp began to win a reputation as an expert on problems of ore deposition. Two years after his appointment at Columbia began, Kemp published the classic *Ore Deposits of the United States* and, as a result, was frequently employed as a consultant by companies exploiting the ore deposits of the western states. Closer to home, Kemp studied—under the aegis of the federal and state surveys— the geology of the Adirondacks and, in New York City, he was a consulting geologist to the Board of Water Supply with regard to the Croton Dam.[12]

Not long after his arrival in Manhattan, Kemp joined the New York Academy of Sciences and soon made his mark both as an organizer of the Section of Geology and Mineralogy and as an officer of the Academy. Kemp frequently served as chairman of the section and for the Academy, he was, at various times, librarian and recording secretary. In 1898 he began his first tenure as vice-president of the Academy; his service to the organization was recognized by the rare distinction of election to the presidency twice, first in 1905 and again in 1910. As an editor of the journal *Economic Geology*, Kemp, in later life, won high visibility among geologists; he was elected president of the American Institute of Mining En-

---

[12] Waldemar Lindgren, "James Furman Kemp: To His Memory," *Economic Geology* 22(1927): 85–87; Robert Peele, "James Furman Kemp," *Engineering and Mining Journal* 122(1926): 872.

gineers, the Mining and Metallurgical Society, and the Society of Economic Geologists.[13]

Arthur Hollick, a second organizer of the Section of Geology and Mineralogy, managed to combine interests in botany and geology to become an expert in paleobotany. Hollick, together with his close friend Nathaniel Lord Britton, was an early member of the Torrey Botanical Club and a protégé of John Strong Newberry. After his graduation from the School of Mines in 1879, Hollick was employed as an assistant sanitary engineer by the New York Board of Health. An avocational interest in geology led to a subsequent appointment at Columbia as a tutor in the Faculty of Pure Science and when Nathaniel Britton had succeeded in establishing the New York Botanical Garden, Hollick received an appointment as curator at the garden with the mandate to increase and supervise the collection of fossil plants. He soon won an international reputation as a paleobotanist; Hollick's knowledge of the Cretaceous and Tertiary fossil plants was unrivalled and his studies of the fossils of Alaska and Puerto Rico won him widespread recognition. His service for the Academy was largely within the Section of Geology and Mineralogy: Hollick served for brief periods as curator and librarian of the Academy but never rose any further.[14]

John James Stevenson was the third stalwart of the section. Stevenson, unlike most of his Academy colleagues, had no connection with Columbia University: he received his undergraduate and graduate degrees from New York University and, after working on the geological surveys of Ohio, Pennsylvania, and Colorado, Stevenson received an appointment as professor of geology at NYU in 1881. His expertise in stratigraphy was concentrated on the Carboniferous layers; Stevenson demonstrated that the New Mexico coal fields were cretaceous and, more notably, that the coal beds in Pennsylvania possessed idiosyncratic features that were invariant over a large area. A founding member of the Geological Society of America, Stevenson was secretary and president of the Society for many years; in addition to his leadership of the Section of Geology, he served as the president of the New York Academy of Sciences from 1896 to 1898.[15]

Kemp, Hollick, and Stevenson—along with Edmund Otis Hovey, a

[13] Lindgren, "James Furman Kemp," 85.

[14] "Arthur Hollick, 1857–1933," *Proceedings of the Staten Island Institute of Arts and Sciences* 7(1932–1933): 11–13; E. C. Jeffrey, "Arthur Hollick, 1857–1933," *Science*, 12 May 1933, 440–441.

[15] Charles Keyes, "Exploratory Coal Stratigraphy of John James Stevenson," *Pan-American Geologist* 42(1924): 161–165; I. C. White, "Memorial of John James Stevenson," *Bulletin of the Geological Society of America* 36(1925): 100–103.

geologist at the American Museum of Natural History—were singularly successful in attracting overflowing audiences to a series of public lectures on geology held in the large auditorium at the American Museum. On 19 October 1903, for example, after the section business was completed, more than 350 "members and their friends" listened to a presentation on the recent eruptions of the Mount Pelée volcano on Martinique. The speaker, Edmund Otis Hovey, had visited the island on two expeditions under the aegis of the American Museum and, at the lecture that evening, he held his audience spell-bound as he detailed the "phenomena of the eruptions . . . the attendant and subsequent aqueous erosion on the slopes of the mountain, the rise and vicissitudes of the new cone of eruption and its wonderful spine or obelisk. The lecture was illustrated with about 95 lantern slides from negatives taken by the author."[16]

Other lectures sponsored by the section were equally successful particularly if they utilized vivid illustrations presented by means of the most modern technological innovations such as lantern slides and the stereopticon. Those lectures which featured politically volatile regions of the world—such as Robert Hill's talk in October 1905 on the "Republic of Mexico, its Physical and Economic Aspects"—were also sure to draw a large audience: Hill's lecture, illustrated by "the stereopticon" attracted a crowd of "371 Members and visitors" to the lecture hall of the American Museum.[17]

For those members of the Section who were less concerned with public display and more with scientific research, the resources of the region provided ample material for the elucidation of stratigraphic theories. Thus, for the final meeting of the Section in the 1909–1910 season, the members organized a field trip to examine the "Helderberg series at Kingston and in making a cross section of the ridge at the old cement mines." This excursion was preceded by a conference featuring Edmund Otis Hovey of the American Museum of Natural History, Douglas W. Johnson from Harvard, and Amadeus W. Grabau and Charles P. Berkey, respectively professors of mineralogy and geology at Columbia. On the second day the geologists assembled for a tour of the "Ashokan Dam and other work being done at the reservoir site by the New York City Board of Water Supply as part of the Catskill Water System."[18]

[16] Minutes of the Section of Geology and Mineralogy, 19 October 1903, in Minutes of the New York Academy of Sciences, 1903, NYAS.

[17] Minutes of the Section of Geology and Mineralogy, 9 October 1905, in Minutes of the New York Academy of Sciences, 1905, NYAS.

[18] Minutes of the Section of Geology and Mineralogy, 2 May 1910, NYAS.

In sum the Section of Geology and Mineralogy was, during the first decade of the century, successful as a forum for laymen and professors alike. Geology, as a science that was not necessarily complex and technical, could appeal to both groups and, as a consequence, the officers of the section could initiate and promote activities and meetings that held the interest of the professoriate and, at the same time, commanded the attention of an audience of avocational geologists.

The Section of Anthropology and Psychology had its origins in a proposal by Nicholas Murray Butler—in 1895 a professor of literature at Columbia but a few years later Seth Low's successor as president of the university—to establish "a section to deal primarily with scientific investigations in the fields of philosophy and philology." Not every member of the Council of the Academy was enthusiastic about Butler's suggestion—philosophy and philology were, after all, dubious candidates for inclusion in the sciences—but, since the proposal was endorsed by seven prominent members of the Columbia professoriate, all of whom had expressed an interest in joining the Academy if the new section were formed, Butler's suggestion was accepted.[19]

At the succeeding annual meeting of the Academy on 24 February 1896, the recording secretary, James F. Kemp, reported that, during the preceding twelve months, there had been "the practical establishment of a new section in Philosophy and Philology which will select an appropriate name and begin activities during the new year. Other departments such as Psychology and Anthropology are as yet not specially grouped in the sections." The latter reference was a consequence of the initiative of a young scientist who had recently joined the Academy. Franz Boas, who was then a lecturer in anthropology at Columbia and an assistant curator at the American Museum, was to have a remarkable effect in subsequent years on scientific life in New York. Boas's ability to utilize the structure of scientific institutions in New York for the advancement of his chosen discipline, anthropology, was unparalleled. His success, especially in his early years in the city, reflects an ability to create institutional niches for a scientific specialty that had been previously slighted. Boas's presence in New York had ramifications for intellectual life in the city that persisted for decades; as a consequence, it is worth our while to examine his early career in detail.[20]

After receiving his doctorate in geography from the University of Kiel

---

[19] Minutes of the New York Academy of Sciences, 16 December 1895, NYAS.
[20] Minutes of the New York Academy of Sciences, 24 February 1896, NYAS.

in 1881, Boas obtained a position as an assistant at the Königliches Museum für Völkerkunde in Berlin where he remained until 1886. In that year Boas made his second journey abroad, to study the native Americans on the coast of British Columbia; on his return east, Boas stayed in New York where he met James McKeen Cattell who straightaway secured the ethnologist a position as assistant editor of *Science*.

For the young German émigré the next decade was occupied by a peripatetic round of fellowships at temporary positions in several anthropological institutions in the United States. In 1888 the British Association for the Advancement of Science agreed to sponsor a series of trips by Boas to study the tribes of British Columbia. After a brief period as a lecturer in anthropology at Clark University, Boas moved in 1892 to Chicago where he collaborated with Frederick Putnam in arranging and cataloguing the anthropological exhibitions at the Chicago World's Fair. Putnam and Boas became close friends and when the former obtained a curatorship at the American Museum of Natural History in New York, he determined to obtain a position for his colleague.[21]

Soon after his arrival in New York, Putnam was submitting his plans for the expansion of the American Museum to Morris Jesup, long-time president and principal benefactor of the Museum. In July 1894 Putnam was able to write to Boas that he had found:

> a wedge for you. In the plans which I have presented to Mr. Jesup is one which he is very anxious to have carried out, that is, making as complete a collection as possible of models illustrating the different tribes of America. . . . I told Mr. Jesup that there was no one better prepared to do this work than you and I thought as you were going to the north-west this fall, and as we had so many garments and objects of various kinds from that region, it would be the best region for us to begin with in the preparation of the ethnological groups. . . . I believe if you could . . . take very accurate measurements, photographs, drawings, etc., so as to have a set of models made illustrating the people and some of their industries, and some phases of their home life with its proper surroundings, that would be a first rate thing for you; and you would then be employed to set up the groups, and in that way you would have your wedge started for a position in the Museum.[22]

Two weeks later Putnam received formal authorization from the Museum to employ Boas on a temporary basis; in answer to Boas's skeptical doubt that there could develop a permanent full-time position for him

---

[21] Robert H. Lowie, "Franz Boas, 1858–1942," *Biographical Memoirs of the National Academy of Sciences* 24(1947): 303–306.

[22] Frederick W. Putnam to Franz Boas, 16 July 1894, Franz Boas Papers, APS.

23. FRANZ BOAS (1858–1942). After leaving Germany in 1886, Boas became assistant editor at *Science*. He was lecturer in anthropology at Clark University until 1892 when he moved to Chicago to work at the Field Museum. In 1896 Boas went to New York to become curator of ethnology at the American Museum of Natural History and lecturer in physical anthropology at Columbia University. Boas joined the New York Academy of Sciences in the same year; he subsequently served on several Academy committees and played an active part in the Puerto Rico survey initiated by the Academy in 1912. Boas was elected president of the Academy in 1911. (*Courtesy of the American Museum of Natural History.*)

at the Museum, Putnam wrote back chidingly that "while your employment at the museum is held in abeyance, there is little doubt in my mind that you will be employed at the compensation you have stated. . . . I do not see, my dear fellow, but what things look bright for you ahead, and that after the cloudy days the sunshine is coming."[23]

As it happened, Boas had little choice in the matter. After the recent economic depression, money was scarce and full-time employment for anthropologists was even scarcer. No doubt Boas's decision to accept the commission from the American Museum was hastened by the alarming news that the salaries of the anthropologists working in the Bureau of Ethnology in Washington had been cut by 15 percent; his friend, Albert Gatschet, reported to Boas that "unsere Salare im B. v. Ethn. sind um 1/6 reduziert worden."[24]

Boas's work for the American Museum so impressed Morris Jesup that, as Putnam was able to report twelve months later, there was a distinct possibility that the Museum would join with Columbia in establishing Boas on a permanent basis. Putnam had been in contact with Seth Low, president of Columbia, and the initial response had been encouraging: "I wrote to President Low about getting you for Columbia College, after a consultation with Mr. Jesup. Mr. Jesup thought if we could manage to keep you in New York through the winter some how or other, that next year would open better for us in many ways, and between Columbia College and the Museum we could be pretty sure of giving you a satisfactory position."[25]

The negotiations between Boas, the Museum, and Columbia dragged on slowly; in the meantime, John Wesley Powell, head of the Bureau of Ethnology, had made Boas an attractive offer to work on the western surveys. There was also a third possibility at Stanford University—perhaps the most alluring of the three choices simply because Boas would be closer to his principal subject of research, the Kwatiutl Indians in the north-west.[26]

In the end, Putnam's influence proved decisive; in 1895 he was able to write to Boas that he was "getting considerable hold on the people in New York, and I think if we can all pull together there we can build up a great anthropological institution which will be worthy of our efforts. . . . Mr. Jesup is anxious to have the cooperation with the Columbia Col-

[23] Putnam to Boas, 3 August 1894, Franz Boas Papers, APS.
[24] Albert S. Gatschet to Franz Boas, 18 August 1894, Franz Boas Papers, APS.
[25] Putnam to Boas, 19 June 1895, Franz Boas Papers, APS.
[26] John Wesley Powell to Boas, 7 June 1895, Franz Boas Papers, APS; Franz Boas to David Starr Jordan, 19 June 1895, Franz Boas Papers, APS.

lege." In the following year, Boas was successful: Jesup had secured an agreement from Seth Low that Columbia would eventually appoint Boas to a teaching position. As a consequence the American Museum offered Boas a position as assistant curator in the department of anthropology; Columbia then made good on its promise by appointing Boas to a lectureship in physical anthropology. Three years later, in 1899, this was elevated to a full professorship. Finally, when Frederick Putnam accepted a chair at Harvard University in 1901, Boas—his anointed successor—was appointed curator of the anthropology department at the American Museum of Natural History.[27]

Once Boas's institutional position within the world of New York science was secure, the young anthropology professor began a systematic campaign to win for his intellectual disciplines—anthropology and ethnology—the wider respect and support that he, Boas, felt they deserved. Consequently he set out—with the help of his associates at Columbia—to win for anthropology a wider publicity within the scientific community. This goal could be attained through no better medium than that society which represented all disciplines: the New York Academy of Sciences. As Boas had been quick to perceive, the Academy—as the leading organization within the Scientific Alliance—served as an effective voice for the city's scientific community; in addition, the Academy had recently inaugurated the annual series of exhibitions that were earning science an unprecedented amount of publicity.[28]

Boas, at his first meeting of the Academy in February 1896, was gratified to hear James F. Kemp report that the "year past has been in many respects the most successful in the history of the Academy. . . . we may feel encouraged that the Academy seems to be advancing more and more toward the place that it ought to occupy on the intellectual life of the city." The publications of the Academy, including the *Transactions* and the *Annals*, were appearing at a regular rate; the membership encompassed the scientific elite of the city and included the organizers of such institutions as the New York Botanical Garden, the American Museum of Natural History, and the New York Zoological Society; and, last but not least, there was a healthy surplus of $11,000 in the Academy's trea-

[27] Frederick W. Putnam to Franz Boas, 19 June 1895, Franz Boas Papers, APS; Lowie, "Franz Boas," 305–306.
[28] For Boas's plans for the development of anthropology as a discipline, see Boas to Nicholas Murray Butler, 15 November 1902 and Boas to Morris K. Jesup, n.d. [1903], in George W. Stocking Jr., *The Shaping of American Anthropology, 1883–1911: A Franz Boas Reader* (New York: Basic Books, 1974), 290–293, 294–297.

sury: "the Treasurer . . . has no official information of any outstanding liabilities except the $105.00 . . . for the Huxley Memorial Fund."[29]

By April 1896, largely as a consequence of muted protests from a small number of members against the concept of philosophy as a science, the Section of Philology and Philosophy had been transformed into the Section of Anthropology, Psychology, and Philology. Since Boas and his close friend, James McKeen Cattell, were wary of being too closely linked to the philologists in the Academy, the section was divided into two sub-sections; A. V. Williams Jackson, a professor of literature at Columbia, was appointed secretary of the sub-section of philology while Livingston Farrand, an instructor in psychology at the university, was appointed secretary of the sub-section of anthropology and psychology. To maintain the necessary degree of cohesion between the two divisions, Franklin Henry Giddings, a professor of sociology at Columbia, was elected the chairman of the section.[30]

Despite the fact that neither Boas nor his colleague, James McKeen Cattell, regularly held official positions within the Section of Anthropology and Psychology (the sub-section of philology was abandoned in 1899), both men dominated their respective disciplines within the Academy for many years. Cattell, who had left his appointment as professor of psychology at Penn to move to Columbia in 1891, had been a student of Wilhelm Wundt at Leipzig where he received his doctorate. Before accepting the chair at Penn, Cattell had also studied for a brief period with Francis Galton in London where he carried out a number of statistical studies in Galton's anthropometric laboratory. Cattell's work at Penn and Columbia reflected both the influence of Wundt's experimental work on human behavior and Galton's reliance on statistical data. Cattell, however, improved on Wundt's approach by re-directing the focus of analysis away from the introspective impressions of the subjects towards parameters that were external to the subject and thus could be quantified. The emphasis of Cattell on the invariability of mental processes enabled him to record data to a greater extent than before; this data then provided him with the raw material necessary for statistical studies. Through his novel combination of experiment and quantification, Cattell reoriented American psychology towards the study of individuals under variant conditions; by his training of numerous graduate students—most notably, Edward L. Thorndike and Robert S. Woodworth—

[29] Minutes of the New York Academy of Sciences, 29 April 1896, NYAS.
[30] Minutes of the New York Academy of Sciences, 24 February 1896, NYAS.

in his methods, Cattell effected a significant and long-lasting influence on the academic approach to psychology.[31]

Within the history of science, however, Cattell is best remembered for his efforts as editor of the weekly journal *Science*. Cattell purchased *Science* from the publishers in 1895 and, by way of his large number of contacts within the New York community and, more generally, the American scientific community, Cattell built the magazine into an indispensable source of information on new intellectual advances in science. At the same time Cattell became one of the principal organizers in New York City of the American Association for the Advancement of Science and, in 1900, he was successful in persuading the AAAS to adopt *Science* as its official publication, thenceforth available to all members. Cattell's synthesis worked wonders for both institutions: the membership of the AAAS quickly doubled and, as a corollary, subscriptions to *Science* rapidly mushroomed. In addition, in 1900 Cattell took control of *Popular Science Monthly* and in 1907 he bought out the magazine *American Naturalist*. For the Academy members, the presentation of papers was thus doubly rewarding because there was always the probability that Cattell would give the occasional synopsis of Academy lectures; in any case, he regularly announced meetings of the Academy in the pages of *Science*.[32]

The prominence of Franz Boas and James McKeen Cattell, during the first decade of the twentieth century, gave the Section of Anthropology and Psychology enormous visibility. Since the two scientists controlled the section either directly or, in later years, through associates who had adopted their methods and ideas, it became virtually mandatory for any graduate student in either discipline at Columbia to join the section and religiously attend the monthly meetings. Both Boas and Cattell frequently presented the results of their latest research at meetings of the section and, in addition, encouraged promising graduate students to give papers before the membership.

Both scientists were very much entrepreneurs of science. Thus, Boas, in addition to his activities at Columbia, the American Museum of Natural History, and the Academy, played a major role in re-establishing the American Ethnological Society. Cattell, for his part, was a leading member of the American Psychological Association. Boas and Cattell

[31] W. B. Pillsbury, "James McKeen Cattell, 1860–1944," *Biographical Memoirs of the National Academy of Sciences* 25(1949): 1–3, 6–8; Edwin G. Boring, *A History of Experimental Psychology*, 2d ed. (Englewood Cliffs, NJ: Prentice-Hall, 1950), 533–534, 537–540.

[32] Pillsbury, "James McKeen Cattell," 4; Boring, *History*, 535. For a trenchant account of Cattell's use of *Science* to restructure fin de siècle American science, see Michael M. Sokal, "*Science* and James McKeen Cattell, 1894 to 1945," *Science*, 4 July 1980, 43–48.

used their influence within these two organizations to ensure that their activities meshed with those of the New York Academy of Sciences. Thus, in October 1903 the Section of Anthropology and Psychology co-sponsored with the American Psychological Association a conference that featured speakers from Dartmouth, Harvard, Columbia, Wesleyan, Penn, and Yale. The following month the section co-sponsored a more modest venture with the American Ethnological Society: a lecture by Clark Wissler—one of Boas's most brilliant students at Columbia—on the symbolic, decorative, and functional art of the Plains Indians. Thus, in a series of cooperative ventures, Boas and Cattell ensured that the establishment of specialist organizations in their respective scientific disciplines never undercut the work of the Academy's Section of Anthropology and Psychology.[33]

Unfortunately this happy congruence was rarely achieved by the leaders of the Section of Astronomy, Physics, and Chemistry, a group that was always in conflict with the Physics Association, a local society of enthusiasts with an avocational interest in physics. Like the other three sections of the Academy, the Section of Astronomy, Physics, and Chemistry relied on key individuals with a strong connection to Columbia. Michael Pupin, a professor of physics at the university, was a stalwart of the section for many years; when he ceased to participate actively in the affairs of the Academy, however, the section underwent a precipitous decline in membership and activity.

Pupin was the quintessential immigrant; according to an autobiographical account, he arrived in the United States with only five cents which he straightaway spent "upon a piece of prune pie." From such humble beginnings, Pupin soon made his mark for, having travelled to Europe to study physics at Berlin and after receiving a Tyndall Fellowship in 1885, Pupin returned to the United States as an instructor in mathematical physics at Columbia College. Conditions for scientific research at Columbia were not good; Pupin recalled that the department of electrical engineering was housed in a "small brick shed. . . . The students called it the 'cowshed,' and the boy who invented the name did not indulge in any stretching of his imagination. . . . The laboratory equipment consisted of a dynamo, a motor, and an alternator, with some so-called practical measuring instruments." Nor was the attitude of Columbia's

[33] Minutes of the Section of Anthropology and Psychology, 20 October 1903, 23 November 1903, in Minutes of the New York Academy of Sciences, 1903, NYAS; Franz Boas, "The Foundation of a National Anthropological Society," *Science*, 23 May 1902; idem., "The American Ethnological Society," ibid., 1 January 1943.

24. MICHAEL PUPIN (1858–1935). Pupin, who taught mathematical physics and electro-
mechanics at Columbia, is best remembered for his invention of the loading coil, an innovation that, by distributing inductance uniformly along a telegraph wire, reduces attenu-
ation and distortion. Pupin was elected president of the New York Academy of Sciences
in 1916; his autobiography, *From Immigrant to Inventor*, won a Pulitzer Prize in 1924. (*Courtesy
of Columbiana, Columbia University.*)

trustees very auspicious; the college's governors let no opportunity slip by to tell the young professor that "any additional equipment . . . would have to be bought from contributions outside of the university."

Fortunately for Columbia, Pupin was imaginative, hard-working, and ambitious. Within a short period of time he had organized his colleagues into giving a course of popular lectures on physics to "business men and lawyers, who were either interested in the electrical industries, or expected to become interested." Gradually Pupin found himself drawn into a network of political and economic power linked to the physical expansion of New York City. In 1893, for example, Pupin became close friends with William Barclay Parsons, an engineer then involved in supervising the installation of the electrical power transmission system in the New York subway.

Pupin, like Franz Boas, was appreciative of the benefits that a membership in the New York Academy of Sciences could generate. Pupin was soon actively committed to the Academy and played a leading part in the Section of Astronomy, Physics, and Chemistry. Not the least of his advantages gained through the Academy was a friendship with James McKeen Cattell, editor of *Science*; when Pupin delivered a talk at the section in April 1895 on recent advances in electromagnetic theory he found an available publication outlet in Cattell's magazine: Pupin's paper appeared in the issue of *Science* of 28 December later that year. Similarly, after Pupin gave a talk before the Academy on 6 April 1896 on secondary X-ray radiation, a condensed account of his lecture soon appeared in *Science, Electricity,* and other journals.[34]

Shortly after his 1896 talk before the Academy, Pupin contracted pneumonia; his wife also succumbed to pneumonia and her death a few months later left Pupin depressed and moody. As a consequence, his activities became sharply curtailed. Even after a long recuperation at his country home in Norfolk, Pupin never regained the enthusiasm and energy which had marked his early years in New York. Although he remained at Columbia and continued with his research on radio transmission he had effectively resigned from the Academy; he was elected president for one year but Pupin treated it as a purely honorary office and rarely attended meetings of the Council.[35]

Consequently leadership of the Section on Astronomy, Physics, and Chemistry passed to the hands of Charles Lane Poor, a professor of

[34] Michael Pupin, *From Immigrant to Inventor* (New York: Charles Scribner's Sons, 1923), 1, 280, 286, 309.

[35] Bergen Davis, "Michael Idvorsky Pupin, 1858–1935," *Biographical Memoirs of the National Academy of Sciences* 19(1938): 310–311.

physics at Columbia. Poor was steadfast, reliable, and competent but he never brought to his position the flair and imagination that Pupin had so frequently displayed. More seriously Poor was never able to deal with two other city organizations that, by his own admission, had diminished the ranks of his own section: "the competition of the Chemists' Club and the Physicists Association is such as to draw away to those organizations all the actual workers and students in their sciences."[36]

By 1912 attendance at meetings of the Section of Astronomy, Physics, and Chemistry had fallen so drastically that the section officers began an informal discussion amongst themselves about a possible solution to the crisis. By the fall of 1912 the situation had become so acute that Poor and Charles C. Trowbridge, the secretary of the section, decided to bring the question up for discussion at a full meeting of the Council of the Academy. When Trowbridge introduced the matter on 7 October, he found that—while none of the other three sections shared his problem—the members were, nevertheless, concerned with "getting satisfactory programmes and interesting the scientific and general public in its work. This led to a general discussion as to the policy of the Academy in the past and future and as to its present needs."

The subject proved controversial and complex; owing to the lateness of the hour and because Trowbridge's item was the last point on a very full agenda, the chairman, Emerson McMillin, proposed that they re-open the subject at a later date. Consequently the members adopted a "motion to the effect that the chairman of each section be requested to appoint a committee of three from the active members of his section to report at the next meeting of the Council regarding its condition and to make recommendations as to its future work."[37]

With such a broad mandate, it was inevitable that the members of the Academy should become progressively involved in a wide-ranging discussion amongst themselves on the nature of the organization, its purpose and goals. As a consequence, the forthcoming meeting of the Council—now scheduled for 19 November—was effectively opened up to all the leading members of the Academy regardless of their formal position vis-à-vis the individual sections. In anticipation of a large attendance, Emerson McMillin moved the forthcoming Council meeting from the Academy's cramped quarters at the American Museum of Natural History to a conference room at the Union League Club.

[36] Minutes of the Council of the New York Academy of Sciences, 19 November 1912.
[37] Minutes of the Council of the New York Academy of Sciences, 7 October 1912.

On the evening of 19 November 1912, a host of scientists gathered to assess the past and present and to plan for the future. In addition to McMillin, most of the Academy luminaries were present: Franz Boas, Clark Wissler, and James McKeen Cattell represented the Section of Anthropology and Psychology; Thomas Hunt Morgan, Nathaniel Lord Britton, and Henry Fairfield Osborn came as delegates from the Section of Biology; James F. Kemp was present to share his experiences as the chairman of the Section of Geology and Mineralogy; and Charles C. Trowbridge and Charles Lane Poor represented the Section of Astronomy, Physics, and Chemistry.

Poor was the most despondent member present at the meeting that evening; his introductory remarks gave the gathering an unfortunate shading of pessimism: "attendance at the meetings of the Section . . . is discouragingly small, often not more than one to three in addition to the officers . . . the regular stated meetings are a failure. The speaker recommended that the Section be allowed to disband."[38]

For many members of the Council present that evening, the problem outlined by Poor was indicative of the diversification of the Academy's audience. On the one hand, E. B. Southwick believed that the "Academy's meetings were too exclusive" and spoke in favor of "broadening the scope of the Academy's work and making it more popular in character." In reply, James Kemp remarked that while "specialists ought . . . to be willing to give popular resumes of the progress of science," nevertheless it was important to "continue sectional meetings." The tension between specialization and popularization was clearly marked in the activities of the Academy and, as many speakers pointed out, it was exacerbated (for the Academy) by the growth in the previous two decades of innumerable specialist societies that either were locally based or, if they were national organizations, possessed thriving and energetic chapters in New York City.

Clark Wissler, an anthropologist at Columbia and a protégé of Boas, reminisced that when, as a graduate student, he had first attended an Academy event, he had received a "profound impression . . . as to the serious and elevated character of the papers and their discussions . . . the effect was stimulating intellectually." Wissler also remembered that after the talks the Academy members would "adjourn to a nearby cafe . . . [this] was perhaps even more inspiring through the familiar conversation and discussion that took place."

The members of the Council clearly acknowledged the particular and

[38] Minutes of the Council of the New York Academy of Sciences, 19 November 1912.

unique situation of the Academy: first, what we might call the external problem, that is, the "present tendency . . . toward a rather sharp subdivision into professional societies," as J. Edmund Woodman, a professor of geology at NYU, put it. Second, there was the internal problem, namely that the Academy no longer possessed an undifferentiated audience but instead had to address several constituencies; as Edmund Otis Hovey expressed it: "the three classes of persons to be depended upon for any organization like ours [include] . . . professional workers . . . amateurs and others with a general interest . . . [and] students." Few members present that evening, however, had any answer to the situation; Thomas Hunt Morgan cautioned that the Academy should refrain from "diffusing itself over as much ground as at present," but his suggestion did not go over well with the many members who looked for an expansion, rather than a contraction, of the Academy's activities.

It fell to Nathaniel Lord Britton, president of the New York Botanical Garden, to make a proposal that was both realistic and ambitious. Britton had long perceived that the Academy could only take on new life as a scientific organization if it carried out original research that would, at one and the same time, excite the enthusiasm of its own members and win a wider support outside its own ranks. Any proposed project had to be as intellectually inclusive as possible since those members of the Academy interested in geology, say, were not likely to participate in a proposal restricted, say, to botany (and, of course, vice versa). Finally it would be all to the best, naturally enough, if the Academy's research could tap into the pockets of the wealthy New York philanthropists who had already contributed so much to Columbia, the American Museum, and the Botanical Garden but not, as yet, to the Academy.

For Nathaniel Lord Britton, the future health of the Academy could only be secured by "going beyond the scientific meetings which have been held so long, its publications and its occasional small grants in aid of research, and entering into a field of active investigation, centering its energies on some one enterprise." Britton had discussed his plans beforehand with those members of the Council amenable to his favored project; hence, when he proposed his idea of a "physical and natural history survey of Porto Rico," few voices were raised in opposition although there were demands for more information.

Britton explained that he envisaged a comprehensive survey of the island, lasting four years, and taking cognizance of its geology, botany, and zoology. He anticipated that the Academy would spend two thousand dollars annually for a period of four years with the expectation that the Academy would obtain "additional funds by subscription." The results of the survey would appear in the Academy's *Annals*, the investigators sent down to Puerto Rico would be expected to report their progress to the relevant section of the Academy, and the collections obtained were to become the property of the Academy.

Although Franz Boas cautioned that the Academy should "not duplicate [work] . . . already in progress" and tactfully pointed out that the "anthropology of Porto Rico had already been cared for," most members at the meeting that evening enthusiastically adopted Britton's suggestion. James Furman Kemp stated that the "Porto Rico plan appealed strongly to him because he thought it a good field in the various natural sciences," while Edmund Otis Hovey described it as "very attractive and hopeful." Britton realized, however, that he would need an explicit vote of confidence from the most influential members of the Council; he was not to be disappointed—Emerson McMillin, president of the Academy and an investment banker on Wall Street, had already promised Britton that, should he win the Academy's support, he, McMillin, would contribute generously to its funding. The project was secured, therefore, when Henry Fairfield Osborn, in his closing remarks in summary at the end of the meeting, explicitly singled out Britton's plan as "admirable for its effect upon the scientific world in general and the Academy in particular, and seems extremely practicable." The members of the Council—imbued with a sense of having spent a very fruitful and productive evening in reviewing the state of the Academy—adjourned just before midnight, tired but happy.[39]

Britton's choice of Puerto Rico as an object of study for the New York Academy of Sciences was linked to the political status of the island. Since the expulsion of the Spanish administration by the United States in 1898, Puerto Rico had become increasingly influenced by political and economic decisions emanating from Washington. Resistance to colonial rule was not slow to appear: in 1904 a new political party, the Unión de Puerto Rico, was organized by the charismatic Luis Muñoz Rivera; the Unionists promptly endorsed the principle of self-government of Puerto Rico as an independent nation while preserving the island's status as a protectorate of the United States. This political position, which tempered the desire for independence with an acknowledgment that the influence of the United States was not to be wished out of existence, reflected an ambiguity on the part of the general population to the new administration.[40]

[39] Minutes of the Council of the New York Academy of Sciences, 19 November 1912.
[40] For an account of the political history of Puerto Rico during the first two decades of United States administration, see Arturo Morales Carrión, *Puerto Rico: A Political and Cul-*

One consequence of North American influence was the rapid construction of an infrastructure that included harbor improvements, the irrigation of the land, and the construction of highways (all of which served the economic development of the island); a second result was the creation of educational institutions that included rural primary schools, urban high schools, and a national university.[41]

The decision by the New York Academy of Sciences to conduct a scientific survey of the island was a consequence of the cultural development of Puerto Rico and was predicated on an expectation of support and assistance from the new administration. In addition, Puerto Rico seemed a propitious choice for the Academy because, as Robert Hill, a scientist associated with the United States Geological Survey, had pointed out at the time of the 1898 conflict, so little was known, in a scientific sense, of even the principal features of the island: "there has been little or no systematic exploration of it. There is no record of any topographic or geological survey by which either the details of its relief or its exact area is known. Neither has its geology, flora, or fauna been systematically studied. . . . the island is less known in this country than even Japan or Madagascar. This fact is not due to inaccessibility or difficulty of exploration, for hundreds of intelligent people visit it yearly, but merely to the fact that few have taken the trouble to record their observations." In short, the island combined two features that made it the perfect focus for the Academy's purposes: first, an unexplored territory that had the potential for interesting and worthwhile discoveries and, second, the presence of an administrative structure that would provide Academy scientists with invaluable logistical and technical assistance.[42]

In March 1913 Nathaniel Lord Britton visited the island to meet with prominent scientists associated with the University of Puerto Rico. Established by the colonial administration in 1903, the University of Puerto Rico had been designated by the United States Congress as a land-grant

tural History (New York: W.W. Norton, 1983), 129–199. A more pointed analysis is given by Manuel Maldonado-Denis, Puerto Rico: A Socio-Historic Interpretation, trans. Elena Vialo (New York: Random House, 1972), 65–147. See also Henry Wells, The Modernization of Puerto Rico: A Political Study of Changing Values and Institutions (Cambridge, MA: Harvard University Press, 1969), 63–93.

[41] Morales Carrión, Puerto Rico, 173–176; Maldonado-Denis, Puerto Rico, 72–79.

[42] Robert T. Hill, Cuba and Porto Rico (New York, 1898), 148–149. The imbrication of metropolitan science and peripheral context (evident in the Academy's survey of Puerto Rico) is the subject of an instructive analysis of German physics and astronomy in Samoa, Argentina, and China during the same period; see Lewis Pyenson, Cultural Imperialism and Exact Sciences: German Expansion Overseas, 1900–1930, Studies in History and Culture, vol. 1 (New York: Peter Lang, 1985), 1–31, 295–316.

college and, beginning in 1908, was the beneficiary of funds according to the stipulations of the Morrill-Hatch Act. As a consequence of this support, the university's College of Agriculture at Mayagüez was in a flourishing condition, at least by comparison with the university's other branch, the impecunious College of Liberal Arts. With eighteen faculty members teaching courses in sugar chemistry, agriculture, engineering, and economics, and with an enrollment, in 1912, of 126 students, the College of Agriculture was a modest, yet successful, locus of science; consequently Britton was optimistic that he would find a corps of volunteers at the college willing to facilitate both the scientific aspirations of the Academy as well as the necessary political maneuvers with the island's legislature.[43]

In his conversations with the university faculty, Britton also discovered what he had previously anticipated, that while a small amount of initial work had been carried out on the natural history of the island, most of it was available only in relatively obscure journals that were generally inaccessible even to the small community of scientists associated with the university. Britton found, moreover, that the various scientific studies were episodic and incomplete; a comprehensive account of the island's natural history awaited an author. The New York scientist also remarked that Puerto Rico possessed no collections of any sort; accordingly the Academy would be charged with the task of assembling specimens in geology, botany, and zoology.

Britton, as the director of the New York Botanical Garden, was intimately aware of the logistical problems of mounting scientific surveys in remote and distant countries. His particular genius for solving organizational tasks led him, during his two-month stay, to make contacts with the leading scientists and scientific institutions on the island. He was also perceptive enough to appreciate that there was a network of organizations that would provide invaluable aid and assistance for the Academy scientists. At the University of Puerto Rico, Britton introduced himself to Frank Lincoln Stevens who served both as the director of the university's College of Agriculture and as Dean of the Faculty of Science. Britton was especially gratified to find that the College of Agriculture had "been successfully established, beautifully housed and thoroughly equipped with modern scientific methods." In a long discussion with Stevens at the agricultural college, Britton was pleased to learn that the Academy's scientific survey would "be cordially welcomed in the colony,

[43] John Joseph Osuna, *Education in Porto Rico* (New York: Teachers College, 1923), 252–255.

that the University would gladly cooperate, [and] that the keen interest of the insular government would certainly be aroused." Happily enough, Britton experienced the same response when he talked with officials at the island's two other scientific institutions; the staff at the Sugar Planter's Experimental Station and at the Agricultural Experiment Station expressed enthusiasm and support for the anticipated scientific survey.

More prosaically, as Britton noted in a report to the Council of the Academy in May 1913, travel around the island had been immensely improved since 1898; the sugar companies and the American administration had constructed an "elaborate system of stone roads . . . since the American occupation, now reaching to nearly all parts of the island. These roads also make possible much more complete and accurate collections and observations." Britton, in his report to the Academy, saved the best for last: he had been informed, on reliable authority, that the "insular government would . . . put into the work two dollars for every one dollar put in by the Academy." Inspired by this unexpected generosity and enthused by Britton's glowing report, Emerson McMillin, the president of the Academy, immediately announced that he would match the government's offer by subscribing "two dollars for every one dollar."[44]

As a consequence, matters began to move speedily towards the implementation of the proposal. On the basis of Britton's report, the Academy advertised among the membership for plans of work to be undertaken in Puerto Rico. A special committee of the Academy—known as the Extension Committee—was set up under the leadership of Britton; at their first meeting on 24 October 1913, members of the Extension Committee unanimously resolved not only to recommend that the Academy "appropriate $500 annually for five years, commencing in 1914, for the purpose of this investigation," but also determined to draw up plans for contacting the "Government of Porto Rico, in order to ascertain what cooperation could be expected for this investigation."[45]

The success of the scheme depended on the willingness of the Puerto Rican government to give financial support to the survey; a special committee on the scope of the Academy's activities had endorsed the survey with an important qualifier: "provided that funds can be raised outside in addition to those which are available in the Academy income." Since

[44] Minutes of the Council of the New York Academy of Sciences, 5 May 1913, NYAS.

[45] Minutes of the Council of the New York Academy of Sciences, 6 October 1913, NYAS; Minutes of the Extension Committee, 24 October 1913, in Minutes of the Council of the New York Academy of Sciences, 1913, NYAS.

the Academy had liquid assets amounting to only $1555.51 the need to obtain other sources of support was paramount. Accordingly, in a letter to the governor of the island, Edmund Otis Hovey asked the Puerto Rican government to consider making an annual grant of $5000 for a period of five years for "field-work, reduction of observations and statistics, typewriting, illustration and printing . . . and facilities for dredging by the use of a steam vessel." Hovey pointed out that the Academy survey would be of great benefit to Puerto Rico; since it would encompass geology, meteorology, oceanography, archaeology, botany, and zoology, the survey would possess scientific, educational, and economic advantages for many years to come. As an added inducement, Hovey also offered to return a "series of the specimens obtained . . . to Porto Rico to form the basis of a natural history museum"; in addition, the Academy would be willing to publish enough copies of the completed survey to "supply all Porto Rico schools and libraries."[46]

Hovey's plea for financial support was followed by a visit to the island by Henry E. Crampton, the corresponding secretary of the Academy, who discussed the survey with the governor of Puerto Rico and several other important members of the legislature. By May 1914 the legislature had given the proposal due consideration and—much to the gratification of Hovey and his colleagues—was able to report that the members had met in special session and approved the full amount.[47]

An appeal to private industry was less successful. Hovey had postponed his requests to the Puerto Rican sugar companies until the grant from the legislature was assured; then, armed with proof that the survey had serious support from a variety of institutions both in the United States and on the island, Hovey searched for a sugar company that would either contribute financially or give some other form of aid. He wrote, for example, to William Schall, president of the South Porto Rico Sugar Company, to inquire if "your company [would] be disposed to aid the Survey . . . by furnishing a steam vessel for oceanographic investigations and dredging, for a period of two or three months each year?" Surprisingly, in light of the modesty of the request, support from this quarter was not forthcoming; however, the governor of the island, Arthur Yager, was more accommodating and in June 1914, Yager was able to report that he had obtained the promise of the "only boat in Porto

[46] Edmund Otis Hovey to Arthur Yager, n.d. [22 December 1913], Puerto Rico Correspondence, NYAS.

[47] Edmund Otis Hovey to Emerson McMillin, 6 March 1914; Edmund Otis Hovey to Arthur Yager, 15 May 1914; J. W. Bonner to Arthur Yager, 22 May 1914, Puerto Rico Correspondence, NYAS.

Rican waters that is suitable and available for the uses of your investigators in their oceanographic work."[48]

Back in the United States, as word circulated among the scientific community that the survey of Puerto Rico was about to begin, individuals and institutions not previously connected with the project came forward to offer their services and, in several cases, to suggest lines of research that would dovetail with work already in progress. Most notably there was a report from Oliver L. Fassig, a meteorologist connected with the United States Department of Agriculture, who, having recently returned from a four-year residence in Puerto Rico, was able to relate his surprise, on his arrival on the island, at "how little had been done on the Island in the way of a physical and biological survey during the 15 years of occupancy of the Island by our Government. My study of the climate of Porto Rico made me especially anxious to secure a good topographic map of the Island—but there is no such map in existence."[49]

Buoyed by the promise of support from the Puerto Rico legislature, groups of scientists from New York began arriving on the island throughout 1914. The survey initially encompassed not only the principal island of Puerto Rico but also some of the smaller islands such as St. Thomas and St. Croix. The decision to take an expansive survey was based, in large part, on the results of an exploration of the region in February 1914 by a group that included Nathaniel Lord Britton; his wife, Elizabeth Britton, an eminent scientist in her own right and an international authority on mycology; John F. Cowell, director of the Buffalo Botanical Garden; and Frank E. Lutz, an assistant curator in invertebrate zoology at the American Museum of Natural History. This small band of explorers, during its two-month stay in the region, carried out "botanical and entomological collections in the northern and western parts of Porto Rico and in the small islands Desecheo and Mona, which yielded several thousand specimens and much information."[50]

With the grant from the island legislature, together with the funds of the Academy and the private contributions from such members as

[48] Edmund Otis Hovey to William Schall, 11 May 1914, Puerto Rico Correspondence, NYAS; Arthur Yager to Edmund Otis Hovey, 9 June 1914, Puerto Rico Correspondence, NYAS.

[49] Oliver L. Fassig to Edmund Otis Hovey, 8 June 1914, Puerto Rico Correspondence, NYAS.

[50] Nathaniel Lord Britton, "Botanical Explorations in Porto Rico and Islands Adjacent," Journal of the New York Botanical Garden 15(1914): 95–96; idem., "History of the Survey," in Scientific Survey of Porto Rico and the Virgin Islands, New York Academy of Sciences, vol. 1, pt. 1 (New York, 1919), 1–10.

Emerson McMillin, the Academy was able to launch an appeal to the con-
clave of scientific institutions in New York City for the support of research
on the island; as the Puerto Rico survey became a reality, it won both
financial and logistical assistance from a variety of institutions. Thus, in
the summer of 1914, a group of zoologists connected with the American
Museum of Natural History made the first extensive survey of the fauna
of Puerto Rico. Roy W. Miner, an assistant curator of invertebrate zoology
at the American Museum, investigated the marine invertebrates and
myriopods in the waters off the main island; Harry G. Barber, a leading
member of the New York Entomological Society, made a similar survey
of the insects and arachnoids; while a third member of the group, John
T. Nichols, an assistant curator of fishes at the American Museum of Natural History, investigated the ichthyology of the region.[51]

The reports of the initial surveys were so favorable that, in subsequent
months, a multitude of investigators turned their attention and energy
to various aspects of the Academy survey. Indeed, during the first two
years, the Puerto Rico Survey expanded at an almost exponential rate so
that by the summer of 1916, a total of twenty-three different groups had
travelled to Puerto Rico to explore the botany, entomology, geology, ichthyology, mycology, anthropology, paleontology, and archeology of the
island. The large majority of the expeditions were generally successful;
only the attempt of Edwin T. Hodge, during the summer of 1915, to investigate the "supposed petroleum oil shales in the western part of the
island," produced a negative result. Even in this isolated case there was
something of value to report for Hodge went on to make a "detailed geological study of the Coamo region. . . . He also made a study of the
thermal springs of the island."[52]

The fecundity of the survey was alluring enough to attract not just the
resources of the scientific institutions from New York City but also, on
several occasions, the support of organizations from other areas of the
country and, in some cases, from Europe. Thus when Nathaniel Britton
announced that plans were underway for a second botanical expedition
in the early part of 1915 under the joint leadership of the New York
Academy of Sciences and the New York Botanical Garden, both the
Academy of Natural Sciences in Philadelphia and the Buffalo Botanical

[51] Britton, "History of the Survey," in *Scientific Survey*, 1–10. See also Minutes of the Extension Committee, 24 October 1913, in Minutes of the Council of the New York Academy
of Sciences, NYAS.
[52] Britton, "History of the Survey," in *Scientific Survey*, 4. See also Edwin T. Hodge,
"The Geology of the Coamo-Guayama District, Porto Rico," in *Scientific Survey of Porto Rico
and the Virgin Islands*, New York Academy of Sciences, vol. 1, pt. 2 (New York, 1920), 222.

Garden volunteered their support. Subsequently Nordal Wille, the director of the Botanical Garden of Christiana in Norway, expressed an interest, and when the party sailed for Puerto Rico it consisted of prominent botanists from all five sponsoring institutions. The expedition was a great success; it extended over the whole of the western region of the island and resulted in large collections of plants for each of the sponsors.[53]

For those members of the Council of the Academy who had listened to Britton's initial proposal at the meeting in December 1912, the Puerto Rico survey exceeded their greatest hopes and expectations. Britton, by seizing on a project that was both intellectually diverse and able to attract substantial funding, had ensured a growing reputation for the New York Academy of Sciences. Britton was exceptional in his ability both to pinpoint challenging projects that would capture the imagination of his peers and to ensure that the requisite organizational and administrative tasks were successfully completed.

Nothing could better illustrate his acumen than the rapid publication of the initial results of the Academy survey. Not long after the survey officially commenced, Britton became aware that the survey could continue for a considerably longer time than either he or his colleagues had initially anticipated. The expansion of the survey served the interests of all the protagonists: the Puerto Rican legislature, the scientific institutions in New York, the faculty at the College of Agriculture, the individual scientists, and the New York Academy of Sciences. Future support for the survey beyond that already promised was contingent, however, on the rapid dissemination of the initial results. To this end, Britton made sure that reports of the scientific surveys were published in the appropriate outlets and, as a consequence, articles by the various survey participants appeared in the *Journal of the New York Botanical Garden*, the *Bulletin of the American Museum of Natural History*, and, of course, the *Annals of the New York Academy of Sciences*. More general essays on the aims and achievements of the survey were promoted through the pages of *Science* and, beginning in 1919, the Academy began a separate series of volumes dedicated exclusively to reports of the scientific results of the survey.[54]

Thus, only a few years after the initial field-work, a valuable series of papers appeared on the geological physiography of Puerto Rico together with reports on the rock formations, structural features, and mineral resources of the island. This geological survey, undertaken by the faculty

[53] Nathaniel Lord Britton, "Further Botanical Explorations of Porto Rico," *Journal of the New York Botanical Garden* 16(1915): 103–104.
[54] Britton, "History of the Survey," in *Scientific Survey*, 1–10.

in the Department of Geology at Columbia University, was significant on account of the belief that Puerto Rico, as a representative island in the Greater Antilles, would provide a reliable guide to the stratigraphy of the entire region. The latter included the Antilles and Central America which, as Douglas Semmes, a recent recipient of a Columbia doctorate, pointed out in his report to the Academy, "have remained . . . almost a *terra incognita* as regards their geological structure and history. Unfortunately, little study has . . . been devoted to this critical region which connects the two Americas, and until more accurate information regarding it is available our ideas of the two continents must remain largely conjectural." With the notion, therefore, that the stratigraphy of the island would serve as a valuable guide to the geology of the Caribbean region, a principal investigator was assigned to one of seven regions on the island with a mandate to provide a complete geological and topographical map; each of the seven reports differed in their particulars yet they gave sufficient corroborative detail that a remarkably consistent picture of the island's geology could be constructed.[55]

With the extension of the geological survey to the Virgin Islands a few years later, the Academy scientists were able to report that the physiography of the region was remarkably uniform; after a prolonged period of vulcanism and subsequent sedimentation, the area comprising Puerto Rico and the Virgin Islands had experienced three cycles of erosion. The first cycle, which formed the "upper peneplane of Porto Rico" was ended by uplift; the second cycle destroyed the earlier peneplane and "produced an old erosional surface approximately 700 feet below the first"; while the third cycle, which was terminated by submergence, resulted in the formation of a lower peneplane. Thus the fundamental geological structure of the region was created; during the conclusion of the Tertiary period, this structure was subjected to a differential warping and as a consequence the western part of Puerto Rico had become elevated. Howard Meyerhoff, a professor of geology at Smith College who made several field trips to the Virgin Islands during the 1920s, was able to conclude in his report of 1927 that "the entire Porto Rico-Saint Croix-Virgin Islands area developed as a unit until the late Tertiary dissection of the coastal plain."[56]

55 Douglas R. Semmes, "The Geology of the San Juan District, Porto Rico," in *Scientific Survey of Porto Rico and the Virgin Islands*, New York Academy of Sciences, vol. 1, pt. 1 (New York, 1919), 36; Charles P. Berkey, "Introduction to the Geology of Porto Rico," ibid., 26–27.

56 Howard A. Meyerhoff, "The Physiography of the Virgin Islands, Culebra and Vieques," in *Scientific Survey of Porto Rico and the Virgin Islands*, New York Academy of Sciences, vol. 4, pt. 2 (New York, 1927), 213–216.

For those members of the Academy concerned with anthropology, the Puerto Rico Survey was equally productive. Franz Boas, who had been skeptical of Britton's initial proposal, had, three years later, become one of the most enthusiastic proponents of the scheme. Boas, always the artful opportunist, quickly realized that the survey would provide an ideal opportunity for field-work for his assistants and graduate students at little or no expense. Accordingly, in May 1915, he led a small party of Columbia anthropologists—including Herman Karl Haeberlin, J. Alden Mason, and Robert T. Aitken—to the island; this group, with the assistance of officials from the Puerto Rico Department of Education, carried out a series of studies on the relationships between development and environment. From his studies with school-children and with "the soldiers of the Porto Rican regiment," Boas was able to make a tentative claim that, from his work on the island at least, "it would seem that a remarkably strong environmental influence upon the racial type of man may be observed."[57]

In addition to his own work in anthropology, Boas also directed the research efforts of the folklorists and archaeologists in the party. According to a report presented by Boas at a meeting of the New York Academy of Sciences, J. Alden Mason, the principal folklorist, had "accumulated many hundreds of folk tales, riddles, rhymes, ballads, songs, which will give us a clear insight into the traditional literature of the island. . . . the material, when worked out and published, will have not only great value for the study of Romance philology and comparative literature, but will also furnish reading matter for the rural schools, attractive and interesting to the children, because based on their own historic environment." The archaeologists were equally industrious, discovering several burial grounds and village sites of ancient communities; subsequent efforts to persuade the Puerto Rican legislature to preserve a particularly important site at Capa as a national monument proved fruitless, although Boas did report to the Academy that the group's efforts were continuing.[58]

In subsequent years the survey seemed to acquire its own momentum: a steady stream of scientists traveled to Puerto Rico to investigate the natural history of the island; back in New York the survey results appeared at a regular rate in the special series of the *Annals of the New York Academy of Sciences*. The progress of the survey was only occasionally

[57] Britton, "History of the Survey," in *Scientific Survey*, 4–5; "Records of Meetings: Report of the Porto Rico Committee," *Annals of the New York Academy of Sciences* 26(1916): 460.
[58] "Records of Meetings," 460.

interrupted when members of the island legislature began to question the appropriations made to the Academy; such questions generally concerned the relevance of the scientific results to the island's economy. Thus in 1916 when Herbert J. Spinden, a representative of the Academy, arrived in Puerto Rico, he learned, much to his consternation, that "no allowance is made for the coming year" by the legislature. After talking with the auditor, J. W. Bonner, about the appropriation, Spinden was able to report to the Academy that there was some unease among the politicians about the archaeological and anthropological investigations: "the Auditor . . . is not quite sure how archaeology fits the requirements of the fund that is supposed to deal with the natural resources of the Island. In fact the hot weather seemed to be a little too much for General Bonner and he said he hoped the scientific work this year would result in a report on reforestation and soil analysis and that all the money would not be spent taking down folk songs on a phonograph."[59]

The reluctance of the legislators to fund the work of Franz Boas on the folklore and ethnology of the island was eventually soothed away by a letter from Nathaniel Britton to the governor explaining the future plan of the Academy's work and the relevance of the anthropological investigations to the scientific survey. The appropriation was granted that year but, as Henry E. Crampton remarked, the concern of the legislature for practical results remained: "I rather fear that Brother [J. Alden] Mason's work was not entirely appreciated by the local authorities, but as a matter of fact in technical respects it is extraordinarily valuable. However, it is difficult to educate an official like some who might be mentioned so that they can see the real value of such results. The trouble is that they all want to see results in the way of dollars and cents value."[60]

The annual appropriation from the legislature continued uninterruptedly until 1923 when, as a consequence of a feud between the political parties and the outgoing governor, the legislative machinery came to a sudden halt; this was especially frustrating for Nathaniel Britton and James F. Kemp who had spent several days in January of that year lobbying for a $5000 appropriation for the survey. The two scientists, during their stay on the island, had had reason to feel considerable satisfaction at their efforts for they had obtained the "promised support of the proposed bill by the Commissioners of Agriculture and Education, and the leaders of the two main political groups in the House." Unfortunately

---

[59] Herbert J. Spinden to Henry E. Crampton, 27 April 1916, Puerto Rico Correspondence, NYAS.

[60] Henry E. Crampton to Basil H. Dutcher, 9 May 1916, Puerto Rico Correspondence, NYAS.

this lobbying effort was rendered of little import for, shortly after Britton and Kemp left the island, a fierce struggle broke out between the two principal political parties and the governor and "in order to paralyze his activities, they met the constitutional requirements by assembling about once a week and immediately adjourning without transacting any business."[61]

The political contretemps was eventually resolved but the approval of the Academy appropriation for 1923 was still in doubt. Fortunately for the New York scientists, they possessed a valuable friend in Carlos Chardón, the new Commissioner of Agriculture. Chardón had received a doctorate from Cornell University and was a keen botanist who had been largely instrumental in the establishment of a natural history museum at San Juan. As he informed Britton, he was also keen to establish a "Botanical Garden here in Porto Rico. . . . the idea has not been very well received in our Legislature but I am doing my best to get them interested in such an institution." His scientific background and his personal knowledge of the United States made Chardón particularly receptive to the wishes of the Academy. His influence was a valuable asset for, when it seemed that the 1923 appropriation would be rescinded, Chardón undertook a persistent lobbying campaign that won the full amount—five thousand dollars—for the Academy.[62]

Chardón's influence was also decisive later in the year when Britton put in an additional request for $3000 to "expedite the publication of the remaining geology papers." The legislature refused the request but, at Britton's prompting, Chardón was quick to suggest to the governor of the island that the Academy receive $2000 for the "printing of the pamphlets" from a fund reserved for "special appropriations." This measure, along with a further appropriation of $1000 for the purchase of botanical and geological specimens, won the approval of the governor and the Academy thus received its appropriation of $3000.[63]

The skill displayed by Britton in cultivating the friendship of influential and important officials in San Juan was put to good use when the Academy extended its field of operations to three small islands that had been purchased in 1917 by the United States from Denmark. The expan-

[61] Nathaniel Lord Britton to Ralph W. Tower, 27 January 1923; James F. Kemp to Ralph W. Tower, 23 May 1923, Puerto Rico Correspondence, NYAS.

[62] James F. Kemp to Ralph W. Tower, 23 May 1923; Carlos Chardón to Nathaniel Lord Britton, 6 July 1923, Puerto Rico Correspondence, NYAS.

[63] Nathaniel Lord Britton to Carlos Chardón, 26 September 1923, 7 July 1924; Chardón to Britton, 9 October 1923, 28 November 1923, 30 June 1924, Puerto Rico Correspondence, NYAS.

sion of the Puerto Rico Survey to the islands of St. Thomas, St. Jan, and St. Croix led to a proposal in 1922 to extend it to include the entire Virgin Islands. Edmund Otis Hovey and Frank E. Lutz, both curators at the American Museum of Natural History who had already carried out geological and zoological surveys for the Academy in Puerto Rico, first suggested this expansion of the survey in April 1922; the Puerto Rico Committee of the Academy was willing to listen to the suggestion of Hovey and Lutz but, as everyone agreed, it was contingent on "assistance . . . for this work from the Government of the Virgin Islands."[64]

By May 1923, after a visit to St. Thomas and St. Croix by James F. Kemp and Nathaniel Britton, the Academy—having received official notification from Henry H. Hough, the governor of the Virgin Islands, of his support for the survey—decided to reserve the fourth volume of the series of *Annals* for "documents on the Geology and Paleontology of the Virgin Islands." More specifically, James Kemp was able to announce preparations for an archeological survey of Puerto Rico and the Virgin Islands; this survey was to be a venture co-sponsored with the Academy by the Natural History Museum of Copenhagen in Denmark. During the next few years, the Academy was also able to announce plans for studies on the mammalogy of the Virgin Islands by Harold E. Anthony, curator of biology at the American Museum of Natural History, and on the physiography of the islands by Howard Meyerhoff. In 1926 Fred J. Seaver and Carlos Chardón completed a mycological survey of Puerto Rico and the Virgin Islands while Alexander Wetmore, a research scientist at the Smithsonian Institution, also completed work on the ornithology of the Virgin Islands.[65]

The survey of Puerto Rico and the Virgin Islands, which Nathaniel L. Britton had originally anticipated as a project of four years duration, lasted until the mid-1940s. Britton, who remained in charge of the project until his death in 1934, lived to see the bulk of the work successfully completed. Indeed by the 1930s the survey, which had proved to be the most ambitious project ever undertaken by the New York Academy of Sciences, had become an almost routine affair. The legislatures of Puerto Rico and the Virgin Islands continued to provide generous and uninterrupted support; as a consequence scientists from a variety of institutions produced a series of reports on every aspect of the islands. Britton, who

[64] Minutes of the Puerto Rico Committee, 28 May 1917, 18 April 1922, NYAS.

[65] Minutes of the Puerto Rico Committee, 31 May 1923, 14 January 1926, 24 May 1926, NYAS. See also Nathaniel Lord Britton to Philip Williams, 5 July 1924, Puerto Rico Correspondence, NYAS.

continued his field-work in Puerto Rico past his seventy-second birthday, could, in 1934, write with considerable pride of the series of volumes on the survey published by the Academy that "nearly all the information brought together, through field, laboratory, museum and library work, on which these volumes are based, has been brought together . . . through the cooperation of over fifty expert investigators, who have worked without remuneration; this is a remarkable achievement; no other part of Tropical America has had its natural features, plants and animals so completely studied."[66]

No individual played a greater role in the conception and execution of the survey than Nathaniel Britton. From his first suggestion of the project at the meeting of the Council of the Academy in December 1912 to his death in 1934 Britton remained in control of almost every aspect of the survey. The New York Botanical Garden has proved to be the most enduring monument to Britton's acumen as an entrepreneur of science; the survey of Puerto Rico and the Virgin Islands also stands as a testimonial to Britton's extraordinary organizational and administrative talents.

[66] Nathaniel Lord Britton to José Padín, 10 January 1934, Puerto Rico Correspondence, NYAS.

6

The Dissemination of Knowledge
1934–1970

DURING THE 1930s the membership of the New York Academy of Sciences reflected the preoccupation of the Academy with the Puerto Rico survey. Thus, while the Section of Astronomy, Physics, and Chemistry had, over the previous two decades, atrophied and eventually disappeared, the Section of Geology and Mineralogy had flourished. The physicists and chemists, by necessity, had had little connection with the work of the survey while the geologists, botanists, and zoologists in the Academy had come to regard the survey as a useful source of employment. The concentration of the Academy's activity in natural history thus led to an appreciable overlap between the membership of the Academy and the scientific staff at the American Museum of Natural History. The location of the Academy's offices, moreover—in two large rooms within the American Museum—greatly facilitated the friendly cooperation between the two institutions.

For the Academy, it was a research assistant in the department of invertebrate zoology, Eunice Thomas Miner, who proved to be the most valuable recruit to the Academy's ranks. Miner, a graduate of Boston University, joined the Academy in 1935. Her husband, Roy Waldo Miner, a curator of zoology at the Museum, had persuaded her to join the Academy on account of the Puerto Rico survey; the scientists at the Museum and the officers of the Academy anticipated that, despite the recent death of Nathaniel Lord Britton, the natural history survey would continue for at least another decade.

Eunice Miner's decision to join the Academy was propitious for, once she had discovered that the Academy was one of the oldest scientific societies in New York, she set her aim on rebuilding it and, more important, on increasing its significance for a more widely extended circle of scientists. Her enthusiasm for the task was evident; in October 1939 the Scientific Council of the Academy, impressed by her diligence and energy, appointed Eunice Miner to the position of executive secretary.[1]

Upon her appointment Eunice Miner lost little time in giving the Academy a renewed sense of vigor and energy. She was assisted in her task by the relatively prosperous condition of the organization; despite the recent deaths of two of its most distinguished members, Nathaniel Lord Britton and Henry Fairfield Osborn, the Academy was in a flourishing condition. Thus, at the annual meeting of 16 December 1935, the treasurer, Harold E. Anthony, was able to report that, despite the recent depression, the "investments of the Academy, everything considered, have survived these troubled financial times with no more losses than must be expected in any list of diversified holdings. . . . the principal and interest have stood up very well with favorable prospects of a substantial recovery of such losses as have been suffered. . . . the Academy should be able to materially strengthen its investments during the coming year."[2]

The financial stability of the Academy was complemented by its continuing research work on the geology, anthropology, and botany of Puerto Rico and the Virgin Islands and by the presentation of popular lectures on science to a growing audience. During 1937, for example, each of the three sections held ten public meetings; in addition, the Academy, in cooperation with the Museum, held two scientific meetings that exceeded all expectations: "two General meetings were held in conjunction with the American Museum of Natural History, 1185 persons being present at the first and 861 at the second. Four Smokers were also held under the auspices of the various sections with a gratifying attendance at each."[3]

The particular contribution of Eunice Miner to the continued success of the New York Academy of Sciences consisted in radically increasing the size and scope of its membership and activities. Her later reminiscence of the Academy's condition when she joined in 1935 is certainly tendentious—"there were 317 people listed on the books, but only one was actually recorded as a dues-paying member. . . . no one was handling the job of maintaining active memberships and recruiting new members"—but undoubtedly reflects her impatience at the routinism of the Academy, a routinism that she quickly began to shatter.

[1] Harry Atkins, "Eunice Thomas Miner: A Life in Science," *The Sciences* 7(1967): 41–42; Minutes of the New York Academy of Sciences, 2 December 1935, 2 October 1939, NYAS.

[2] Summary of the Report of the Treasurer, 30 November 1935, in Minutes of the New York Academy of Sciences, 16 December 1935, NYAS.

[3] Report of the Recording Secretary, 15 December 1937, in Minutes of the New York Academy of Sciences, 15 December 1937, NYAS.

As a condition of her appointment as executive secretary, Miner obtained the approval of the Council of the Academy for a series of membership drives. Her initial efforts relied more on a gregarious nature than on the scientific merits of the organization; Miner's account of the early years is apocryphal, but nicely captures, nevertheless, the essence of her leadership: "I particularly remember the first meeting my husband and I attended. I don't recall the specific topic, but the speaker was a geologist. In attendance to hear the paper were exactly four people: the section head, my husband, myself, and a janitor. Because the janitor was less interested in geology than the rest of us, we invited the speaker and the section head to our apartment, which at that time was just across the street from the museum. That was really the first of many dinners we gave at which members of the Academy presented papers. Before too long we were having as many as 80 people at our meetings, but to be perfectly honest . . . I suspect some of the turnout could be ascribed to gastronomic, as well as scientific, enthusiasm."[4]

Within a few years the Academy was flourishing anew. In 1938 the Section of Physics and Chemistry was successfully re-established; within a few months the section, as though to prove its virility, sponsored a two-day conference on electrophoresis. This event, which was held at the end of October 1938, was, as the recording secretary claimed in his annual report, a "new step in progressive activities of the Academy" principally because of its specialized nature. Thus attendance was limited only to "active workers in the field" and the proceedings were later published by the Academy.[5]

Other indicators of Academy growth also reflected the leadership of Eunice Miner. The *Annals* of the Academy, which not only continued to focus on the scientific survey of Puerto Rico and the Virgin Islands but also began to reflect a broader range of scientific concerns, greatly increased in popularity so that, during 1939, the sales of the *Annals* increased by a factor of four. As a consequence of the membership drive, almost five hundred new members were recorded in 1940; this increment easily surpassed the total number of members of the Academy in 1935. In the following year the recording secretary, Duncan A. MacInnes, was able to report that the Academy "has . . . held more important conferences, and increased its membership, of well known scientific workers,

4 Atkins, "Eunice Thomas Miner," 43.

5 Duncan A. MacInnes, "Introduction to the Conference on Electrophoresis," *Annals of the New York Academy of Sciences* 39(1939–1940): 107–109; Report of the Recording Secretary, 14 December 1938, in Minutes of the New York Academy of Sciences, 14 December 1938; Minutes of the New York Academy of Sciences, 3 October 1938, NYAS.

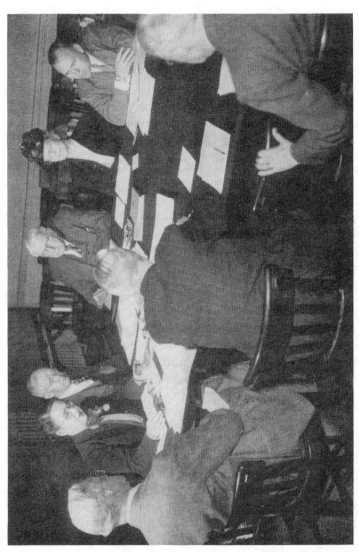

25. MEETING OF THE COUNCIL OF THE NEW YORK ACADEMY OF SCIENCES, 1948. The members of the Council in 1948 were (from the head of the table, clockwise): Eunice Thomas Miner, executive director; Harden F. Taylor, president; Roy Waldo Miner, editor; Clairette P. Armstrong, councilor; Charles R. Schroeder, councilor; E. Clifford Williams, treasurer; Hans Molitor, vice-president; and George B. Pegram, recording secretary. This photograph is taken from a promotional brochure, *The New York Academy of Sciences – Past, Present, Future* (1948), 4. (*Courtesy of the New York Academy of Sciences.*)

to a greater degree than in any previous year" while the editor of the *Annals*, Erich M. Schlaikjer, was able to claim that the Academy "has published more than in any other single year in . . . [its] history." Last but not least, a fifth section was formed in 1941; like the other four sections, the new Section of Oceanography and Meteorology was led and organized by members of the Columbia professoriate.[6]

The rapid expansion of the activities of the Academy during the 1940s was, for some scientists on the Council of the Academy, a mixed blessing; to those members active in the organization before 1935 the fraternal club of previous years had seemingly been replaced by an impersonal organization that apparently accepted every applicant irrespective of his or her social standing and professional credentials. A more serious problem, one perceived by every member of the Academy, was the relationship between the Academy and the American Museum of Natural History; in 1948, for example, the total membership of the Academy was already four thousand and it was evident to the officers that the administration of the Academy required a larger headquarters than the two rooms provided by the Museum.

As a consequence, at the beginning of 1948, the Academy prepared to launch a fund drive of one million dollars for the purchase of a new building. The campaign, which was formally announced in November 1948, aimed not only to supply the funds for a new headquarters, but also to hire a permanent administrative staff. For the previous thirteen years Eunice Miner had had little assistance with the many mundane organizational tasks that were essential to the smooth functioning of the organization. One million dollars would—it was hoped—enable the Academy not merely to "purchase and recondition a centrally located building" but also, in subsequent years, to "expand its program into the fields of astronomy, astrophysics, experimental medicine and public health, and mathematics."[7]

Despite the very best efforts of the Scientific Council there is little indication that the Academy was successful in raising the total amount and, since the American Museum of Natural History was eager to re-

[6] Report of the Librarian, 14 December 1938, in Minutes of the New York Academy of Sciences, 14 December 1938; Report of the Recording Secretary, 11 December 1940, in Minutes of the New York Academy of Sciences, 11 December 1940; Report of the Recording Secretary, 10 December 1941, in Minutes of the New York Academy of Sciences, 10 December 1941; Report of the Editor, 10 December 1941, in Minutes of the New York Academy of Sciences, 10 December 1941, NYAS.

[7] "Opens $1,000,000 Drive of Academy of Sciences," *New York Times*, 16 November 1948. See also "Dr. La Mer Heads Science Academy," *New York Times*, 16 December 1948.

claim the rooms occupied by the Academy, it seemed that making provision for the anticipated expansion of coming decades would pose a thorny problem for the Academy. Eunice Miner, who had been promoting the fund drive by pleading her case before wealthy philanthropists in New York City, had the good fortune to capture the attention of Norman Woolworth, scion of the family that owned a network of chain stores around the country. Woolworth, who owned an ornate five-story building on Sixty-third Street, was apparently so impressed by Miner's eloquence, energy, and enthusiasm that, on learning of the Academy's search for a new home, simply donated his mansion with the sole requirement that the Academy pay all the necessary legal fees involved in the transfer.

On her first visit to the mansion, Miner realized that her hopes had been exceeded beyond any expectation. Located on the south side of Sixty-third Street between Fifth and Madison avenues and just a few yards from Central Park, the Academy's new home was situated in one of the most prosperous parts of Manhattan. The building itself was the epitome of elegance: in the foyer and main halls the floors were constructed of black and gold marble specially imported from Tuscany and Spezia; the Italian Renaissance style was emphasized by the sixteenth century Florentine mantel that stood in the entrance hall; and throughout the building the doors were constructed of oak spiked with bronze ornamentation. Eunice Miner noted with quiet satisfaction that the library, built entirely of English carved oak, was eminently suited to impress future visitors to the Academy with the erudition of the membership. Everything was done to perfection—there was even a central courtyard that served to give the new Academy building an atmosphere akin to a cloister—the Academy was now not merely a scientific organization but also a refuge and a sanctuary from the ceaselessly hectic streets of Manhattan.[8]

Enough money had been raised during the fund drive for the Academy to refurbish the entire building from top to bottom and to install the most modern furniture and fittings in the administrative offices on the second and third floors. A series of rooms on the fourth floor was set aside to receive the "duplicating and stencil equipment . . . devoted to preparing the academy's journal" while the necessary structural alterations were carried out to provide the Academy with "three conference rooms, with a seating capacity of 200 each." Last but not least, the portrait of Samuel Latham Mitchill—donated to the Lyceum of Natural History

    [8] "Scientists Get Woolworth Home in 63d Street as $1,000,000 Gift," New York Times, 2 October 1949.

by the painter, Henry Inman, in 1830—was hung in the entrance hall above the mantel.

On 11 April 1950 the members and friends of the Academy gathered at the new headquarters for the official inauguration of the Woolworth mansion. Moses L. Crossley, the president of the Academy for 1950, in his opening speech of welcome to the assembled scientists, expressed the hope that with its own building the New York Academy of Sciences would soon become the "greatest scientific center in the world." In a more modest vein, George B. Pegram, vice-president of Columbia University, who was present to dedicate the new home of the Academy, remarked that this new acquisition would "mark a turning point in the work of the academy," while the main speaker, Detlev W. Bronk, president of Johns Hopkins University, restricted his remarks to a plea for the unfettered advance of scientific thought. The heightened tensions of the Cold War and the spread of McCarthyism were inimical to the pursuit of truth: the "poisons of international tensions and national unrest" should be fought by a reaffirmation by the scientific community of the "universal right to know as a basic human right."[9]

The ceremonies on Sixty-third Street that day were relatively low-key; it was certainly true that they only partially reflected the satisfaction of Miner and her colleagues in the acquisition—for only the second time in the Academy's long history—of a permanent home. Norman Woolworth's gift instantaneously changed the Academy's status as a perpetual supplicant to other scientific institutions in the city—most notably the American Museum of Natural History—and, at long last, gave the organization a permanent measure of independence and self-sufficiency.

The acquisition of the new building on Sixty-third Street gave fresh impetus to the Academy's program of activities, most notably, to the series of conferences that had been initiated during the 1930s. During the next two decades, largely on account of the vigor of the Academy's Section of Biology, a series of important meetings on biomedical issues were sponsored by the Academy. On account of the interest in the Academy's affairs by the medical community and by research scientists involved in the discovery and manufacture of new pharmaceutical drugs, the Academy served as a forum for the evaluation of the new antibiotics that were then proving effective in conquering a wide variety of diseases. As early as 1946, for example, the Academy convened the "first large scientific assembly on antibiotics": this conference, which began on 17 Jan-

[9] "Freedom of Inquiry for Science Urged: Dr. Bronk of Johns Hopkins University Denounces the 'Trend Toward Secrecy'," *New York Times*, 12 April 1950.

uary and lasted for three days, was notable not only for its priority in bringing together research workers from many different fields but also for the various reports presented to the conference on the efficacy of antibiotics, in particular streptomycin, in combatting tuberculosis. The 1946 meeting, which took place only two years after the discovery of streptomycin, marked an important precedent for the Academy; in subsequent years, the Academy meetings proved valuable in evaluating the effectiveness of many of the new antibiotic drugs.[10]

Since the discovery of penicillin in 1928 by Alexander Fleming and the subsequent realization of the clinical potential of penicillin against bacteria by Howard Florey and Ernst Chain, many scientists on both sides of the Atlantic had tried to uncover further antibiotics that would reinforce or complement the potency of penicillin against disease. Most notably there was Selman Waksman, a soil microbiologist at the New Jersey Agricultural Experiment Station at Rutgers University, who, in 1943, discovered the first of the new antibiotics, streptomycin. Waksman's discovery possessed significance most obviously in a clinical sense; other actinomycetes had been previously discovered but they were generally too toxic to be employed in the fight against disease. Streptomycin, however, was effective against both gram-positive and gram-negative organisms, and, most notably, against the tubercle bacillus. The appearance of an antibiotic that could apparently vanquish tuberculosis caused a considerable stir amongst the scientific community, and very soon the hunt was on for other antibiotics.[11]

At the Lederle Laboratories, for example, Benjamin Duggar, a former professor of plant physiology at the University of Wisconsin, successfully isolated the antibiotic aureomycin in 1945. *Streptomyces aureofaciens*, which earned its name on account of its golden-yellow color, was distributed for testing to physicians at Johns Hopkins University, Harlem Hospital, and the College of Physicians and Surgeons at Columbia Univer-

[10] Selman A. Waksman, *My Life with the Microbes* (New York: Simon and Schuster, 1954), 215. The conference proceedings were published as "Antibiotics: Part I. Microbiological; Part II. Pharmacological," *Annals of the New York Academy of Sciences* 48(1946–1947): 31–218.

[11] Hubert A. Lechevalier, "The Search for Antibiotics at Rutgers University," in *The History of Antibiotics*, ed. John Parascandola (Madison, WI: American Institute of the History of Pharmacy, 1980), 113–116. The discovery of streptomycin was first announced in Albert Schatz, Elizabeth Bugie, and Selman A. Waksman, "Streptomycin, a Substance Exhibiting Antibiotic Activity Against Gram-Positive and Gram-Negative Bacteria," *Proceedings of the Society for Experimental Biology and Medicine* 55(1944): 66–69. For an informal account of the discovery of streptomycin, see Julius H. Comroe Jr., "Pay Dirt: The Story of Streptomycin," *American Review of Respiratory Diseases* 117(1978): 773–781, 957–968.

sity and, within the next two years, preliminary results were reported to the research staff at Lederle.[12]

In the early part of 1948, Duggar approached the New York Academy of Sciences with a request to hold a conference on the use and properties of aureomycin; after financial support for the proposed meeting had been guaranteed by Lederle and after the Section of Biology had agreed to bear the brunt of the organizational details, the Academy convened the conference on 21 July 1948. After an introduction by Duggar who, in his remarks to the assembled scientists, described the process of the discovery of aureomycin and its relationship to the other antibiotic organisms, the various research groups gave extended summaries of their findings. Alson E. Braley and Murray Sanders reported that, in their application of aureomycin to external diseases of the eye, the new antibiotic had proved eminently successful; with regard to the treatment of trachoma and inclusion conjunctivitis, for example, aureomycin provided prompt and effective treatment. A team of physicians at Harlem Hospital led by Louis T. Wright reported tentative success in the treatment of lymphogranuloma; thirty-five patients who had contracted this relatively obscure disease had been treated; although therapeutic progress was variable, Wright was able to conclude that "this antibiotic is a superior, specific form of therapy."[13]

The clinical tests at the College of Physicians and Surgeons, Harlem Hospital, Johns Hopkins, and the other medical facilities that had received the drug from Lederle were not conclusive enough to warrant an enthusiastic reception for the new antibiotic. Experimental tests by the scientists at Lederle, however, were more successful in proving the drug's efficacy. Sam C. Wong and Herald Rea Cox, for example, used aureomycin in tests on mice and guinea pigs infected with a variety of diseases; aureomycin was effective against spotted fever, typhus, psittacosis, and Q fever but had no effect on rabies, influenza B, encephalomyelitis, and MEF–1 poliomyelitis.[14]

[12] William L. Laurence, "Chemical Attacks Stubborn Diseases: Venereal Malady and External Eye Ills are said to Yield to Aureomycin, from Mold," *New York Times*, 22 July 1948. See also Helmuth M. Böttcher, *Miracle Drugs: A History of Antibiotics*, trans. Einhert Kawerau (London: Heinemann, 1963), 184–187.

[13] Benjamin M. Duggar, "Aureomycin, a Product of the Continuing Search for New Antibiotics," *Annals of the New York Academy of Sciences* 51(1948–1951): 177–181; Alson E. Braley and Murray Sanders, "Aureomycin in Ocular Infections," ibid., 284; Louis T. Wright et al., "The Treatment of Lymphogranuloma Venereum and Granuloma Inguinale in Humans with Aureomycin," ibid., 329.

[14] Sam C. Wong and Herald R. Cox, "Action of Aureomycin against Experimental

While subsequent tests showed that aureomycin was effective against many other diseases, its transcendent value derived from its efficacy against organisms against which both penicillin and streptomycin were useless. As a consequence aureomycin was soon hailed as one of the most valuable antibiotics ever discovered and the American Cyanamid Company (which owned Lederle Laboratories) began large-scale production of the drug only months after the July conference at the New York Academy of Sciences.[15]

For American Cyanamid the production of aureomycin resulted in profits that exceeded all expectations. After the addition of aureomycin as a feed supplement was found to increase the yield of dairy products from farm animals, demand increased exponentially; and, when the federal government began to use aureomycin to treat wounded soldiers fighting in Korea, American Cyanamid was forced to build a second production plant. By 1950 annual sales of American Cyanamid were $325 million; much of the company's profits derived from sales of aureomycin which, in 1952, reached a peak of $61 million.[16]

On 24 June 1949, less than a year after the conference on aureomycin, the New York Academy of Sciences sponsored a conference at the American Museum of Natural History on the chemotherapy of tuberculosis. One significant section of the meeting considered the use of synthetic drugs, most notably the sulfonamides, in combatting tuberculosis; a second section, which reviewed the therapeutic value of natural drugs, concentrated on the use of antibiotics. Selman Waksman, who served as the chairman of the meeting that day, recalled in his introductory remarks that, only ten years previously, it had been unimaginable that tuberculosis could be successfully treated: "one could hardly dare to mention this subject before a scientific or medical gathering, except in a mere whisper, for fear of being declared a visionary." Waksman was particularly enthused with the results obtained through the use of a new antibiotic, neomycin. One paper, presented to the meeting by a research team from Charles Pfizer & Co., a pharmaceutical company based in Brooklyn, reported that preliminary tests with neomycin had shown that it possessed a "relatively low degree of toxicity" and, in addition, was "highly active against . . . both streptomycin-sensitive and streptomycin-

Rickettsial and Viral Infections," *Annals of the New York Academy of Sciences* 51(1948–1951): 301–303.

[15] Editorial, "Science in Review: Effectiveness of New Antibiotic, Aureomycin, Demonstrated Against Virus Diseases," *New York Times*, Sunday, 25 July 1948, sec. 4.

[16] Tom Mahoney, *The Merchants of Life: An Account of the American Pharmaceutical Industry* (New York: Harper & Brothers, 1959), 178–179.

resistant tubercle bacilli." Thus neomycin was the ideal antibiotic to be used in combination with streptomycin; the tubercle bacilli that were resistant to the latter drug could be knocked out by subsequent doses of neomycin.[17]

Selman Waksman, in his coda to the conference, pointed out that, while the initial tests did show resistance on the part of some strains of tuberculosis to neomycin, these strains "did not appear to be the same strains that showed resistance against streptomycin." As a consequence, it seemed likely that a combination of the two drugs would effectively eliminate tuberculosis: "before long . . . we will talk about tuberculosis as we do now about pneumonia."[18]

Waksman's prediction proved premature; his hopes for neomycin rested on its apparent superiority to streptomycin—neomycin was more stable, did not permit the rapid growth of resistant tubercles, and was more active. Unfortunately, subsequent tests showed that neomycin had a high toxicity and in fact proved even more toxic than streptomycin; neomycin, like all aminoglycosidic antibiotics, attacks the eighth cranial nerve. As a consequence neomycin was soon abandoned as a possible cure for tuberculosis. Nevertheless, while neomycin was never a panacea for tuberculosis, it did prove profitable for its manufacturer, Charles Pfizer & Co. Neomycin proved effective as a preoperative intestinal antiseptic, could be used to treat salmonellosis and enteritis in farm animals, and was extremely effective against a wide variety of dermatological afflictions.[19]

For Charles Pfizer & Co., however, it was a soil-derived antibiotic, terramycin, that proved to be the most profitable antibiotic developed during the 1950s—a drug that dwarfed neomycin and almost every other antibiotic in terms of sales and that transformed Pfizer into a huge multinational company. Terramycin, one of the first antibiotics to be found through the use of paper chromatography, was first isolated in a Pfizer laboratory in November 1949. Gladys Hobby, who had previously carried out tests on neomycin, evaluated the new antibiotic by way of informal

[17] Selman A. Waksman, "Drugs of Natural Origin: Introductory Remarks," *Annals of the New York Academy of Sciences* 52(1949–1950): 750; Gladys L. Hobby, Tulita F. Lenert, and Nancy Dougherty, "The Evaluation of Neomycin and other Antimicrobial Agents of Bacterial and Fungal Origin, and Substances from Higher Plants," ibid., 778.

[18] William L. Laurence, "New Mold Drug for Tuberculosis Successfully Passes Animal Tests," *New York Times*, 26 June 1949. See also Selman A. Waksman, "Historical Background," in *Neomycin: Its Nature and Practical Application*, ed. Selman A. Waksman (Baltimore: Williams & Wilkins Co., 1958), 1–6.

[19] Hubert A. Lechevalier, "The 25 Years of Neomycin," *CRC Critical Reviews in Microbiology* 3(1975): 376–377, 380–381, 384–385, 389.

contacts among physicians working in New York hospitals. According to an informal history of Pfizer, the drug was first tested on influenza patients in Harlem Hospital: "the tests exceeded the most optimistic expectations. Toxicity was very low, the patient's temperature plunged from its high levels, and improvement was rapid."

A few months later, on 22 March 1950, the Food and Drug Administration issued its approval for the use of terramycin and almost immediately Pfizer began to prepare for the marketing of the drug. The Pfizer executives, aware that the company had discovered an extremely efficacious drug that seemed to have few side effects, were determined not to make the mistake of manufacturing terramycin and selling it for commercial distribution to other manufacturing companies. This route had been taken with penicillin; in 1946 Pfizer was producing eighty-five percent of all penicillin manufactured in the United States and, since Pfizer was solely a pharmaceutical manufacturer, it had sold penicillin directly to such companies as Lilly, Parke-Davis, Burroughs-Wellcome, and Upjohn. When the latter companies subsequently began manufacturing penicillin, the Pfizer sales quickly disappeared. The decision to distribute terramycin commercially meant the overnight creation of a marketing division. On the same day that the FDA gave its approval for the sale of the drug twenty detail men began telephoning hospitals and physicians around the country; as John McKeen, the president of Pfizer, recalled those early days, the company "called all the wholesalers, all the retailers, all the large hospitals in the United States, and in almost every single instance we received an order for Terramycin and mailed it out. The thing just snowballed."[20]

Less than three months later, at the Barbizon-Plaza Hotel in Manhattan, three hundred scientists, physicians, and pharmacists met at a conference held under the aegis of the New York Academy of Sciences to discuss the benefits of the new antibiotic. The gathering, which lasted for two days, was chaired by Chester S. Keefer, a physician at the Evans Memorial Hospital in Boston; the keynote speaker was Henry Welch, the head of the antibiotic division of the Food and Drug Administration. Welch, who was also the principal editor of *Antibiotics and Chemotherapy* and *Antibiotic Medicine and Clinical Therapy*, two journals owned by MD Publications, reported that the "new antibiotic has proved as effective as penicillin, streptomycin, aureomycin and other compounds." Other speakers at the Academy conference discussed various aspects of the new drug and a consensus seemed to be held that terramycin could be

[20] Samuel Mines, *Pfizer . . . An Informal History* (New York: Pfizer Inc., 1978), 115-119.

"particularly effective when germs have become resistant to the hereto-fore available antibiotics."[21]

For Pfizer the Academy conference served as an imprimatur that, combined with the FDA approval earlier in the year, helped to convince physicians and hospitals around the country that terramycin was superior in many respects to such antibiotics as streptomycin and aureomycin. The subsequent commercial success of terramycin and the later development and marketing of new antibiotics enabled Pfizer to reap unprecedented profits; by 1957 the company's annual sales were more than $200 million, it employed 11,300 employees, and its five marketing divisions had 2000 salesmen selling antibiotics to 75,000 customers. Pfizer had 14 overseas plants and sold nearly $80 million in antibiotics on foreign markets.[22]

New antibiotics continued to be a major focus of the conferences of the New York Academy of Sciences until the end of the decade; yet as the use of antibiotics became increasingly prevalent so physicians began to report that the new drugs were not entirely without risk. The most puzzling phenomenon associated with the more popular antibiotics such as aureomycin and terramycin was the intermittent inability of the drug to effect a cure or to prevent a relapse; some physicians, moreover, believed that the use of antibiotics only masked the effects of the disease and consequently inhibited proper treatment. The pharmaceutical companies, which had often touted each successive antibiotic as a miracle drug that would act as a universal panacea, were obviously concerned that an increasingly skeptical public would eventually reject the pharmacological route; in addition the often gullible acceptance by physicians of each new drug and the relaxed attitude of the FDA in testing new drugs for long-term toxicity could prepare the way for a subsequent disaster.[23]

As early as 1952 the New York Academy of Sciences was sponsoring meetings in the city that brought together members of the medical community, research workers from the major pharmaceutical companies, and representatives of government regulatory agencies. On 17 January

---

[21] "Terramycin Accepted: Efficacy of New Antibiotic is Reported by U.S. Spokesman," New York Times, 17 June 1950; Milton Silverman and Philip R. Lee, Pills, Profits, and Politics (Berkeley, CA: University of California Press, 1974), 113. The conference proceedings were published as "Terramycin," Annals of the New York Academy of Sciences 53(1950–1951): 221–460.

[22] Mahoney, Merchants of Life, 237–238.

[23] For a judicious discussion of the social impact of antibiotics, see Harry F. Dowling, Fighting Infection: Conquests of the Twentieth Century (Cambridge, MA: Harvard University Press, 1977), 187–192.

1952, for example, almost two hundred scientists convened at the Barbizon-Plaza Hotel to hear reports on the efficacy of antibiotics in the treatment of tropical diseases. As part of the proceedings, Charles W. Mushett, a research scientist at Merck & Co. who also served as chairman of the Section of Biology at the Academy, spoke at length on the mechanisms of antibiotic use; Mushett warned that an indiscriminate use of streptomycin, chloromycetin, and aureomycin might interfere with the body's natural immune system. The present level of understanding of the use of antibiotics interpreted the action of the drugs as a process of inhibition, that is, they did not kill the germs outright but held the "infection in check" provided that a sufficiently high level of antibiotics was in the blood stream. If the antibiotic were suddenly discontinued the patient "may suffer a relapse . . . because the normal development of antibodies to combat invading germs has been checked, along with the spread of infection."[24]

As an example of this phenomenon, Theodore E. Woodward, the principal investigator representing a research group at the University of Maryland Medical School, cited the treatment of typhoid fever through the use of chloramphenicol, an antibiotic manufactured by Parke, Davis & Company. To reduce the propensity of chloramphenicol to interfere with the body's immune system, Woodward reported that the Maryland team had used the drug only intermittently; this procedure gave the physician the opportunity to develop natural immunity in the patient against the disease: "intermittent therapy . . . may allow adequate antigenic stimulus."[25]

The 1952 conference on antibiotics was less concerned with social or ethical problems related to the increasing use of prescription drugs than with the many technical problems associated with the prescription of antibiotics. A conference of the Academy held in October 1956 on the use of tranquilizers took a more philosophical tack; the keynote speaker, Aldous Huxley, used his time at the podium to speculate on a future without disease. Huxley's address before the Academy was somewhat typical (of him): the writer predicted vaguely that the use of "tranquilizing drugs used to alleviate mental conditions" would result in a reexamination of social mores and ethics.[26]

[24] "Drawbacks Found in Antibiotics' Use: Drugs may Seriously Affect Body's Own Development of Immunity, Doctors Hear," New York Times, 18 January 1952.

[25] Theodore E. Woodward et al., "Treatment of Typhoid Fever with Antibiotics," Annals of the New York Academy of Sciences 55(1952): 1049.

[26] "'Behavior' Drugs now Envisioned: Aldous Huxley Predicts they will bring Reexamining of Ethics and Religion," New York Times, 19 October 1956.

Within a few years, this essentially benign view of the effect of prescription drugs on society was radically altered by a series of disasters that served to alert the general public to unanticipated dangers. In 1960 physicians who had prescribed the drug triparanol began reporting that their patients were suffering skin damage and the growth of cataracts on the eyes. The manufacturer, William S. Merrell Co., a pharmaceutical firm based in Cincinnati, had submitted triparanol to the Food and Drug Administration in July 1959 and had received approval for its sale ten months later. When reports of the side effects of triparanol became widespread the FDA, early in 1962, re-examined the records provided by Merrell and found that incorrect reports had been submitted by the company to the FDA that flatly contradicted the conclusions of two other pharmaceutical manufacturers—Merck & Co. and Upjohn—that the drug was toxic. In April 1962 Merrell withdrew triparanol from the market, in December the following year the company was indicted on criminal charges, and a large group of patients filed a class-action suit. Merrell eventually paid $50 million in damages, three executives were given six-month suspended sentences, and the company was fined $80,000.

The William S. Merrell Co. was also involved, albeit indirectly, in one of the most tragic cases to involve prescription drugs. In 1958 Chemie-Grunenthal, a pharmaceutical company based in the Federal Republic of Germany, promoted the drug thalidomide as a sedative that seemed to have none of the customary side-effects—grogginess, for example—that were then common to sleeping pills. When thalidomide was submitted to the FDA in 1960 for approval in the United States, the application was delayed (ostensibly on the grounds that the request was incomplete). In the same year reports of phocomelia, an extremely rare disease that involves the birth of children with deformities, began appearing in West Germany. Chemie-Grunenthal withdrew thalidomide from the European market in November 1961 and William S. Merrell Co. (which had obtained the license from Chemie-Grunenthal to distribute the drug in North America) withdrew thalidomide from the Canadian market in March 1962 but, by that time, the damage had been done; approximately ten thousand children were born with phocomelia. Fortunately the FDA had never approved the drug for distribution in the United States; the FDA officer in charge of the application, Frances Kelsey, had noticed a correlation of slight peripheral neuritis with the use of the drug and had blocked approval of thalidomide on technical grounds.

The two cases of triparanol and thalidomide prompted calls for the strengthening of the Food and Drug Administration as a regulatory agency and, in a less specific sense, engendered among the general public a climate of mistrust about the claims of pharmaceutical companies. The thalidomide tragedy, in particular, prompted the passage of Senate Bill 1552 which was sponsored by Estes Kefauver, a senator from Tennessee and the Chairman of the Senate Subcommittee on Antitrust and Monopoly. This bill, which was supported by such pharmaceutical companies as Eli Lilly Company and Merck, Sharp & Dohme, strengthened the powers of the FDA by stipulating that a drug should be both safe and effective, that advertising should list all contraindications, and that manufacturing plants should be open regularly to inspection.[27]

The general air of controversy surrounding prescription drugs in the 1960s did not entirely by-pass the New York Academy of Sciences. The Academy was never directly involved in any of the debates but as a sponsor of numerous conferences on the effects of antibiotics, tranquilizers, sulfa compounds, anticoagulants, and oral contraceptives, the Academy inevitably became the focus for disputes involving, at various times, the federal government, the pharmaceutical companies, the medical community, scientists working in university research centers, and, last but not least, patients anxious to obtain drugs to alleviate such afflictions as arthritis and cancer.

One of the most controversial Academy conferences during the decade took place in March 1966 on dimethyl sulfoxide (DMSO). Widely used as a commercial solvent, dimethyl sulfoxide had been discovered to possess the ability to penetrate body tissues quickly and, at the same time, to "carry" other drugs with it into the body. Researchers at the University of Oregon Medical School also found that DMSO appeared to have "marked anti-inflammatory and pain-killing properties of its own." The curious ability of DMSO to travel rapidly throughout the body was first noticed by a laboratory assistant at the University of Oregon who, spilling a small amount of the liquid on his hand, noticed, a few minutes later, a "sweet or oysterlike taste. This indicated that the compound had spread through his body." Researchers at the university medical school described the drug as having many applications; when tested on patients, dimethyl sulfoxide was effective as a tranquilizer and as a painkiller and alleviated the symptoms of such ailments as the "common cold, headache and arthritis . . . [and] the pain of skeletal-muscular injuries including sprains and bruises." Most significant of all, DMSO had the "ability in animal experiments to enhance the absorption of at least one cancer-treating drug."[28]

The commercial potential of such a multi-purpose drug led to the

[27] Silverman and Lee, *Pills, Profits, and Politics*, 89–94, 94–98, 113–115.
[28] Robert K. Plumb, "Multipurpose Drug Reported on Coast," *New York Times*, 18 De-

rapid signing of an agreement between the Oregon State Board of Higher Education (which oversaw the University of Oregon) and the Crown Zellerbach Corporation (which had supplied the university with DMSO) to divide equally all future profits from the commercial distribution of the drug. Further research demonstrated not only that DMSO had other medical uses, such as the relief of respiratory allergies and the alleviation of bursitis, but also that it was valuable as an aid to the diffusion of agricultural chemicals and nutrients to crops and had applications in the treatment of animals. In short, dimethyl sulfoxide had all the attributes of a "miracle drug."[29]

For the Food and Drug Administration, mindful of the recent scandal surrounding thalidomide and aware of the mandate given by Congress to tighten controls on the manufacture and distribution of new drugs, the reports on DMSO poised an especial challenge. The effusive publicity given to dimethyl sulfoxide as a cure for a wide variety of ailments was a challenge because DMSO was freely available to the general public: DMSO had been used for years in industry as a solvent and there was little obstacle to obtaining even the purified form. Thus it was inevitable that the FDA should come under sustained pressure from a variety of interest groups to approve the drug as quickly as possible: pressure from the six pharmaceutical companies (Squibb, Schering, Syntex, Merck, Geigy, and Wyeth) licensed to market the drug; pressure from the medical community which was concerned over reports that patients were buying industrial grade DMSO; and pressure from patients who were anxious to use DMSO without running afoul of the law. At the very least, urgent action was imperative; reports were already arriving of "peddlers . . . [selling DMSO] outside arthritis clinics."[30]

In November 1965 reports from Wyeth Laboratories, a division of one of the pharmaceutical companies licensed to market DMSO, indicated that, in tests on laboratory animals, DMSO caused changes of the "refractive index of the animals' eyes." The Food and Drug Administration, on 11 November, immediately ordered a halt to the clinical testing of the drug on human patients and, to show that it meant business, began seizing supplies of DMSO that were being illegally sold by drug-stores.[31]

cember 1963; idem., "New Drug Hailed in Initial Testing: All-Purpose Agent is Studied in Humans on the Coast," New York Times, Sunday, 2 February 1964, sec. 1.

[29] Plumb, "Multipurpose Drug," New York Times, 18 December 1963; John A. Osmundsen, "Miracle Drug," New York Times, Sunday, 28 February 1965, sec. 4.

[30] Harold M. Schmeck Jr., "Scientists Decry Use of New Drug: Many Persons Testing DMSO on Themselves with no Supervision by Doctor," New York Times, 14 August 1965.

[31] Harold M. Schmeck Jr., "Testing of a Drug on Humans Halts: Changes in Eyes of Ani-

This zealous action by the officials of the FDA did not, however, allow the agency to escape censure by members of the House of Representatives when a Congressional hearing met in March 1966 to investigate the implementation of the 1962 Kefauver legislation on drug production and distribution. James L. Goddard, who had been appointed the new commissioner of the FDA on 17 January with a mandate to enforce the 1962 legislation, acknowledged that the FDA had allowed improper testing of DMSO to go ahead; Goddard, who appeared before the Congressional subcommittee on 9 March, promised to expand his investigative force and to scrutinize new products submitted by pharmaceutical companies with greater care.[32]

Goddard's influence as commissioner of FDA had already been demonstrated: on 1 February the agency established a separate category for barbiturates and amphetamines to indicate that "special control and accounting procedures [were] . . . required." Five weeks later the FDA banned the "manufacture of hundreds of brands of antibiotic lozenges on the ground that they had not been shown effective against sore throats as claimed" and on 18 March Goddard announced that special controls were to be placed on sixteen popular drugs including the tranquilizers valium, librium, and placidyl. Even more draconian was the announcement that all drugs approved by the FDA between 1938 and 1962 had to be re-submitted to the agency: "drug makers [must] show not only that their product is safe, but also that it does what they claim."[33]

While the necessity for drug regulation might have seemed to some self-evident after the thalidomide tragedy, in fact the new regulations of the FDA stirred up considerable debate not primarily on the grounds of efficacy or need but on more philosophical questions relating to the liberty of the individual. The medical community, through its representative organization, the American Medical Association, had long contested any suggestion of the nationalization of medicine along the lines effected by Aneurin Bevan in Britain in 1948; the AMA was also adamantly opposed to restrictions placed on the right of physicians to conduct clinical tests of new drugs.

The debate over drug regulation by the federal government reached its climax at a conference sponsored by the New York Academy of Sci-

mals Given DMSO Brings Curb on Trials with People," *New York Times*, 12 November 1965; "Experimental Drug Confiscated Here," *Philadelphia Inquirer*, 4 December 1965.

[32] Jane E. Brody, "Drug Agency Head Concedes Laxity: Tells House Unit Testing of 2 Preparations was Faulty," *New York Times*, 10 March 1966.

[33] Walter Sullivan, "Drugs Approved before '62 Face Rescreening," *New York Times*, 19 March 1966.

ences. Held at the Waldorf-Astoria and attended by several hundred physicians from around the world, the March 1966 conference on the use of dimethyl sulfoxide featured seventy-nine presentations by research workers and clinicians. The meeting, which had been organized six months previously, gained a particular significance by virtue of its coincidence with Senate hearings on the 1962 Kefauver drug legislation. While the conference had originally been planned by its organizer, Chauncey D. Leake, a former president of the AAAS and a professor of pharmacology at the University of California, as a forum for the exchange of information on the effects of DMSO, its serendipitous coincidence with the Senate hearings had the effect of putting pressure on the FDA at a crucial moment. While Joseph F. Sadusk Jr., a medical director at the FDA, was reporting to the Senate committee that twenty-four patients had suffered "double vision, decrease in vision, conjunctivitis, pain, vitreous opacity, increased relucency, and scotomas" after being treated with DMSO by private physicians, the clinicians gathered at the Waldorf-Astoria were reporting that, while they too had found deleterious effects on the eyes, they were convinced that these results were not sufficiently proven for the FDA to continue its ban on clinical testing of DMSO.[34]

Thus Dan Gordon, an ophthalmologist at the New York Hospital, in a presentation at the Academy conference on applications of DMSO on patients, reported that "the results were so variable and unpredictable . . . [that] no statistical conclusions could be drawn." Other reports to the Academy conference discussed the metabolism of DMSO, its absorption and distribution through the body, and its therapeutic value when combined with other drugs. Eduardo Ramírez, a physician at the Universidad Peruana in Lima, reported that DMSO was useful in treating schizophrenics on account of its ability to alter the "permeability of the blood-brain barrier, the neuronal or the vesicle membrane," while John T. Mallams, a radiologist at Baylor University at Dallas, reported to the Academy conference that DMSO seemed to be useful in treating heart attack victims.[35]

The issue before the participants at the conference was not so much the efficacy of dimethyl sulfoxide—even Arthur Ruskin, a deputy di-

[34] "Charge, Countercharge over Controversial DMSO," *Medical World News*, 8 April 1966, 29.

[35] Dan M. Gordon, "Dimethyl Sulfoxide in Ophthalmology, with Especial References to Possible Toxic Effects," *Annals of the New York Academy of Sciences* 141(1967): 399; Eduardo Ramírez and Segisfredo Luza, "Dimethyl Sulfoxide in the Treatment of Mental Patients," ibid., 665; J. W. Finney et al., "Protection of the Ischemic Heart with DMSO Alone or DMSO with Hydrogen Peroxide," ibid., 231–241.

rector of the FDA who took part in the conference, admitted that there was no conclusive proof linking DMSO with the twenty-four reports of eye damage in patients—but rather the extent of the control by the federal government over the testing of new substances by physicians. The restriction of DMSO was a consequence of the insistence by Congress that there should be no more disasters like that of thalidomide; the FDA, which took its orders from Congress, was keen to ban any drug at the slightest suspicion that it might have harmful side-effects. For the physicians, however, the expanded powers of the FDA represented an unwarranted invasion of their professional integrity; the Food and Drug Administration had no business interfering with the self-regulation of physicians.[36]

In his remarks at the conference organized by the New York Academy of Sciences, Chauncey Leake, who chaired the proceedings throughout, forcefully expressed the sentiments of many of the physicians present; Leake, in an explicit rebuff to the FDA, claimed that physicians, as "trustworthy and dedicated members of a sophisticated society . . . [were] qualified to decide whether or not a certain drug should be administered." According to Leake, the role of the federal government should involve not the regulation of the medical community but the dissemination of information on new drugs; the physician, employing his professional expertise, would use this information to make a decision on the efficacy of a new drug.[37]

James Goddard, the commissioner of the FDA, readily acknowledged the resistance of the medical community to his regulatory powers; he also knew of the close, almost symbiotic, relationship that existed between the pharmaceutical companies and a large number of clinicians. In particular Goddard pointed to the common practice of using clinical facilities in large hospitals to test new drugs; this system, which involved the payment of grants to physicians by pharmaceutical companies to test new drugs, was clearly open to abuse. Proposals to alleviate the problem, most notably the establishment of an impartial institute to test new

[36] "Charge, Countercharge," *Medical World News*, 8 April 1966, 29. See also Harold M. Schmeck Jr., "New Data Shed Light on the Baffling Drug DMSO," *New York Times*, 15 March 1966; idem., "DMSO to be Tried on Heart Victims: Chemical Helped Animals Survive Massive Attack," *New York Times*, 16 March 1966; "DMSO is Suggested in Malaria Control," *New York Times*, 17 March 1966. For a synoptic overview of the impact of federal regulation, see Jerome E. Schnee, "Governmental Control of Therapeutic Drugs: Intent, Impact, and Issues," in *The Pharmaceutical Industry: Economics, Performance, and Government Regulation*, ed. Cotton M. Lindsay (New York: John Wiley & Sons, 1978), 9–21.

[37] Sullivan, "Drugs Approved," *New York Times*, 19 March 1966.

drugs, had foundered on the reluctance of drug companies to reveal trade secrets which could be leaked to competing pharmaceutical firms. Goddard, naturally enough, rejected such schemes and persisted in demanding the stringent application of FDA regulations on new drugs.[38]

For the New York Academy of Sciences—which had been taken unawares by the controversy surrounding the conference on DMSO—the unfortunate coincidence between the Senate subcommittee hearings and the Academy meeting (a coincidence that gave the impression of a tendentious sympathy for the medical community and against the FDA) provided the stimulus for the later adoption of more stringent guidelines for Academy conferences and publications. A consequence of the DMSO meeting was the decision by the Academy to put a greater distance between itself and the pharmaceutical companies; the Academy, in subsequent years, only agreed to sponsor a conference if the organizers had obtained the necessary support from several institutions.

The controversy surrounding the DMSO conference was, regardless of the merit of the arguments of each protagonist, a suitable indicator of the vitality and energy of the New York Academy of Sciences in the 1960s. Under the leadership of Eunice Miner the Academy had transformed itself from a small scientific group with a strictly local impact into an organization with thousands of members who participated not only through the many sectional meetings but also through the approximately twenty international conferences held every year.

The success of the Academy's principal activities—the sectional meetings, the publication of the *Annals*, and the international conferences—was the spur for the launching of a campaign for a World Science Center. Eunice Miner, the indefatigable leader of all Academy projects, first seized on the idea of a Science Center as early as 1959; Miner's concept involved the centralization of meeting-rooms, libraries, and communications facilities for a wide variety of "societies, foundations, institutions, corporations and other organizations affiliated with or allied to science."[39]

Not until 1964—after Miner had extensively canvassed the scheme among prominent leaders of New York's political and cultural institutions—did the planned Science Center become a matter of public knowledge. The president of the Academy that year, J. Joseph Lynch, was a

[38] A perceptive contemporaneous analysis of the issue of regulation and control can be found in Walter Sullivan, "Drugs Approved Before '62 Face Rescreening," *New York Times*, 19 March 1966.

[39] Eunice Thomas Miner to Margaret Mead, 13 May 1960, NYAS Folder (1959–1965), Box E100, Organizations File, Margaret Mead Papers, Library of Congress (hereafter cited as LC).

staunch supporter of Miner and had previously agreed that, when his term of office expired at the end of the year, he would continue as the head of the building campaign. Lynch, a Jesuit priest who taught seismology at Fordham University, had studied in the Netherlands and at Oxford University; after his ordination in Dublin in 1926 he had moved to the United States where he commenced a teaching career. In addition to his prominent position within the leadership of the New York Academy of Sciences, Lynch was also a leading member of the American Association for the Advancement of Science and the American Geographical Society. Apparently there was no contradiction between his scientific work and his religious beliefs for, as he told a reporter on his election to the presidency of the Academy: "the laws of nature are written deep in the folds and faults of the earth. By encouraging men to learn those laws one can lead them further to a knowledge of the Author of all laws."[40]

The campaign for the World Science Center began auspiciously in August 1964. Miner and Lynch had been careful to canvass an impressive array of supporters; their efforts were capped by the endorsement of Robert F. Wagner, mayor of New York, who heralded the news of the World Science Center as a "great step forward in the furtherance of natural scientific investigation in all its disciplines . . . [and] a tremendous development for the people of New York City, our educational institutions, our science-oriented businesses, and our youth." Wagner's endorsement, which was invaluable in attracting the attention of the city's newspapers as well as stimulating the interest of other scientific institutions that might participate in the project, came with a promise that the city would fall in enthusiastically with the project: "please be assured that my administration will do everything that it properly can to aid you and the Academy in this enterprise."[41]

The location of the new building seemed equally auspicious. The Academy had arranged to buy a site on the east side of Broadway between Sixty-third and Sixty-fourth streets; the land was owned by Columbia and on 9 September 1964 the title to the land passed from the university to the Academy. It was a bold step; at a press conference held to give details on the World Science Center, J. Joseph Lynch announced that the Academy would construct not only a 32-story main building but a "second, smaller building adjacent to the Center [that] will house an 1,800-seat auditorium." The Science Center itself would have three smaller auditoriums "equipped with simultaneous translation facilities

[40] "Fordham Seismologist: John Joseph Lynch," New York Times, 5 December 1963.
[41] Robert F. Wagner to J. Joseph Lynch, 5 August 1964, NYAS folder (1959–1965), Box E100, Organizations File, Margaret Mead Papers, LC.

for international conferences, with demonstration laboratories and with closed circuit television." Lynch noted, in his remarks to the press, that the new site was directly opposite Lincoln Center; it was easily accessible from all parts of the city; and, last but not least, the proposed Science Center would be a considerable addition to an area that already contained many of New York's most prominent cultural institutions. In sum, it was, as a reporter for the *Real Estate Weekly* remarked, "one of the most significant Manhattan free sales in some years."[42]

A recurrent theme in subsequent announcements of the campaign emphasized that the Academy, which had witnessed an exponential expansion of all its activities in the past decade, had outgrown its present headquarters in the Woolworth mansion on Sixty-third Street. The Academy, during the 1960s, was sponsoring almost thirty conferences annually and was distributing to its membership and to libraries around the world almost forty thousand copies of the *Annals* each year. In 1961 the Academy had begun publication of a magazine, *The Sciences*, that was distributed to the twenty-three thousand members; in addition the number of Academy sections had recently grown to sixteen. In short, it was evident to all that the Academy would greatly benefit from a larger headquarters.

Eunice Miner, who was anticipating, after more than thirty years service for the Academy as executive director, that she would soon hand over the reins to a successor, was hopeful that the Science Center would be ready by the Academy's sesquicentennial in 1967. With anticipated assistance from the New York state legislature as well as the support promised by Robert Wagner as mayor of the city, Miner looked to attract funding from private industry and from those other scientific organizations that would use the World Science Center as a headquarters. In her appeal to these various constituencies the matriarch of the Academy gave emphasis not only to the present but also to the future consequences of scientific development: "science has only scratched the surface of the potential benefits to come. The slightest endeavor in scientific research ultimately expands on a universal basis for the benefit of mankind."[43]

Unfortunately the enormous cost of the proposed building—an anticipated twenty-five million dollars—and the reluctance of the state legisla-

[42] "Science Group buys Land for Center," *New York Times*, 10 September 1964; Joseph R. Hixson, "A Skyscraper Science Center: Planned for Broadway and the 60s," *Herald Tribune* (New York), 24 August 1964; "Science Center Pact Signed," *Real Estate Weekly*, 17 September 1964. See also "Academy of Sciences Will Build a 21-Story Center at Lincoln Sq.," *New York Times*, 24 August 1964.

[43] James L. Kilgallen, "Science Center Dream Ready to Come True," *Journal American* (New York), 17 September 1964.

26. THE WORLD SCIENCE CENTER. Planned to open during the sesquicentennial year of the Academy, this proposed World Science Center building was never completed, largely on account of financial difficulties. Situated opposite Lincoln Center, it was intended to serve as the headquarters for numerous scientific organizations. (*Courtesy of the New York Academy of Sciences.*)

ture to act on a crucial piece of legislation created hesitancy on the part of sympathetic corporations and individuals to commit major sums of money to the project. The governor of New York, Nelson Rockefeller, was keenly interested in the success of the World Science Center; in a letter to the president of the Academy, Rockefeller wrote that the Science Center would "fill a highly important need in our City and State. . . . I am well aware of the benefits that will accrue from the more rapid communication among scientists that the World Science Center will bring about." Rockefeller was as good as his word; in the summer of 1965 he helped shepherd an amendment to the Dormitory Act through the Senate and Assembly that would have provided for partial state funding for the Science Center. The funds from Albany, however, could, under the terms of the original legislation, only be released at the discretion of the state commission charged with overseeing the execution of the Dormitory Act. Part of the requirement stipulated to the Academy in the early part of 1966 by the commission demanded that the Academy raise $250,000 from "membership sources alone . . . within ninety days." For the Academy it mattered little that the commission's sudden requirement was a consequence of political maneuvering in Albany among the different groups concerned; after asking the general membership for financial support of the World Science Center throughout the previous two years, it proved impossible to raise the necessary sum in so short a period.[44]

This blow was followed, a few months later, by a second setback. The recent inauguration of the Metropolitan Opera Hall at Lincoln Center—a facility designed to accommodate almost four thousand people—had contributed to immense traffic jams in the vicinity of Lincoln Center; on nights when the Philharmonic Hall, the New York State Theater, and the Vivian Beaumont Theater were all in use, almost eleven thousand people congregated at Lincoln Center. As a consequence of this seemingly intractable problem, the City Planning Commission announced tentative plans to build an underground garage on Broadway between Sixty-third and Sixty-fourth streets. In an interview with the *New York Times*, a spokesman for the City Planning Commission announced that "the city would acquire the land by condemnation proceedings."[45]

[44] Nelson A. Rockefeller to J. Joseph Lynch, 6 October 1964, NYAS Folder (1959–1965), Box E100, Organizations File, Margaret Mead Papers, LC; Eunice Thomas Miner and Emerson Day to Margaret Mead, 23 August 1965, NYAS Folder (1959–1965), Box E100, Organizations File, Margaret Mead Papers, LC; Circular letter from Margaret Mead to the Academy membership, 5 April 1966, Box E100, Organizations File, Margaret Mead Papers, LC.

[45] Don Sullivan, "Lincoln Center Weighs Means to Counter Traffic Congestion," *New York Times*, 17 October 1966.

For the New York Academy of Sciences it was small consolation that, in the same report, the spokesman for the City Planning Commission emphasized that the "project was 'only in the talking stage' and . . . that no target date, even for a recommendation, has been fixed for it" for, as the Academy quickly realized, the article in the *Times* was cause for a rumor to spread that the World Science Center would have to be abandoned. As J. Joseph Lynch informed the Academy's Board of Trustees at a meeting two days after the appearance of the *Times* article, the announcement of the City Planning Commission "had become a serious deterrent to the efforts that were being made to obtain additional funds, especially with those foundations and corporations where a close appeal for major donations was under consideration." The eventual demise of the World Science Center was a consequence of unfavorable circumstances; the officers of the Academy, towards the end of 1966, reluctantly accepted the unavoidable fact that insufficient support for the project meant an indefinite postponement of their ambition.[46]

The cancellation of the Science Center, in a paradoxical manner, served to display the resilience of the Academy, for, in the early months of the following year, the plans for the celebration of the sesquicentennial of the founding of the Academy were set in motion. Eunice Miner, in a circular letter to the membership, noted that fifty years previously, the centennial celebration had been cancelled because the "nation was at war and a national spirit of austerity made it impossible to celebrate such large events. As we move into our sesquicentennial, our nation is again at war, but . . . having missed the celebration of our Centennial, we should double our efforts to make up for the loss with a Sesquicentennial Celebration that will be long remembered."[47]

The Vietnam War and the widespread opposition within the United States to the government's foreign policy did not leave the Academy entirely unscathed. Both Lyndon Baines Johnson and Secretary of Defense Robert McNamara had to decline invitations to speak at the sesquicentennial celebration on account of prior engagements. Unfortunately for the Academy a conference held at the Waldorf-Astoria as part of the celebration coincided with an address inside the hotel by Secretary of State Dean Rusk before the National Association of Manufacturers; a large and hostile crowd that had gathered outside the Waldorf-Astoria was, as

[46] Sullivan, "Lincoln Center," *New York Times*, 17 October 1966; Minutes of the Board of Trustees of the New York Academy of Sciences, 19 October 1966, NYAS.

[47] Circular Letter from Eunice Thomas Miner to the membership, 12 December 1966, NYAS.

the reporter from the *New York Times* wryly remarked, uttering "cries of discontent."[48]

The invective directed at Rusk did not otherwise disturb the sesquicentennial celebrations. On the first day, Tuesday, 5 December, the gathering was addressed by, *inter alios*, Nelson Rockefeller (on the relationship between science and government), Marshall McLuhan (on communications in the electronic age), and by the vice-president of General Electric, Hilliard W. Paige (on earth orbiting satellites, lunar and interplanetary exploration). During the second day of the conference the speakers discussed the future of science and its implications for society; interestingly enough, the proceedings sparked a certain amount of controversy on the platform over the benefits of science. Glenn T. Seaborg, the chairman of the Atomic Energy Commission, provocatively "depicted abundant nuclear energy as ultimately bringing about a golden age," but René Dubos, a Nobel laureate and professor of environmental biomedicine at Rockefeller University, immediately countered this assertion with the claim that "energy, as presently used, adds to the devastation and makes the environment increasingly unfit for human life."[49]

It fell to Margaret Mead, vice-president of the New York Academy of Sciences and curator of ethnology at the American Museum of Natural History, to give an expanded critique of the discontent that dominated American life in the final years of the decade. Mead, who spoke on "Man and the Culture of Tomorrow," attributed the upheavals of the 1960s to the rapid pace of technological change and development; in the past, there had been opportunity for successive generations to mature but now, at a time when social institutions disappeared as quickly as they had arrived, there was no mechanism for the orderly transfer of power and authority to the younger generation. As a consequence, everything was dissolving into chaos: "the young realize that things will not be corrected in time . . . [there is] the cry of the citizen against a war for which he did not vote [and] the cry of the student against a curriculum in which he has no hand in shaping." The sesquicentennial celebrations in 1967 also included an "academic procession of representatives from about 100 universities and colleges" and, at the conclusion, a more informal birthday party in the banquet room of the Waldorf-Astoria.[50]

---

[48] Minutes of the Scientific Council of the New York Academy of Sciences, 27 October 1966, NYAS; Walter Sullivan, "Technology Held a Friend and Foe: Scientists Differ on Atom as Key to Golden Age," *New York Times*, 7 December 1967.

[49] Sullivan, "Technology Held a Friend and Foe," *New York Times*, 7 December 1967.

[50] Sullivan, "Technology Held a Friend and Foe," *New York Times*, 7 December 1967;

For the general membership of the Academy the sesquicentennial events of 1967 were a symbol of the Academy's renewed growth and prosperity; many members, however, shared a sentiment that the real celebration of the Academy's stature—one that had greater significance for the organization—came almost exactly one year later when, on the occasion of her retirement as executive director, the Academy held a gala tribute in honor of Eunice Miner. In the thirty-two years of her stewardship of the Academy, the organization had grown from a strictly local group of some three hundred members to an organization of 26,000 scientists from around the world. The international flavor of the Academy's activities was nicely captured at the symposium held in Miner's honor on 4 December 1968; Yuji Shibata, president of the Japan Academy of Sciences, Julius Speer, president of the German Research Association, and Grga Novak, president of the Yugoslav Academy of Sciences and Arts, each spoke on the conditions of science in their respective countries. Scientific institutions in the United States were also represented: Frank Fremont-Smith of the Smithsonian Institution spoke in appreciation of Eunice Miner's contribution to the sciences in America, Albert Szent-Györgyi of the Marine Biological Laboratory at Woods Hole spoke on the intellectual relationships between the sciences in the twentieth century, and to end the program on a fitting note, Margaret Mead, a close friend of Miner ever since they had worked together at the American Museum of Natural History as research assistants, gave a talk to the assembled scientists that evoked a spirit of comradeship that had endured for more than three decades.[51]

The departure of Eunice Miner quickly demonstrated her importance for, in the two years after her retirement, the Academy experienced considerable constitutional difficulties. The principal problem arose from the exceptional quality of Miner's leadership; for three decades she had presided over the Academy's affairs by sheer force of will and, as a consequence, had knitted the various constitutional bodies of the Academy, most notably the Board of Trustees and the Scientific Council, into a unified administration. As Edmund Blake, a trustee of the Academy, put it, Eunice Miner had "provided the strong leadership which welded the diverse elements together. However, this was accomplished entirely by her personality and not by an organization of well-defined and good

---

Walter Sullivan, "Academy of Sciences Observes an Anniversary," *New York Times*, 6 December 1967.

[51] Program of Events in Honor of Eunice Miner, 4 December 1968, General Activities Box (1968–1970), NYAS.

administrative leadership support. When she left the scene, a large vacuum occurred."[52]

The principal difficulty arose out of a conflict between the Scientific Council, the Board of Trustees, and the chairmen of the seventeen sections. The Board of Trustees, which had been established in 1959 as an advisory body to the Scientific Council to "handle business matters and give good business advice," had gradually expanded its mandate. When Eunice Miner retired, the trustees initiated the search for a new executive director without informing the Scientific Council. The latter body, which consisted of the officers of the Academy who were, by and large, scientists and physicians, naturally resented this *coup de main* by the businessmen and corporate executives who sat on the Board of Trustees. In time, however, both organizations perceived the superfluity of two administrative groups and, not long after the dispute had first broken out, harmony was restored by their merger into a single Board of Governors.[53]

[52] Edmund J. Blake Jr. to Margaret Mead, 7 August 1968, Box E100, Organizations File, Margaret Mead Papers, LC.

[53] Report of a Meeting of the Committee on Organization and Rules, 12 August 1968.

Epilogue

IN RECENT DECADES there has been a significant increase in the interest of the literate public in science and scientific affairs. This interest, fueled by the increasing domination of modern life by science and technology and exemplified by such diverse phenomena as the exploration of space, the ubiquity of the personal computer, and advances in medical care, has stimulated an unprecedented concern with the impact of science on society. Science is now no longer the province of a small elite; in the contemporary world science has become accessible to a vast audience through popular magazines, books, and television. For the New York Academy of Sciences, the heightened interest of an enlarged audience for science has resulted in an enormous expansion of membership, activities, and publications.

During the past twenty years the Academy has maintained its primary purpose, the publication of the *Annals* and the consequent dissemination of scientific research to an international community of scientists. The Academy has sponsored approximately eighteen conferences each year on a variety of topics covering all of the major medical and scientific disciplines including such diverse specialties as neurobiology, psychology, mathematics, organic chemistry, anthropology, and material sciences. Most of the papers presented at the Academy conferences have subsequently been published in the *Annals*; in 1981 a more systematic effort was initiated by the Academy to publish also the proceedings of non-Academy conferences, a move prompted by the conviction that, in this way, the membership would become more aware of advances in science that would not otherwise come to its notice. Thus, in the past few years, the Academy has acquired series on, *inter alia*, Enzyme Engineering; Biochemical Engineering; and the Texas Symposia on Relativistic Astrophysics. The growth of Academy activities is clearly evident in the publication of the *Annals*: during 1972, fourteen volumes were published; seventeen years later the Academy published thirty-three volumes with a total of fourteen thousand pages. A less precise measure of success has been the distribution of its publications in an international market: in 1986 the *Annals* were exhibited at book fairs in Moscow, Frankfurt, and Beijing and were distributed to the eight thousand Academy members living outside the United States. A second major publication of the Academy, the magazine *The Sciences*, has earned a growing reputation for the presentation of science in a lively and accessible manner. In recent years the success of *The Sciences* has earned it the National Magazine Award in addition to awards from the Society of Publication Designers and the American Association of Museums.

Science in the modern world is conspicuous not only for its ubiquity and size but also for its fragmentation into increasingly esoteric specialties. For the Academy this phenomenon has meant a growth in the number of its sections which, in the present decade, range from anthropology to science education and include, *inter alia*, economics, geological sciences, inorganic chemistry, microbiology, neuroscience, polymer science, and psychology. During the 1980s the twenty-four sections have held an annual total of approximately one hundred and seventy lectures; these evening presentations have been attended by a total audience of ten thousand each year. Speakers have included such luminaries as Isaac Asimov, Edward Teller, Donald Johanson, Barry Commoner, and Victor Weisskopf; the list of subjects has ranged from the arcane minutiae of specialized research to considerations of the effect of science on society. In the latter respect the focus of the Academy's attention over the past fifteen years has been pronounced: the biomedical sciences section has sponsored series of talks on the acquired immune deficiency syndrome; the environmental sciences section has held meetings on low-level ionizing radiation, hazardous waste, and the health effects of electrical and magnetic fields; the engineering section has presented lectures on problems of pollution control; and the science and public policy section has featured speakers on Agent Orange, United States arms control policies, and legal issues connected with new technologies.

Two committees of the Academy, the women in science committee and the human rights committee, both founded in the 1970s, have been particularly concerned with emphasizing an activist role for the Academy in the wider world. The women in science committee, established in 1977, has found a distinct resonance among the membership. Seminars and symposia on the status of women scientists in engineering, computer science, immunology, pharmacology, and health sciences have recorded enthusiastic responses; members of the committee have testified before the Committee on Labor and Human Resources of the United States Senate; and, last but not least, the committee has worked for the release of women scientists imprisoned in Latin America. The latter project has served as a complement to the work of the Academy's human rights committee which, over the past decade and a half, has espoused the cause of scientists exiled or imprisoned in Uruguay, Chile, South Africa, Argentina, El Salvador, Poland, and the Soviet Union. The Academy, in conjunction with such organizations as the National Academy of Sciences and the American Association for the Advancement of Science, has sponsored fact-finding missions to El Salvador and Uruguay to report on the murder and imprisonment by the armed forces of physicians and health workers. The human rights committee has also focussed considerable attention on the Soviet Union, most notably, in protesting the internal exile of Andrei Sakharov in 1980 to the closed city of Gorky and in publishing the work of dissident scientists who have been removed from academic positions.

A concern for the rights of scientists around the world, reflects, at least in part, the belief that science, in its universality, knows no boundaries. The cosmopolitan character of the Academy is a relatively recent phenomenon; it has found expression not only in the membership (twenty percent of the members live outside the United States) but also in its conferences which attract speakers from around the world. This growing presence of the Academy on the international stage has not, however, resulted in a diminution of its role on the local scene. In this respect the Academy has expanded its educational activities within the city and the state with an eye to combatting a perceived failure of the American educational system to develop a literate scientific public. Thus, in 1974, the Academy, at the request of School District No. 4 in Manhattan, initiated a program that aimed to bring members of the Academy into high schools to talk about science; with the financial assistance of interested corporations, scientists from industry and academe went to high schools to demonstrate their specialties. Within three years, other school districts in the Bronx, Queens, and Manhattan had indicated their desire to participate in the scheme and the Academy, under the auspices of the educational advisory committee, formally created the Scientists in Schools Program that, by 1983, reached out to all school districts in the metropolitan area. A second innovation in science education began in 1979 when the Academy initiated a summer internship program that placed a small group of high school students into paid research positions. This project, formally known as the Science Research Training Program, began by sending students to work in such local institutions as the American Museum of Natural History, New York University, Mount Sinai Hospital, and City College. By 1984 the program, with the help of a grant from the state legislature, had spread to Westchester, Herkimer, Rockland, and Oneida counties and had sparked interest in the creation of similar programs in other regions of New York State. Finally, and closer to home, the Junior Academy of Sciences, an organization for high school students modelled after the Academy, enrolls approximately fifteen hundred members; the Junior Academy offers a variety of lectures, symposia, and field-trips.

In the late twentieth century, the New York Academy of Sciences is a vastly different institution from the organization established in 1817 by Samuel Latham Mitchill and his small coterie of disciples at the College of Physicians and Surgeons. In one regard, this comes as no surprise: the Academy has been primarily a reflection of its intellectual and social context and, as science has changed over the years, so the Academy has gradually altered its activities, membership, and structure. Yet it would be wrong to imagine that this process was effected in any purely mechanistic fashion for, as I have attempted to show in the preceding pages, the conscious choices and strategies adopted by individuals had a significant part to play in determining the institutional structure of science in New York City. Max Weber's statement that individuals are "endowed with the capacity and the will to take a deliberate attitude toward the world" has lost none of its force; within the necessary framework provided by a material world and its past, the actions of individuals have possessed considerable force in the shaping of social and intellectual change.[1]

---

[1] Max Weber, "Die 'Objektivität' sozialwissenschaftlicher und sozialpolitischer Erkenntnis," *Archiv für Sozialwissenschaft und Sozialpolitik*, n.s., 1(1904): 55.

Select Bibliography

ABERBACH, ALAN DAVID. *In Search of an American Identity: Samuel Latham Mitchill, Jeffersonian Nationalist*, American University Studies, vol. 46. New York: Peter Lang, 1988.

ALDRICH, MICHELE. "New York Natural History Survey, 1836-1845." Ph.D. diss., University of Texas-Austin, 1974.

ALLEN, GARLAND. *Thomas Hunt Morgan: The Man and his Science*. Princeton, NJ: Princeton University Press, 1978.

BAATZ, SIMON. "Philadelphia Patronage: The Institutional Structure of Natural History in the New Republic, 1800-1833." *Journal of the Early Republic* 8(1988): 111-138.

BALTZELL, E. DIGBY. *Puritan Boston and Quaker Philadelphia: Two Protestant Ethics and the Spirit of Class Authority and Leadership*. New York: Free Press, 1979.

BATES, RALPH S. *Scientific Societies in the United States*, 2d ed. Cambridge, MA: Massachusetts Institute of Technology, 1958.

BELL, WHITFIELD J., JR. "The American Philosophical Society as a National Academy of Sciences, 1780-1846." *Proceedings of the Tenth International Congress of the History of Science* 10(1962): 165-177.

BENDER, THOMAS. *New York Intellect: A History of Intellectual Life in New York City.* New York: Alfred A. Knopf, 1987.

——. *Toward an Urban Vision: Ideas and Institutions in Nineteenth Century America.* 1975; reprint, Baltimore: Johns Hopkins University Press, 1982.

BERKELEY, EDMUND and DOROTHY SMITH BERKELEY. *George William Featherstonhaugh: The First U.S. Government Geologist.* Tuscaloosa, AL: University of Alabama Press, 1988.

BÖTTCHER, HELMUTH M. *Miracle Drugs: A History of Antibiotics.* Translated by Einhert Kawerau. London: Heinemann, 1963.

BROWN, CHANDOS. *Benjamin Silliman: A Life in the Young Republic.* Princeton, NJ: Princeton University Press, 1989.

BROWN, WILLIAM ADAMS. *Morris Ketchum Jesup: A Character Sketch.* New York: Charles Scribner's Sons, 1910.

BROWNE, JULIUS HENRI. *The Great Metropolis: A Mirror of New York.* Hartford, CT, 1869.

BRUCE, ROBERT V. *The Launching of Modern American Science, 1846–1876.* New York: Alfred A. Knopf, 1987.

BURGESS, JOHN W. *Reminiscences of an American Scholar: The Beginnings of Columbia University.* New York: Columbia University Press, 1934.

COLBERT, EDWIN H. and KATHARINE BENEKER. "The Paleozoic Museum in Central Park, or the Museum that Never Was." *Curator* 2(1959): 137–150.

COON, HORACE. *Columbia: Colossus on the Hudson.* New York: E.P. Dutton & Co., 1947.

COSENZA, MARIO EMILIO. *The Establishment of the College of the City of New York as the Free Academy in 1847: A Chapter in the History of Education.* New York: College of the City of New York Press, 1925.

CRAMPTON, HENRY E. *The Department of Zoology of Columbia University, 1892–1942.* New York: Columbia University Press, 1942.

DAIN, PHYLLIS. *The New York Public Library: A History of its Founding and Early Years.* New York: New York Public Library, 1972.

DALTON, JOHN C. *History of the College of Physicians and Surgeons.* New York, 1887.

DALZELL, ROBERT F., JR. *Enterprising Elite: The Boston Associates and the World They Made,* Harvard Studies in Business History, No. 40. Cambridge, MA: Harvard University Press, 1987.

DESMOND, ADRIAN J. "Central Park's Fragile Dinosaurs," *Natural History* 83(October 1974): 64–71.

DOLAN, ANNE MARIE. "The Literary Salon in New York, 1830–1860." Ph.D. diss., Columbia University, 1957.

DOWLING, HARRY F. *Fighting Infection: Conquests of the Twentieth Century.* Cambridge, MA: Harvard University Press, 1977.

DUPREE, A. HUNTER. *Asa Gray, 1810–1888.* Cambridge, MA: Harvard University Press, 1968.

——. *Science in the Federal Government: A History of Policies and Activities.* 1957; reprint, Baltimore: Johns Hopkins University Press, 1986.

FAIRCHILD, HERMAN LE ROY. *A History of the New York Academy of Sciences.* New York, 1887.

FLEMING, DONALD. *John William Draper and the Religion of Science.* Philadelphia: University of Pennsylvania Press, 1950.

FOORD, JOHN. *The Life and Public Services of Andrew Haswell Green.* New York: Doubleday, Page & Co., 1913.

FRANCIS, JOHN W. *Old New York or Reminiscences of the Past Sixty Years.* New York, 1858.

FULTON, JOHN. *Memoirs of Frederick A. P. Barnard.* New York, 1896.

GEIGER, ROGER L. *To Advance Knowledge: The Growth of American Research Universities, 1900–1940.* New York: Oxford University Press, 1986.

GREENE, JOHN C. *American Science in the Age of Jefferson.* Ames, IA: Iowa State University Press, 1984.

——. "The Development of Mineralogy in Philadelphia, 1780–1820." *Proceedings of the American Philosophical Society,* 113(1969): 283–295.

HALL, COURTNEY ROBERT. *A Scientist in the Early Republic: Samuel Latham Mitchill, 1764–1831.* New York: Columbia University Press, 1934.

HALL, PETER DOBKIN. *The Organization of American Culture, 1700–1900: Private Institutions, Elites, and the Origins of American Nationality.* New York: New York University Press, 1984.

HAMMACK, DAVID C. *Power and Society: Greater New York at the Turn of the Century.* 1982; reprint, New York: Columbia University Press, 1987.

HARRIS, JONATHAN. "DeWitt Clinton as Naturalist." *New-York Historical Society Quarterly* 56(1972): 265–284.

HEATON, CLAUDE EDWIN. *A Historical Sketch of New York University College of Medicine, 1841–1941.* New York: New York University Press, 1941.

HELLMAN, GEOFFREY. *Bankers, Bones & Beetles: The First Century of the American Museum of Natural History.* Garden City, NY: Natural History Press, 1968.

HILL, ROBERT T. *Cuba and Porto Rico.* New York, 1898.

HOPKINS, VIVIAN C. "The Empire State—DeWitt Clinton's Laboratory." *New-York Historical Society Quarterly* 59(1975): 7–44.

HOWE, WINIFRED E. *A History of the Metropolitan Museum of Art.* New York: Metropolitan Museum of Art, 1913.

INKSTER, IAN. "Robert Goodacre's Astronomy Lectures (1823–25), and the Structure of Scientific Culture in Philadelphia." *Annals of Science* 35(1978): 353–363.

JAHER, FREDERIC COPLE. *The Urban Establishment: Upper Strata in Boston, New York, Charleston, Chicago, and Los Angeles.* Urbana, IL: University of Illinois Press, 1982.

JAMES, MARY ANN. *Elites in Conflict: The Antebellum Clash over the Dudley Observatory.* New Brunswick, NJ: Rutgers University Press, 1987.

JONES, THEODORE FRANCIS, ed. *New York University, 1832–1932.* New York: New York University Press, 1933.

JULY, ROBERT W. *The Essential New Yorker: Gulian Crommelin Verplanck.* Durham, NC: Duke University Press, 1951.

KASS, ALVIN. *Politics in New York State, 1800–1830.* Syracuse, NY: Syracuse University Press, 1965.

KENNEDY, JOHN MICHAEL. "Philanthropy and Science in New York City: The American Museum of Natural History, 1868–1968." Ph.D. diss., Yale University, 1968.

KEPPEL, FREDERICK PAUL. *Columbia.* New York: Oxford University Press, 1914.

KEVLES, DANIEL. *The Physicists: The History of a Scientific Community in Modern America.* New York: Vantage Books, 1979.

KOHLSTEDT, SALLY GREGORY. *The Formation of the American Scientific Community: The American Association for the Advancement of Science, 1848–60.* Urbana, IL: University of Illinois Press, 1976.

——. "International Exchange and National Style: A View of Natural History Museums in the United States, 1850–1900." In *Scientific Colonialism: A Cross-*

Cultural Comparison, edited by Nathan Reingold and Marc Rothenberg. Washington, D.C.: Smithsonian Institution Press, 1987.

KOHLSTEDT, SALLY GREGORY and MARGARET ROSSITER, eds. *Historical Writings on American Science*. Osiris, 2d ser., 1(1985).

LARSON, ROBERT LOURIE. "Charles Frederick Chandler: His Life and Work." Ph.D. diss., Columbia University, 1950.

LINDSAY, COTTON M., ed. *The Pharmaceutical Industry: Economics, Performance, and Government Regulation*. New York: John Wiley & Sons, 1978.

LURIE, EDWARD. *Louis Agassiz: A Life in Science*. Chicago: University of Chicago Press, 1960.

LYDENBERG, HARRY MILLER. *History of the New York Public Library: Astor, Lenox and Tilden Foundations*. 1923; reprint, Boston: Gregg Press, 1972.

LYNCH, DENNIS TILDEN. *"Boss" Tweed: The Story of a Grim Generation*. New York: Boni & Liveright, 1927.

MCALLISTER, ETHEL M. *Amos Eaton, 1776–1842: Scientist and Educator*. Philadelphia: University of Pennsylvania Press, 1941.

MACK, EDWARD C. *Peter Cooper: Citizen of New York*. New York: Duell, Sloan and Pearce, 1949.

MAHONEY, TOM. *The Merchants of Life: An Account of the American Pharmaceutical Industry*. New York: Harper & Brothers, 1959.

MALDONADO-DENIS, MANUEL. *Puerto Rico: A Socio-Historic Interpretation*. Translated by Elena Vialo. New York: Random House, 1972.

MATHEWS, JAMES M. *Recollections of Persons and Events*. New York, 1865.

MAZARAKI, GEORGE ALEXANDER. "The Public Career of Andrew Haswell Green." Ph.D. diss., New York University, 1966.

MERRILL, GEORGE P., ed. and comp. *Contributions to a History of American State Geological and Natural History Surveys*. Smithsonian Institution, United States National Museum Bulletin no. 109. Washington, D.C., 1920.

MILLER, HOWARD S. *Dollars for Research: Science and its Patrons in Nineteenth-Century America*. Seattle: University of Washington Press, 1970.

MORALES CARRÍON, ARTURO. *Puerto Rico: A Political and Cultural History*. New York: W.W. Norton, 1983.

NEVINS, ALLAN. *Abram S. Hewitt*. New York: Harper & Brothers, 1935.

NEVINS, ALLAN and MILTON HALSEY THOMAS, eds. *The Diary of George Templeton Strong*, 4 vols. New York: MacMillan Co., 1952.

NODYNE, KENNETH R. "The Founding of the Lyceum of Natural History." *Annals of the New York Academy of Sciences* 172(1970): 141–149.

———. "The Rise of DeWitt Clinton and the Municipal Government in the Development of Cultural Organizations in New York City, 1803–1817." Ph.D. diss., New York University, 1969.

NORWOOD, WILLIAM FREDERICK. *Medical Education in the United States before the Civil War*. Philadelphia: University of Pennsylvania Press, 1944.

OLESON, ALEXANDRA and SANBORN C. BROWN, eds. *The Pursuit of Knowledge in the Early American Republic: American Scientific and Learned Societies from Colonial Times to the Civil War*. Baltimore: Johns Hopkins University Press, 1976.

OSUNA, JOHN JOSEPH. *Education in Porto Rico.* New York: Teachers College, 1923.

PAULY, PHILIP J. "The Appearance of Academic Biology in Late Nineteenth-Century America." *Journal of the History of Biology* 17(1984): 369–397.

PORTER, CHARLOTTE M. "The Concussion of Revolution: Publications and Reform at the early Academy of Natural Sciences, Philadelphia, 1812–1842." *Journal of the History of Biology* 12(1979): 273–292.

——. *The Eagle's Nest: Natural History and American Ideas, 1812–1842.* University, AL: University of Alabama Press, 1986.

PRESTON, DOUGLAS J. *Dinosaurs in the Attic: An Excursion into the American Museum of Natural History.* New York: St. Martin's Press, 1986.

PUPIN, MICHAEL. *From Immigrant to Inventor.* New York: Charles Scribner's Sons, 1923.

RAINGER, RONALD. "Vertebrate Paleontology as Biology: Henry Fairfield Osborn and the American Museum of Natural History." In *The American Development of Biology,* edited by Ronald Rainger, Keith R. Benson, and Jane Maienschein. Philadelphia: University of Pennsylvania Press, 1988.

REDFIELD, JOHN HOWARD. *Recollections of John Howard Redfield.* n.p., 1900.

REINGOLD, NATHAN, ed. *Science in Nineteenth-Century America: A Documentary History.* Chicago: University of Chicago Press, 1964.

ROBBINS, CHRISTINE CHAPMAN. *David Hosack: Citizen of New York.* Memoirs of the American Philosophical Society, no. 62. Philadelphia, 1964.

RODGERS, ANDREW DENNY. *John Torrey: A Story of North American Botany.* Princeton: Princeton University Press, 1942.

ROPER, LAURA WOOD. *FLO: A Biography of Frederick Law Olmsted.* Baltimore: Johns Hopkins University Press, 1973.

RUDY, S. WILLIS. *The College of the City of New York: A History, 1847–1947.* New York: City College Press, 1949.

SILVERMAN, MILTON and PHILIP R. LEE. *Pills, Profits, and Politics.* Berkeley, CA: University of California Press, 1974.

SHAFER, HENRY BURNELL. *The American Medical Profession, 1783–1850.* New York: Columbia University Press, 1936.

SHRADY, JOHN, ed. *The College of Physicians and Surgeons: A History,* 2 vols. New York: Lewis Publishing Co., n.d. (1903).

SLOAN, DOUGLAS. "Science in New York City, 1867–1907." *Isis* 71(1980): 35–76.

SOKAL, MICHAEL M. "*Science* and James McKeen Cattell, 1894 to 1945." *Science* (4 July 1980): 43–48.

SPANN, EDWARD K. *The New Metropolis: New York City, 1840–1857.* New York: Columbia University Press, 1981.

STEWART, IAN R. "Central Park, 1851–1871: Urbanization and Environmental Planning in New York City." Ph.D. diss., Cornell University, 1973.

STOCKING, GEORGE W., JR. *The Shaping of American Anthropology, 1883–1911: A Franz Boas Reader.* New York: Basic Books, 1974.

STONE, BRUCE WINCHESTER. "The Role of the Learned Societies in the Growth of Scientific Boston, 1780–1848." Ph.D. diss., Boston University, 1974.

STOOKEY, BYRON. *A History of Colonial Medical Education in the Province of New York, With its Subsequent Development (1767–1830)*. Springfield, IL: Charles C Thomas, 1962.

SWETT, STEVEN C. "The Test of a Reformer: A Study of Seth Low, New York City Mayor, 1902–1903." *New-York Historical Society Quarterly* 44(1960): 5–41.

THACKRAY, ARNOLD. "Natural Knowledge in Cultural Context: The Manchester Model." *American Historical Review* 79(1974): 672–709.

THACKRAY, ARNOLD et al. *Chemistry in America, 1876–1976: Historical Indicators*. Boston: D. Reidel Publishing Co., 1985.

THOMAS, MILTON HALSEY. "The Gibbs Affair at Columbia in 1854." M.A. thesis, Columbia University, 1942.

TOMKINS, CALVIN. *Merchants and Masterpieces: The Story of the Metropolitan Museum of Art*. New York: E.P. Dutton & Co., 1970.

VEYSEY, LAURENCE R. *The Emergence of the American University*. Chicago: University of Chicago Press, 1965.

WAKSMAN, SELMAN A. *My Life with the Microbes*. New York: Simon and Schuster, 1954.

WREN, DANIEL A. "American Business Philanthropy and Higher Education in the Nineteenth Century." *Business History Review* 57(1983): 321–346.

WELLS, HENRY. *The Modernization of Puerto Rico: A Political Study of Changing Values and Institutions*. Cambridge, MA: Harvard University Press, 1969.

ZACHOS, J. C. *The Political and Financial Opinions of Peter Cooper*. New York, 1877.

MANUSCRIPT SOURCES

ACADEMY OF NATURAL SCIENCES, PHILADELPHIA
Isaac Lea Correspondence
Minutes, Academy of Natural Sciences
Lewis David von Schweinitz Collection

AMERICAN PHILOSOPHICAL SOCIETY, PHILADELPHIA
Franz Boas Papers
Reuben Haines III Papers

BOWDOIN COLLEGE, BRUNSWICK, ME
Parker Cleaveland Papers

COLUMBIA UNIVERSITY, NEW YORK CITY
Columbiana, Low Library

GENERAL THEOLOGICAL SEMINARY, NEW YORK CITY
John McVickar Papers

HARVARD UNIVERSITY, CAMBRIDGE, MA
Historic Letter File, Gray Herbarium

HISTORICAL SOCIETY OF PENNSYLVANIA, PHILADELPHIA
Ord-Peale Correspondence, Peale Papers

LIBRARY OF CONGRESS, WASHINGTON, D.C.
Margaret Mead Papers

MASSACHUSETTS HISTORICAL SOCIETY, BOSTON
John Collins Warren Papers

MANUSCRIPT SOURCES

MUSEUM NATIONAL D'HISTOIRE NATURELLE, PARIS
Adolphe Brongniart Correspondence

NEW YORK ACADEMY OF SCIENCES
Minutes of the Board of Trustees
Minutes of the Council
Minutes, Council of the Scientific Alliance
Minutes, Lyceum of Natural History
Minutes, New York Academy of Sciences
Minutes of the Puerto Rico Committee
Minutes of the Section of Biology
Minutes of the Section of Geology and Mineralogy
Puerto Rico Correspondence

NEW YORK BOTANICAL GARDEN, NEW YORK CITY
John Torrey Correspondence
Nathaniel Lord Britton Papers

NEW-YORK HISTORICAL SOCIETY, NEW YORK CITY
Albert Gallatin Papers

NEW YORK STATE LIBRARY, ALBANY, NY
Miscellaneous Letters

ROYAL SOCIETY OF LONDON
William Buckland Correspondence

YALE UNIVERSITY, NEW HAVEN, CT
Silliman Family Manuscripts

Index

References to illustrations are printed in italic type

Academy of Music, *90*, 91–93

Academy of Natural Sciences, 3, 17, 18, 73; compared to Lyceum of Natural History, 118; as democratic organization, 9; founding of, 16; as model for Lyceum of Natural History, 9, 19, 21; publishes journal, 34; and Puerto Rico survey, 209–210; sponsors lecture-series, 18

Adet, Pierre Auguste, 12

Agassiz, Louis, 74; establishes Museum of Comparative Zoology, 97–98

Agricultural Experiment Station (Puerto Rico), 206

Aitken, Robert T., 212

Akerly, Benjamin, 24–25

Albany Institute, 49

Albany Lyceum of Natural History, 49

Allen, George, 89

Allen, John A., 147

Allen, Timothy F., 125, 127

American Academy of Arts and Sciences, 4, 74; as patrician organization, 9

American Academy of the Fine Arts, 5–6, 37–38

American Association for the Advancement of Science, 67, 73–75, 120–121, 249; establishment of, 74; and New York Academy of Sciences, 128–131, 136

—— New York meeting, 128–131, *132*, 133–137; Biology Section, 135–136; Physics Sec-

tion, 133–135; significance of, 130, 135–136, 137; speech by Frederick Barnard at, 133

American Chemical Society, 119, 120, 158; establishment of, 119, 121–124; influence of, 124; opposition to, 120, 121–124; and Scientific Alliance, 148–149, 173

American Chemist, 119

American Ethnological Society, 196–197

American Geographical Society, 149

American Institute, 45, 52

American Institute of Mining Engineers, 122

American Journal of Science and Arts, 30–32, 35, 71, 72

American Mathematical Society: and Scientific Alliance, 171–172, 173

American Medical Association: and federal regulation of drugs, 234; first meeting of, 68–69; opposition to formation of, 69

American Mineralogical Journal, 30

American Monthly Magazine and Critical Review, 25, 32

American Museum of Natural History, 96, 117, 118, 140, 143, 149, 150, 168, 173, 177, 179; establishment of, 104–105; and New York Academy of Sciences, 221; and popularization of science, 171, 174; and Puerto Rico survey, 209; and Scientific Alliance, 174; scientific research at, 171; support for, 97

American Ornithologists' Union, 149

259

260 ANNALS NEW YORK ACADEMY OF SCIENCES

American Philosophical Society, 3, 5, 73; as national scientific society, 2; as patrician organization, 9, 16
American Psychological Association, 196–197
American scientific community: size of, in 1819, 32
American Society for the Diffusion of Knowledge, 45
Annals of the Lyceum of Natural History, 29, 35–37, 73; costs of publication of, 36–37
Annals of the New York Academy of Sciences, 219, 221, 247–248
Anthony, Harold E., 215, 218
antibiotics: aureomycin, 224–226; chloramphenicol, 230; conferences on, 223–229; neomycin, 226–227; penicillin, 224, 226, 228; streptomycin, 224, 226, 227; terramycin, 227–229
Archaeological Institute of America, 148–149
Armstrong, Clairette, 220
Asimov, Isaac, 248
Association of American Geologists, 67, 74
Association of American Geologists and Naturalists, 74
Astor Library, 159–160; unites with Lenox Library and Tilden Trust, 163–164
Audubon, John James, 33
Authors' Club, 46
Avery, Samuel P., 153

Bache, Alexander Dallas, 109
Bancroft, George, 85
Banks, Joseph, 15
Banvard, John, 98
Barber, Harry G., 209
Bard, Samuel, 11
Barnard, Frederick A.P., 110, 129, 131; and AAAS, 109, 133; biography of, 108–109, 111; at Columbia, 109, 111–112, 117; compares Columbia to City College, 112; and reform at Columbia, 109, 111
Barnes, John, 18
Barnum, P.T., 98
Baudoine, Ezekiel R., 20, 24
Beck, John B., 20
Beck, Lewis C., 53
Bedford, Gunning S., 69
Bellevue Hospital, 93
Bennett, James Gordon, 79

Berkey, Charles P., 189
Bickmore, Albert, 97–98
Bigelow, John, 162
Binney, Horace, 4
Blake, Edmund, 244
Blunt's American Coast Pilot, 72
Boas, Franz, 192; and American Museum of Natural History, 191, 193–194; appointed professor at Columbia, 194; biography of 190–191; as entrepreneur of science, 196–197; and New York Academy of Sciences, 194, 201; and Puerto Rico survey, 203, 212, 213
Bodley, Rachel L., 119–120
Bolton, H. Carrington, 147, 162; and Lyceum of Natural History, 120; opposes formation of American Chemical Society, 123; organizes Priestley centennial meeting, 119–121
Bonner, J. W., 213
Boston, 2; as cultural center, 3–4; scientific societies in, 74
Boston Society of Natural History, 74
Botanical Garden of Christiana, 210
Botanical Club of New York. See Torrey Botanical Club
Bowne, Jane, 16
Boyd, George W., 51
Braley, Alson E., 225
Brevoort, Henry, Jr., 40
Brevoort, J. Carson, 77
British Association for the Advancement of Science, 72, 74, 128–129, 191
Britton, Elizabeth Knight, 142–143, 208
Britton, Nathaniel Lord, 139, 144, 188; establishes New York Botanical Garden, 143, 145–147; and New York Academy of Sciences, 201; organizes Puerto Rico survey, 202–203, 204–206, 209–210, 214–216; and Scientific Alliance, 141–142, 147–150, 172, 173; and Tilden Trust, 159–160, 161–162, 163; and Torrey Botanical Club, 125; visits Puerto Rico, 204–206, 208
Brongniart, Adolphe, 35
Bronk, Detlev W., 223
Bronx Society of Arts and Sciences, 124
Brooklyn Entomological Society, 136, 174
Brooklyn Institute of Arts and Sciences, 149, 154

264 ANNALS NEW YORK ACADEMY OF SCIENCES

Lawrence, Abbott, 74
Lavoisier, Antoine, 11, 12
Leake, Chauncey D., 235, 236
LeConte, John, 22
Lederle Laboratories, 224–226
Ledyard, Lewis Cass, 163
Leeds, Albert, 123
Leidy, Joseph, 101
Leggett, William H., 125, 127
Lenox, James, 163–164
Lenox Library, 159–160; unites with Astor Library and Tilden Trust, 163–164
Le Roy, Peter V., 127
Lincoln Center, 239, 241
Linnaean Society of New England, 4
Linnaean Society of New York, 124, 139, 141, 149–150; and American Museum of Natural History, 174; and Scientific Alliance, 148
Linnaean Society of Philadelphia, 3
Love, E. G., 172
Low, Seth, 129, 146, 161, 163, 164, 179, 193–194; as fundraiser, 153–154; inauguration speech of, 152; and New York Academy of Sciences, 166; and science in New York, 154; and Scientific Alliance, 151, 154, 173
Lutz, Frank E., 208, 215
Lyceum of Natural History, 11, 25–26, 73, 75, 76; and Broadway hall, 43–46, 54, 55; building fund, 38, 43, 57, 77, 80–81; and Central Park, 83–86; changes name, 118; changing role of, in urban context, 105, 117–119; and College of Physicians and Surgeons, 19, 20–21; and Columbia, 88–89, 91; committee of publication, 32, 34–35, 36–37; comparison of, to Academy of Natural Sciences, 118; and Cooper Union, 82–83; destruction of, by fire, 92–93; economic crisis of, 53–55; establishment of, 9, 17, 19; lecture series, 22, 49, 54; and New York geological survey, 48, 50, 51–52, 74–75; and New-York Institution, 21–22, 37–38; and New York University, 38, 40, 63–64, 81, 83, 89; and Paleozoic Museum, 99, 103–104; and Priestley centennial meeting, 120; receives charter from state legislature, 25; scientific expedition of, 23–24. See also New York Academy of Sciences
Lynch, J. Joseph, 237–239, 242

MacCracken, Henry M., 129, 161
MacInnes, Duncan A., 219
Maclure, William, 34, 35, 36
MacNeven, Francis, 27
Mallams, John T., 235
Manly, Basil, 108
Marcy, William, 52
Maretzek, Max, 92
Martin, Daniel S., 139, 147
Mason, Cyrus, 63
Mason, J. Alden, 212, 213
Mathews, James M., 39, 40, 41
Maxwell, Hugh, 39
McKeen, John, 228
McLean, John, 12
McLuhan, Marshall, 243
McMillin, Emerson, 200, 206, 209; and Puerto Rico survey, 203
McMurtrie, William, 172
McNamara, Robert, 242
McVickar, John, 40
McVickar, William A., 109
Mead, Margaret, 243, 244
Mechanics' Institute, 43, 45, 52
medical community (New York): factional disputes within, 21
medicine: relationship of, to science, 21
Mercantile Library, 159–160
Metropolitan Museum of Art, 96, 104
Meyerhoff, Howard, 211, 215
Michelson, Albert A., 133–135; and experiment on luminiferous ether, 134–135
Miner, Eunice Thomas, 217, 220, 222, 223, 237, 242, 245; appointed executive secretary of New York Academy of Sciences, 218; organizes World Science Center campaign, 237; tribute to, on retirement, 244
Miner, Roy Waldo, 209, 217, 220
Mitchill, Samuel Latham, 10, 13, 16, 21, 22, 23–24, 26, 29, 118, 250; biography of, 11–12; elected president of Lyceum of Natural History, 20; establishes Lyceum of Natural History, 19; political career, 12; professor at College of Physicians and Surgeons, 12, 25, 27–28; and Reuben Haines, 17–18; as scientific entrepreneur, 9, 12. Works: *Medical Repository*, ed., 11–12, 23; *Synopsis of Chemical Nomenclature and Arrangement*, 11

Wilson, Edmund Beecher, 180, *182*; appointed professor at Columbia, 183; and New York Academy of Sciences, 183, 185, 186

Winthrop, Theodore: *Cecil Dreeme*, 41

Wissler, Clark, 197, 201

Wolfe, John David, 96

Wong, Sam C., 225

Woodhouse, James, 12

Woodman, J. Edmund, 202

Woodward, Theodore E., 230

Woodworth, Robert S., 195

Woolworth, Norman, 222

Working Women's Protective Association, 96

World Science Center, 237–239, *240*, 241–242; description of, 238–239; lack of support for, 239–242

Wright, Louis T., 225

Yager, Arthur, 207–208

Yale University (Yale College), 3, 4, 32; Sheffield Scientific School, 76

Zabriskie, Martin, 69